François Gény and modern jurisprudence

UNDER THE AUSPICES OF
THE CENTER OF CIVIL LAW STUDIES
LOUISIANA STATE UNIVERSITY LAW SCHOOL

François Gény and modern jurisprudence

JARO
MAYDA

LOUISIANA STATE
UNIVERSITY PRESS
*Baton Rouge and
London*

Manufactured in the United States of America

Design: Dwight Agner
Typeface: Linotype Caledonia
Composition: Modern Typographers, Inc.
Printing: Thomson-Shore, Inc.
Binding: John H. Dekker & Sons, Inc.

LIBRARY OF CONGRESS CATALOGING IN PUBLICATION DATA

Mayda, Jaro.
François Gény and modern jurisprudence.

Bibliography: p.
Includes indexes.
1. Jurisprudence. 2. Gény, François, 1861–1959.
3. Law—Interpretation and construction. I. Title.
K230.G462M39 340.1 78–17864
ISBN 0–8071–0389–6

TO

MARUJA'S MOTHER

AND MINE

Contents

Foreword

François Gény was one of the leading jurists in France around the turn of the century, but he was way ahead of his time. The full appreciation of the significance of his work came slowly and much later in the modern developments of the civil law. This wave touched Louisiana perceptibly in 1963 when the Louisiana State Law Institute published Professor Jaro Mayda's English translation of Gény's "Méthode d'Interprétation et Sources en Droit Privé Positif."

In the spring of 1969, Professor Mayda delivered the Bailey Lectures to the students at the Louisiana State University Law School on the subject of "François Gény and Modern Jurisprudence," and, under the auspices of the Institute of Civil Law Studies, he conducted a seminar of three round-table sessions on this subject for a group of Louisiana judges, lawyers, and law teachers. The three specific topics were (1) a statement of Gény's thesis; (2) the Swiss experience with "*libre recherche*"; and (3) comparative projections and critique. This program contemplated ultimate publication as a permanent contribution to legal literature, and the present volume is the culmination of that project.

For additional perception in his study and a more penetrating insight of Gény, Professor Mayda communicated and had personal visits with relatives and jurists in France and Switzerland who had known and collaborated with Gény.

The Institute of Civil Law Studies was established under the academic sponsorship of the Louisiana State University Law School as a means of promoting the study of civil law in all its aspects and relationships, with particular emphasis on the Louisiana civil law. One of the primary purposes of the Institute has been to encourage and facilitate research and publication in the civil law. In addition to the publication of a number of doctrinal treatises, and three Special Issues of the Louisiana Law Review, the Institute has collaborated with the Louisiana State Law Institute in several translation and civil code projects.

In 1976 the name was changed to the Center of Civil Law Studies together with a substantial budget for expansion of the program. This made possible the development of a permanent staff, new research and translation projects, collaboration in the civil code revision program of the Louisiana State Law Institute, the establishment of a Louisiana Chapter of the international Association Henri Capitant pour la Culture Juridique Française, and several other activities.

JOSEPH DAINOW
Emeritus Professor of Law
Director Emeritus, Center of Civil Law Studies

Author's Preface

During a research year, 1967–1968, in Paris, to which I make several substantive references in the text and notes, I surveyed rather completely the writers on legal method and what is called in Europe "general theory of law." I found many apparently correct and even brilliant insights. But there was no jurisprudential follow-up. The synthesis seemed to falter on the level of concepts. It was the case of new doctrinal wine being poured into old conceptual bottles. With a few notable exceptions, comparisons outside the national system or its closest "circle" were descriptive, mechanical, clichélike—certainly of no help to the development of comparative jurisprudence.

It reminded me of Gény's critique of his doctrinal environment fifty to seventy years earlier, and of his effort to link legal thought and method with the advanced contemporaneous currents in science and philosophy. Most sciences, even some branches of social science, have greatly advanced since then; our lives have been changed by their practical application in the form of various technologies. Jurisprudence as the scientific-theoretical base for the social technology which is the practice of law in the broadest sense, has on the contrary stayed outside this mainstream, put pretty much in the same place.

I said this during my Parisian year,* rather loudly, considering the professional standards of *noblesse oblige* which make for pleasant tribal relations, if not also always for dialectic rigor. And I kept wondering whether some contemporaneous writing in jurisprudence could not have critically benefited from the comparative analysis of Gény's doctrine and of the still unfinished job, if it had been more accessible than it was in fact—hidden in the translator's introduction to the American edition of the *Méthode d'interprétation* (1963). Also, as my own research progressed, I felt that the first formulation of what I thought Gény was telling our generation, and the direction in which jurisprudence should move from there, was susceptible of being usefully elaborated and refined toward an integrated, if not unified, conceptual model of the growth and renewal of legal systems on both sides of the Atlantic.

By a happy coincidence, the Institute of Civil Law Studies at the Louisiana State University had initiated its endowed Bailey Lectures a short time before. The topic and the hospitable auspices came together in the spring of 1969. Unexpected and conflicting academic and professional commitments greatly delayed the elaboration and transformation of the text of the lectures into this volume and the reference apparatus on which it rests. If literature published in the meantime, including the most recent critique of the legal method of the United States Supreme Court,** is any guide, the niche which *François Gény and modern jurisprudence* has pretended to reserve for itself, has not yet been filled.

How well this work fills the void is for others to judge. The intent of the author will be vindicated if the comparative analysis in the first two essays will, apart from pedagogical uses, serve

* "Quelques réflexions critiques sur le droit comparé contemporain" [Roundtable presentation, Société de Législation Comparée, Paris, March 1968]. *Rev. internat. de dr. comp.* XXII(1970)47; "Some critical reflections on contemporary comparative law." *Rev. Jurid. Univ. de P.R.* XXIX(1970)431; in Spanish; *Boletín Méxic. de Der. Comp.* 9(1970)639. The English version is reprinted in K. Zweigert and H. J. Puttfarken (eds), *Rechtsvergleichung—Die Wege der Forschung.* Darmstadt, 1978.

** R. Berger, *Government by judiciary.* Cambridge, Mass., 1977.

as a critical mirror for the doctrine, the sophistication of which is demonstrably proportionate to comparative information; and if the third essay—little more, really, than elements of a prospectus for research toward the operational model of empirical jurisprudence for our time—will stimulate rigorous quantitative and qualitative studies of legal method in a concrete jurisdictional setting. Particularly suited subjects are, of course, the so-called mixed jurisdictions such as Louisiana, where practice has in fact climbed over the historical walls and, thus, has prepared the way for a functional and even elegant jurisprudential synthesis of the interpretation and uses of legislated and decisional laws. The composite result could be only improved, because more assured and soundly founded, administration of concrete legal and social justice.

Structure and reference

The volume presented me also with a formal and structural challenge: how to maintain the readable lecture style and, at the same time, develop the analysis in sufficient detail and pull together all the relevant reference. I have attempted to solve the dilemma by organizing the material on two levels. First, the text is intended to be self-contained. Reference to the bibliography—Index of authors and sources—is noted in the text by arabic superior numbers. Second, the other almost two-thirds of the wordage consists of monographic notes, some of them quite extensive and in some cases—such as the first note on the definition of jurisprudence—in the way of an excursus. The purpose of the notes is as much to elaborate and justify the text as it is to stimulate and facilitate the research of others. An occasional repetition is the price for a modicum of unity and continuity of both the text and the notes. This is intended to favor the student who may prefer to enter the volume sideways, through the conceptual index, rather than reading systematically page by page and note by note. The notes are linked to the text by roman superior numbers.

Besides this apparatus of superior numbers in the text, the following system of reference governs. In the notes, the arabic (and, where necessary, the roman) reference numbers appear in parentheses to distinguish them from other numerals applied conventionally to indicate pages, chapters or volume numbers. Concrete references are cast in a simplified compact form to facilitate scanning. For example, reference (12)345n6 means author/source (12), page 345, note 6. Section numbers are distinguished from page numbers by being italicized. Thus (78)*90* means source (78), section 90.

The bibliographical index of authors and sources contains reference to the page(s) where the source is cited, as well as the page(s), section(s), or note(s) which are cited. These references are distinguished in the following manner: the respective page in this volume is in bold face and separated by a diagonal from the ordinary numerals that locate the citation in the source. For example, **123**/45 means that on page 123 of this volume, the source in question is cited with reference to page 45. In the few instances where no such notation appears following an entry in the bibliographic index, it means that the source was used as general reference rather than with respect to a specific quotation or conception. Page references in the notes are not included in the index.

Acknowledgments

Limiting myself to the shortest possible list, I take a great pleasure in acknowledging the following contributions to the making of this book: Professor A. N. Yiannopoulos of the Louisiana State University School of Law was the perceptive mediator of an idea tossed off in a letter shortly after I returned from Europe in 1968. Professor Joseph Dainow, the author of the Foreword, organized as Director of the Institute for Civil Law Studies the 1969 Bailey Lectures and the related seminars with the Louisiana appellate judges (1969 and 1973). After waiting with patience and understanding for the typescript, he was the principal actor in mediating and making the publishing arrangements. Justice Albert Tate, Jr., an enthusiastic participant in the two seminars and a frequent visitor to the academe, kindly undertook to introduce this work—a task for which his profound practical and theoretical understanding of, and empathy for, the thesis and the need to elaborate and test it in practice, particularly predestine him.

The son of *Doyen* Gény, *M. le Conseiller* Bernard Gény of the French Council of State, provided the missing information for what is, in Appendix I, the only complete bibliography of François Gény's major legal writing in print. Dr. Thomas Daum, Research Assistant at the *Rechtswissenschaftliches Seminar* of the University of Zurich, read the second essay and made helpful comments, corrections and references. Neither he, nor the late Professor Walter Yung of the University of Geneva Faculty of Law, with whom I exchanged on Gény and the Swiss doctrine personally and by correspondence between 1965 and 1970, and to whom the second essay is specially dedicated, are responsible for my analysis and interpretation.

I cannot end with the usual formula which implies that the patience of author's wife need not be strained further and the deprivations caused by the long hours spent in the study are over. Maruja del Castillo, a hard working artist herself, knows better. For her, a sufficient reward is the anticipated pleasure our two mothers, one in Spain, the other in Czechoslovakia, will hopefully experience when they first open this volume dedicated to them.

J.M.

Thanksgiving Day, 1977

Introduction

Professor Jaro Mayda's work is a significant contribution to jurisprudential theory. For American law, it presents the most sophisticated and germinal analysis available of the relationship between judicial and legislative lawmaking. For the first time in English, it makes available to American scholars and judges many insights and views of continental theorists on this subject, which essentially concerns the nature of law in a living society of the Western world.

The both symbiotic and antithetical nature of legislative and judicial function in the formulation and application of a legal rule is brought into focusing perspective by consideration of what, for late twentieth-century American jurisprudential theory, are central queries: When a case is decided, what is law and what is application?; What are the proper limits of judicial power —what, in fact, is the essential meaning of the separation of legislative and judicial powers in a modern democracy? The both far-reaching and subtle implications of these central jurisprudential issues are brilliantly coruscated in this most important work.

As the decades go by, François Gény is receiving increasing recognition for his original perceptions as to these central issues.*

* See e.g.: B. CARDOZO, THE NATURE OF THE JUDICIAL PROCESS 16, 46–47, 119–21, 138–39, 143–45 (1921); J. P. DAWSON, THE ORACLES OF THE LAW 394–95,

It is indeed appropriate that, Professor Mayda has based his own creative analysis and perceptions upon Gény's initial thinking concerning the sensitive relationships between legislation, judicial interpretation, and the extensions and growth of the law as applied in an ever-changing social environment.

The dynamics of Gény's analysis of the relationship of legislation, adjudication, judicial rule-selection, and judicial rule-creation raised new conceptions and fundamental questions concerning the essential nature of law-application by courts and of the law itself as enforced and developed through the judicial process. Gény's insights also, as Professor Mayda demonstrates, implicate a glimmering perception of a phenomenon which until Mayda's analysis many will not recognize as judicial intercession, in which the judge decides in accordance with justice in an absence of (or even seemingly contrary to) governing legal precepts.

The work is organized into three essays and ninety-four "Notes."

The first essay, "Gény's doctrine," includes a précis of his major works and of the praise and critique of him by numerous scholars. This discussion is important in order to obtain some perspective as to Gény's major premises and his place in world thinking. The chapter concludes with the author's excellent analysis of the importance and the originality of Gény's views and of their original contribution to our understanding and to our further exploration of the nature of the judicial process and law itself. It is Professor Mayda's own "further" exploration in the remainder of the work that constitutes his own original and seminal contribution to jurisprudential theory.

The second essay, "The telling test," is a most interesting history and analysis of the jurisprudential application over the

399–400 (1968); W. FRIEDMAN, LEGAL THEORY 328–32, 439 (5th ed., 1967); K. LLEWELLYN, THE COMMON LAW TRADITION 189, 260–21, 422 (1960); 1 R. POUND, JURISPRUDENCE 181–86 (1959); J. STONE, LEGAL SYSTEM AND LAWYERS' REASONINGS 215–23 (1964). Professor Friedmann noted, for instance: "In this writer's opinion, most of the subsequent philosophical discussions of the juridical process are an elaboration or resumption of Gény's pioneer work." Friedmann, Legal Philosophy and Judicial Lawmaking, 61 COLUM. L. REV. 820, 827 (1961).

decades of Article 1 of the Swiss Civil Code. Gény himself had stated that this code article represented a statutory statement of his fundamental view as to the function of the courts in applying law or in reaching justice. Mayda's fascinating study may also illustrate the somewhat disappointing possibility that a judicial bureaucracy (and this includes one of any jurisdiction, including that of an American state) may tend to resist its justice-function, even though explicitly authorized by statute, in favor of deferring to mechanically determined rule. The engrossing study touches on the political-jurisprudential issues of individual-versus-state, rule of law-versus-authoritarianism, and of the pros and cons and fictions and realities of the separation of legislative and judicial power—all issues of the gravest importance for the twentieth and twenty-first centuries and the history of free peoples.

The final essay, "Beyond Gény: The unfinished job," is a brilliant and exciting consideration of the pivotal role of the judge in the formulation and application of legal rules, whether the latter are rooted in legislative or decisional law, and of the judge's duty in the exceptional case to apply no previous rule. For me, the important perceptions included new insights into viewing the law-in-being as involving a sharing rather than a separation of law-creating powers between the legislature and the judiciary, at least in the development of private-law precepts, and also, by reason of explicit and reasoned formulation, into the judge's duty to do justice without a specific text as being an integral (although exceptional) part of the life of the law. The author's laser beam of ultimate perception is directed not at the routine application or extension of prior precepts, but instead at the necessity of the judge doing particular justice in the exceptional case which is not really within the ambit or congruence of preexisting precepts or extensions of law.

The third essay presents an important and original analysis by Mayda. Inspired by the breakthrough resulting from Gény's initial perceptions as to the existence and justification for judicial "interpretation" to provide nonlegislative precepts to apply in judicial decision, he suggests bases for restatement of the principal conceptual and functional bases of law and the judicial process.

Unlike present models, the restatement should—as to judicial precept-creation or policy-selection—more nearly equate actual practice to articulated theory, should more nearly equate law-word to the social-value tended to be expressed by it.

Process and agency (legislative or judicial) are aspects of law-making; but, in reality, its content may be its most significant feature, as evolved in the light of each jurisdiction's perhaps-differing complex social environment. Comparative empirical studies of the jurisprudence and social factors of Western societies might possibly indicate that the legislative (versus and plus) judicial function in law making is not so much a matter of differing national methodology, as a differing mode by which in each society (through law and its institutions) are expressed similar universal substantive values. This, at least to me, is the connotation of an approach towards unified field theory proposed by Professor Mayda (although he may well disclaim this as implied by his work).

The author opens up the need for a qualitative restatement of definition, comparable to those which in this century have given new perspectives of exponential dimension to the understanding of the physical and biological sciences. The need for a new evaluation of law and investigation into the relationship of the judicial process to law and its essential meaning should focus, he suggests, upon the living legal processes of existing societies and their substantative values and economic and social institutions, rather than upon their abstract theories of justice. Likewise, this third essay contains what to me are seminal perceptions as to accepted legal dogmas and conceptions, which represent a brilliant restatement of judicial process in terms of twentieth-century practice rather than of conceptual theory.

Inspired by the originality of Gény's overview of legal rules and the judicial process as institutions of a living society—which take meaning from its socioeconomic context as well as from verbal formulations—Mayda opens up new vistas by which to evaluate old legal concepts, and upon the basis of which to explore new meanings of law and of the judicial process in their relationship to their social function. In the latter regard, the call for empirical studies of comparative social, economic, and physical data of living societies (as contrasted with existing studies of their metaphysical abstracts) is viewed by Mayda as warranted, in order to verify or not the postulates and hypotheses suggested by his original critique of law and the judicial process, both the traditional models and also his seminal Gény-Mayda one.

In addition to the usual attributions and references, the work includes ninety-four "Notes." Some of these are brief explanatory asides, but many of them are interesting essays elaborating at greater length and in more detail some of the conclusions in the text. The latter are an integral exploration of the postulates and phenomena set forth in the text. The profound supplementary insights and extensions of the text represented by these essays are in themselves a major contribution.

ALBERT TATE, JR.
Associate Justice,
Supreme Court of Louisiana
New Orleans, January 1, 1978

François Gény and modern jurisprudence

ESSAY ONE

Gény's doctrine

A

The title of these essays may seem to be clear, but perhaps it is not or, at least, it does not make a strong prima facie case for the interest and value of the topic. Since the key term of reference in the title is "modern jurisprudence," let me begin with a gloss on these words. This will also put François Gény in the intended context and perspective.

It seems possible to short-cut the exposition by stating what I do not intend to discuss: Gény's contribution to the philosophy of law. It is true that he made a correct estimate of the "meager harvest" general philosophy had offered to law and drew from it the consequent procedural insight.[159] But Gény's substantive philosophizing, centered on the notion of "irreducible natural law," has no original value or relevance for today, no matter how important it appeared to himself and how much it provoked his contemporary critics.

A summary comment along these lines may satisfy the initial need to de-emphasize and restyle the probably most obvious connotation of my topic. But the state of the art is such that to simply distinguish philosophy of law from jurisprudence is not enough to clearly define the latter. An explicit definition is needed.

François Gény

By jurisprudence I mean theory of law. Here the term theory has not a loose colloquial meaning, but the substantive and methodological meaning assigned to it in contemporary sciences. Jurisprudence has then at least four fundamental features: (*a*) it is a system of general concepts, propositions, and principles; (*b*) it is arrived at by means of ordering and testing empirical data with the help of speculative, philosophical hypotheses; (*c*) it aims at finding what governs the operation of law as a system and how the legal system fulfills and rationalizes its purpose in the broader societal framework; (*d*) thus it contributes to the effectiveness of the day-by-day function of law as social technology. Implicit in this composite description is the existence of a self-correcting mechanism that keeps the model up to date in concepts and application.

This is jurisprudence without epithets or philosophical school labels. To add the qualification "modern" as I do in the title is a concession to the fact that in the literature, as well as in general discourse, jurisprudence continues to be identified with conventional philosophy of law; or, at least, its definitions are shrouded in semantics that indicate lack of clarity about its station and mission in the scheme of things.[I]

As an *empirical* discipline, jurisprudence took root not much more than three generations ago. Of course it has come forth from the seamless web of intellectual history. But during the preceding twenty-three centuries—if we start with Socrates rather than only with Aristotle, as is usual[II]—the reflection about law was the métier of *speculative* philosophy. As such, it was marked for life by the dichotomous mold of Aristotelian philosophy and by its syllogistic logic. The first is a continuing source—not only in law—of the so-called reductionism, which is contrary to the modern postulate of complete fact; the second has been made obsolete by experimental logic, which helps to keep the relative, scientific complete fact (or better, probability) up to date. Speculative philosophy also seems never to have entirely recovered from the administration by the Schoolmen.

The distinction I make here between the speculative and the empirical is very sharp indeed. Finer shadings would be appropriate in an essay different in format and focus, but there is a didactic value in drawing the line in this manner. The quantum jump into jurisprudential modernity is so broad that no damage to understanding can come from dramatizing the fact that such apparently opposed members of the fraternity as Thomas Aquinas, the philosopher of natural law, and John Austin, the positivist, are on the same side of the line, together with Immanuel Kant, the master of philosophical fission.

It was only in the last quarter of the nineteenth century and the first quarter of the twentieth that several seminal thinkers switched the thought about law from the speculative and mechanically conceptual onto the social-empirical track:

Rudolph von Jhering spelled out the ideas of individual right as a legally protected interest and of social purpose as the measure of law;

Oliver Wendell Holmes recognized experience as the essence of law and led legal method from the dogmatic to the pragmatic;

Eugen Ehrlich contrasted the law in the books with living law and so laid the groundwork for our understanding of law as a function of society;

John Dewey, a nonlawyer, introduced law to the operational logic of modern science; and

François Gény prepared the way for a thorough reappraisal of the sources and the process of decision in law and outlined the methodology that would make jurisprudence into a "science of action," putting it "among the scientific hierarchy of our times."[157]

To anticipate the reaction of those who, upon different consideration or with reference to less stringent criteria, might feel that this listing slights other meritorious men,[III] let me restate my criteria: the five founders were all *seminal* thinkers, who *consciously* aimed at *empirical* jurisprudence—and, indeed, wrote the right books at the right time.[IV] This makes the difference between their work and the libraries of legal philosophy written during and after the revolutionary half-century that stretches from Jhering's *Zweck im Recht* (1877)[V] to Gény's last volume of *Science et technique* (1924) and Dewey's article "Logical method and law" (1925). This gross philosophical product[VI] contributed little to the progress of jurisprudence, except the small fraction of it that proceeded on the new premise that the proper task of philosophy related to law (as well as to other disciplines) is to frame meaningful questions, or hypotheses, not to look for meaningless answers.

Having fixed the historical and intellectual coordinates of the topic, I hope to have also indicated its inherent value. To devote a series of lectures to Gény seventy years after he published his first and probably most important work, *Méthode d'interprétation,*[157,158] is no exercise in legal papyrology or in history of philosophy. Nor is it a superfluous exercise. Gény is a true classic. He is more talked about than read. His reputation is worldwide, but it rests often on superficial awe rather than on profound understanding. Although he was very much of his time, he came before his time. In a genuine seminal fashion, his doctrine has tended to gain rather than to lose importance with the passing years. He is not merely "still a stimulus for contemporary jurisprudence," as it was too modestly put on the occasion of his centenary.[308] Roscoe Pound was closest to the mark when he wrote me in 1962, shortly before his terminal illness, "The more I think of the matter, the more Gény grows upon me as one of the most satisfactory thinkers on jurisprudence of our time."

I shall start with a composite narrative of Gény's doctrine and then analyze the principal new elements in it, in constant reference to the praise, the critique, and the follow-up by others.

Then, in the second essay, I shall turn to a fascinating and telling confrontation of doctrine and practice: sixty years of Swiss experience under a code, the first article of which expresses Gény's principal contribution, the method of *la libre recherche scientifique* —free objective search for a rule.

Finally, in the last essay, I shall present some comparisons, projections, and hypotheses. They aim "through Gény, but beyond Gény" toward the rational and functional jurisprudence for which he helped to lay foundations. Such a jurisprudence is long overdue, and its systematic construction is becoming increasingly imperative on at least two grounds: philosophically, because the present and growing levels of social stress and conflict require also particularly clear and forward-looking thought about legal policy; technically, as a conceptual and analytical guidance for decision making, which cannot be replaced by any form of communication or data-processing technology.

B

Despite Gény's extensive bibliography (see Appendix A), his doctrine is found principally in two works. The first is the already mentioned *Method of interpretation and sources of private positive law*, published first in 1899 and substantially expanded in 1919 by footnotes and by an epilog of almost two hundred pages. The expressed purpose of the *Méthode* was to inquire into "the nature, function, and hierarchy of formal sources of law" and "the means to supplement them by a free objective search, the processes and proper value of which must be determined."[157]

Gény left us an authoritative restatement of the doctrine of his *Méthode* in two concluding sections (*223–24*) of the second edition. It was designed to answer critics and to clear up misunderstandings. I will extract from it the essence, in Gény's own words, as much as is practical.

Gény's thesis is that judges under the codes have "always and perforce" done more than to apply legislated law with the use of the processes of formal logic. This reality ought to be recognized and its consequences carried out.

They are:

1. Positive law is more than legislated law. Human and social relations cannot be satisfactorily regulated by "several verbal formulae" that could not encompass the whole situation even at the time they were promulgated. (Here Gény of course voices Portalis, the chief draftsman of the Napoleonic codes, whom he extensively quotes.)

2. The contrary thesis—that of the nineteenth-century exegetic positivism—is based on three fictions. First, there is the "fiction of the logically necessary completeness" of the legislated law.[157] Second, this fiction is "corrected by another fiction that isolates

the statute from the authority of its maker" and thus gives it an independent existence. The first fiction, the hermeneutic nature of legislated law (a European continental version of the Blackstonian image of common law as a brooding omnipresence), leads to a technique of interpretation that relies heavily on analogy. This technique is based on the third fiction, that of a presumed legislative intent, although the existence of a gap to be filled by analogy indicates that there was no such intent.

3. The constitutional position of the modern legislature requires that its laws be always fully applied. But "justice and social utility" dictate that the judge use all legitimate resources when he decides. In the absence of applicable legislated law, he must first refer to the other formal source, customary law.

4. When no "appropriate" (that is, clearly and directly applicable) formal norm is available, the judge must seek guidance from doctrine and decisional law as persuasive though not binding, authorities.

5. If all these sources fail him, the judge must *freely search for a rule* on which to base his decision. This search is discretionary, but it must not be arbitrary. It must be *objective*, which means based on the social realities, needs, and values; on the nature of things; in short, on "science" as Gény uses the word. This means that in his exercise of the pretorian power the judge must act as a model legislator would. But his rule is limited to the specific case.[VII]

6. Since "the only justified principle of interpretation is to determine the scope of the text with reference to the time of its enactment,"[158] the so-called interpretation by analogy is in reality not an interpretation, but a response to the absence of any formal norm to be interpreted. Thus it is a legitimate use of judicial discretion, one form of the free search.

7. Only if we discard the fictions and frankly admit the need for the creative method of free search and the existence of its sociological sources will it be possible "to get positive law back on the track."

"Our conclusion tends to affirm," Gény wrote in the last-but-one paragraph of the original edition of the *Méthode*, "that the purely formal and logical elements . . . are insufficient to satisfy the desiderata of law in action. . . . The judicial process must look . . . outside of, and beyond, these elements. This is the essential principle of my thesis, which it will be necessary to reject and destroy if one wants to positively contradict my ideas."

Despite the wrong impressions based on Gény's philosophical reference and scholastic style, his main purpose—as he kept on stressing—was not philosophical. It was "to produce primarily a practical work."[157] His critical focus was on the positivist myth that legislated law is exclusive and self-sufficient and on the complement of the myth, the exegetic method. That was the method of erecting upon the legislative text a system of concepts handled in closed circuit by means of formal logic, independently of the changing world of facts. The appropriately forbidding German word for this method, *Begriffsjurisprudenz*, appears repeatedly in Gény's footnotes, which are full of citations that illustrate and criticize this "conceptual jurisprudence."

In lieu of that, Gény proposed a conception inspired by his idol Jhering and summarized in the famous aphorism "Through the civil code, but beyond it." In this perspective, the legislated law is the alpha but not the omega. It is the structural frame and the principal matter, but not the limiting contour.

Gény's practical strategy was to insist on strict statutory interpretation *ex tunc*—as of the time of the legislation—so as to open the door for the method of judicial free search, unencumbered by any fiction or pretense of finding *ex nunc* the intent of the original legislator in cases where the statute either did not cover the concrete fact situation at all or else dealt with it inadequately.

C

By Gény's own appraisal, the *Méthode* was essentially a negative exercise. The "cracks in the edifice" were "disclosed"; the problems were "raised and tackled,"[157] he wrote in 1919. But the "positive conclusions" suffered a "radical infirmity." Although the need for the method of free search was established, the concrete elaboration was "vague, incomplete, wrong, sometimes contradictory," and "obviously insufficient to provide a firm and comprehensive framework."

The critics concentrated mainly on methodology, on which Gény remained confident through the years that his position continued "very strong," his "negative conclusions . . . unshaken." The fact that they failed to note the "cardinal gap" did not make it any smaller for Gény. His own "remorse over a kind of intellectual laxity" was growing as he saw "too confident disciples use, often indiscriminately, the bits of truth [he had] not without effort extracted from the barely touched mass of legal matter, or the sometimes ill-fitting patches with which [he] only provisionally covered up the deficiencies in the fabric of [his] work."

The outstanding task was to close the "gaping hole," to "pick up and develop in detail all these ideas" that were "barely sensed, uncertain, imperfectly defined, without assurance . . . to outline as clearly as possible the positive direction for the 'free search.'"[159] This job Gény undertook, after a series of warm-up studies, from 1912 on. The result is his *Science et technique en droit privé positif*, four volumes, 1,423 pages in all, published between 1914 and 1924.

After having focused on method, Gény felt that it was now necessary to turn to "law as such . . . essentially practice based on knowledge." He wrote, "Jurists hardly seem aware of the need and obligation" to understand "how we in fact work, and how we should work. . . . Even the broadest minds who do not turn back before the task of abstraction or generalization . . . have almost without exception neglected to analyze their own research procedures, which they practice instinctively." He explained:

> Questions are seldom raised, and always only incidentally. . . . We are told that such theoretical problems are without influence on the actual development of law, that method is a matter of *pouvoir* [power] rather than *savoir* [knowledge]. . . . The point is not to sacrifice practice to theory, or even to contest the pragmatic superiority of the former over the latter. The question is simply whether enlightened practice does not achieve its goals

> with greater assurance and more fully than blind practice. . . . Either we must take refuge in pure empiricism . . . [or we must] develop a rational theory for law. The task is similar to that in all [contemporaneous] scientific disciplines. . . . Decisive experience indicates that the intimate secret of the life of law cannot be glimpsed from the elevated observation point of abstract speculation, but only in close touch with its concrete processes. . . . Consequently only the jurist provided with the necessary minimum of a philosophical mind has any chance of discovering the innermost mechanism of law that he is to administer. . . . The better research perspective places decisional law, customary and legislative law . . . [in a] comprehensive perspective . . . which shows their relative position in the whole, of which they are only particular functions. . . . This is the spirit of the present study . . . which places law in the midst of other social disciplines. . . . [Methodologically] it is today no more a question—as Taine postulated—of soldering social sciences onto natural sciences. We must treat all science as a whole and in this complex find the proper place for law, while confessing that the sources that nourish law as a scientific discipline remain weak and insufficient.[159,VIII]

I have carefully resisted the urge to give this long composite quotation from Gény more than merely the equivalent meaning in English or to translate it into contemporary idiom. It is obvious that today Gény would say that his ambition was to construct a systemic, operational model of law. Instead, Gény kept on speaking of "legal method." For the purpose of its "more precise formulation," he believed he "found . . . the means . . . in the distinction between *science* and *technique*." This was the "particularly interesting perspective" in which he trusted "the results of [his *Méthode*] will fall in place."

The double-pronged approach that Gény took in *Science* is foreshadowed in *Méthode* in the distinction between, on the one hand, "the conception of science, essentially based on the internal autonomy of reason interpreting objective realities" and, on the other hand, "the implementation, the formal or technical element."[157]

Two complementary concepts were first mentioned in Gény's lectures at the *Collège libre de sciences sociales* in 1910.[156] They are *le donné* and *le construit*. The best short definition for each is based on Gény's summary in 1919, when two volumes of *Science* were published and the third was ready in manuscript. *Le donné* is "data derived from the nature of things and, hence, susceptible of being understood through cognition or sensed through conscience." According to Gény, "Scientific elaboration of law [is] the discovery of these realities which constitute the essence of the legal order." (Consequently, *science* is the system of these data.) *Le construit* is a "product of discretionary will rather than of knowledge. . . . Technical elaboration of law [*technique*] consists of the processes through which man applies his intelligence to the solution of legal problems."[157]

Gény recognized four "principal aspects" or, better, levels of the "raw material," which he chose to call *le donné*: (1) natural data—physical, biological, environmental (*données réelles ou strictement naturelles*); (2) the rules of law developed historically (*données historiques*); (3) the norms of just conduct, which are rationally derived from the "nature of man and his contact with the world" (*données rationelles*); (4) the body of ideals underlying law and based on all the "physical, psychological, moral, religious, economic, and political considerations" (*données idéalles*).

The last category of data consists of the vaguest philosophical postulates. Gény was aware of it and sounded apologetic. The highest operational datum is in fact the third one, the "rational element of justice." Gény compared it to the Roman *jus naturale*, drawing its strength from the historical-normative datum, the Roman *jus gentium*. He considered this *donnée* rationally to be as obligatory as the physical-environmental data are in the natural sphere, "although it could be overlooked in fact."

In sum, the preceding is a catalog of empirical data, cultural and normative patterns and values. Although the *données* represent a hierarchy of norms, from the broadest principles to increasingly specific precepts as they "enclose more exactly the reality," they can at most "sometimes suggest a rule of conduct." The actual confection of a legal norm, Gény polemized with Duguit between the third and the last volumes of *Science*, requires "the intervention . . . of an intellectual effort" by the lawmaker "who articulates the empirical data [*réalités*] with the help of concepts, and then provides them with the characteristic injunction."[159]

This is the field of *technique*, "action more than knowledge, result of will rather than of intelligence." But technique is not an arbitrary activity, since it is subject to "superior directives" flowing from the "stock of moral and economic axioms" derived from the nature of things and centered on the "supreme idea of the objectively just, which represents a balance of interests." To define this admittedly often "vague" and "hazy" datum requires "a constant effort to reconstruct totally the reality of which intellect can gather only fragments." This task requires the contribution of intuition, which "helps to recognize the trend of a given time at a given place" and "the conviction or thrust of the collective will." Thus it not only "offers [the lawmaker a base of] sufficient objectivity," but also "remedies the defects of a purely intellectual [*i.e.*, empirical, analytical] method." The total "social and moral reality . . . can be better sensed than understood."

The decisional process in the courts seemed to Gény to be "the most instructive model" of this "organizing empiricism," which means the interplay of the facts and of the *données*, the "extremely general . . . principles that come from scientific [*i.e.*, systematic] consideration of what is just."[159,IX]

D

Gény's work had an impressive worldwide impact. It was praised, criticized, projected in the work of other scholars, rejected without understanding. I shall discuss all these facets.

To gain some perspective, verbal eulogies and kudos need to be separated from comments that reveal deeper understanding, and short-range reactions need to be contrasted with genuine follow-up. Misunderstandings and failures to pick up and elaborate must be judged in terms of obstacles to communication between Gény and his students.

Gény's first work, the *Méthode*, had an instant impact and evoked almost general praise. The impact is best illustrated by Capitant's assurance, in the second edition of his *Introduction*

(1903),[56] that it was essential to "take into account the spread of ideas provoked by . . . Gény's *Méthode*." (Under Gény's influence, Capitant dropped the "Aubry-Rau doctrine of property as purely deductive and artificial which, as Monsieur Gény demonstrated,[157] makes it useless and dangerous.")

The praise of the *Méthode* ranges from the flowery to simple epithets suggesting true admiration. It comes forth from informed summaries and interpretations. It shows statistically in the number of index entries in major doctrinal works. A good sample are the twenty-two citations in Cardozo's *The nature of judicial process* and the many additional ones in his subsequent works *The growth of law* and *The paradoxes of legal science*.

The scope of the substantive impact of Gény's *Méthode* can be gleaned from the headings one might assign to several interrelated groups of representative appraisals: monopoly of legislated law, exegetic method, modernization of legal method, the unprovided case, legal stability and social change, concrete justice, method and theory.

Some of these appraisals are particularly striking because of who said what. Boulanger, editorial heir to Planiol and Ripert's *Traité élémentaire*, concluded that Gény "put in motion the case against the exegetic school . . . [his] indictment in fact found no contradictor."[39] This testimony was capped by Gény's doctrinal rival, the neo-Thomist Dabin, who considered his "masterly critique" a decisive factor in the "death of the School of Exegesis."[92]

Lambert, a founder of modern comparative law and much better known than Gény at the time he wrote these lines, concluded that, with his "positive nature of things . . . the supreme principle of justice and social utility as applied to a specific society," Gény created "the third and last source of law [in addition to customary and legislated law] . . . to be derived objectively from all the social [and behavioral] sciences that inform the judge or counsel of the actual state of the society and its needs."[241]

Croce emphasized that Gény assigned to "the interpreter a central position in the life of the law [which] takes place below the level of the statute."[87] Thus he made an "epoch-making contribution to the liberalization of legal interpretation."[74] In Llewellyn's admiring terms, Gény demonstrated the "uses [of] an ancient text to handle the most modern cases."[268]

In contrast to the anarchic implications of the German-Austrian "free-law" school, which sprang up shortly after the *Méthode* was first published, Dualde pointed out that, though Gény showed the "gaps in positive law, he did not convert the whole legal system into one big gap."[109]

One of the most comprehensive evaluations comes from Morris Cohen: Gény's thesis, based on "massive learning and overwhelming wealth of illustrative material . . . led to the reconsideration to the relations of law to ethics, logic, and social sciences, and has . . . raised . . . significant philosophical questions as to legal methodology."[74]

Personally most moving may well be the reported sigh of Kantorowicz some twenty-five years after he ignited as Gnaeus Flavius the free-law movement: "I would give everything I have done, and more, to have written . . . *Méthode*."[268]

Another bouquet of epithets illustrates the perhaps most important characteristic of the *Méthode*: the universality of the thesis and its bearing on the center of operation of any developed legal system. Depending on which ingredient in Gény's work the given admirer or critic puts forward of the rest, Gény is called pragmatic and idealist; scientific rationalist and neo-Scholastic; legal sociologist; realist, both in the American sense and in the continental European sense of anticonceptualism; neoclassicist; and, of course, eclectic.[x]

E

As distinguished from the *Méthode*, the reception of *Science et technique* was more mixed.

On the positive side it is difficult but not very important to determine what has caused a greater stir: the so-called minimum conception of natural law (it would be much better described as empirical natural law) or the science-technique classification. The first was a strong source of philosophically oriented neonaturalism, which—perhaps stimulated by Gény's terminology, perhaps inevitably—prostituted the germinal thought because it could not understand its technical core.[XI] The science-technique model found great favor with a group of neoconceptualists of various ulterior orientations, and, perhaps surprisingly, also with Pound.[336]

Both conceptions provoked also a good deal of criticism, much of which has only footnote value. This is true even of big names. Ripert's conclusion that "the value of Gény's classification . . . [is] only analytical and is justified simply by the author's prestige"[353] and Cohen's dismissal of the science-technigue distinction as "artificial and misleading"[74] dissolve with little trace if we permissibly extrapolate Gény's concepts and substitute for his terms the current distinction between policy and law. Villey's special field, history of legal philosophy, should not have impeded him to understand what Gény meant by "*scientifique*" in his formula of "free objective search for a rule" or to note (especially as late as 1962) the crucial turn Gény took toward the empirical-scientific conception of jurisprudence. He could then hardly have accused Gény of submitting to his environment "of exaggerated cult of science."[406]

It is, of course, true of Gény as well as of any other writer that he thought and communicated within a certain context of ideas and words to which he attempted to add. This must mitigate not only Gény's use of the word *scientific* but also his original use of the concept of natural law. In the form of "natural law with a variable content" (Cathrein, Stammler, etc.), the term was widely current around the turn of the century far beyond philosophical circles. In fact, Saleilles' idea of "comparative law"[361] was almost a synonym for this natural law. So was Lambert's "*droit comun legislatif*,"[241] then a notion of a supranational substantive law, which is the direct ascendant of the "general principles of law common to all civilized nations" in Article 38 of the Statute of the World Court, first drafted after the war of 1914–1918.

Nevertheless, most of those who criticized Gény on this account followed strictly party lines or at least let their allergy to the words *natural law* overcome the scholarly urge to examine the matter more profoundly. Standing out in this group is Oliver Wendell Holmes, who unfortunately never realized his intellectual kinship with Gény.[XII]

On the whole, this first cluster of critiques, as well as some positive judgments, tend to fit into the academic folklore, widespread until the war of 1939–1945, that only the founding of a new school, not admitted application, refinement, or synthesis, is a meritorious scholarly activity. The various disciples simply ride Gény's coattails, thus developing a "school." I have already cited Gény's words of concern over their superficiality. Among the critics, the less ambitious merely strain to differentiate, forgetting the eternal truth behind Ripert's words that "opposite schools are never as far apart as they like to think."[353] The more ambitious critics must dismiss Gény in one form or another so as to appear to be original thinkers rather than "merely" creative synthesizers. Cossio, working hard at his "egological school," disposes of Gény derogatorily as an "eclectic";[80] Esser, one of the best contemporaries in this corner of jurisprudence, has no difficulty in recognizing Gény as an originator.[127]

Another common theme of the critics is Gény's middle-of-the-road position. To the traditionalists he was too progressive if not subversive, since he "creates the illusion of defending [traditional ideas] while he destroys them at the very base." To those who saw the new light only under the pressure of overpowering documentation, he was a welcome compromiser and "conciliator."[66] To the genuine or putative progressives, he was "anything but a revolutionary,"[313] he found it difficult to free himself from the roots of the conception in which he was brought up,"[161] or at least he "still attempted to make many concessions to . . . legalism."[127] Most kindly and truly Gény was said to have represented the inevitable admixture of "tradition and innovation."[109, XIII]

This kind of general criticism, some of it mildly gratuitous and showing less than full understanding, is much less serious than the interrelated objections to Gény's positions on (*a*) judicial decisions as a source of law, (*b*) the relative status of the treatise writers, (*c*) hunch judgment, and (*d*) the time frame within which legislated law ought to be interpreted. Critique on these points was made, directly or by implication, by a sizable group of disciples, admirers, and critics, including Lambert, Capitant, Esser, Boulanger, Ascarelli,[12,13] Djuvara,[108] and Liver.[265]

In the matter of decisional law, Gény appears, on the face of his text, at best ambivalent. His final position, hidden in a footnote added to the 1919 edition of the *Méthode*,[158] was that "on this point decisional law represents the true positive law"—the point being that the legislator can often give only the general normative outline and that the details must be filled in through the decisional application of this framework to concrete cases. But, under the constitutional principle of separation of powers, as expressed in Article 5 of the French Civil Code,[XIV] the ruling of the judge (even if not based on legislated law and, therefore, making law) must be only particular, limited to the specific controversy. The development of general law through *jurisprudence constante* (based on a combination of the obligatory force of double cassation under the 1837 statute, which reformed the *Court of Cassation*) and on a de facto *stare decisis*, falls according to Gény under the rubric of customary law rather than being an independent source.[XV]

The position seems strangely out of tune with the contemporaneous trend toward recognizing the de facto judicial lawmaking under the codes as a source of customary law, a trend that began in France and in Germany within the decade before the composition of the *Méthode*.[XVI] Gény seemed, indeed, trapped by his own formalism.

But, contrary to impressions and partly due to Gény's often scholastic mode of developing his argument, the dispute was not about whether decisional law should be recognized as a third formal source of law next to legislated and customary law. Nor was it about whether "we can and should recognize the pretorian power of decisional law," which is "the power to create law in a specific litigation."[158] The real dispute was only about whether decisional law was the contemporary fashion of generating customary law and was hierarchically part of it and equal to it; or whether it was merely a tributary of customary law, no matter how important, and as such was hierarchically inferior to custom and rather the equal of *la doctrine*, the writers.[XVII]

Gény's position on the writers had probably two sources. One was his traditionalist acceptance of the aura of the *École*, whose self-esteem has probably never been higher than in the nineteenth century. This outward respect certainly made it easier for Gény to argue repeatedly how wrong much of the doctrine had been. The second source was the logic of his position on decisional law. Once he denied it the status of a formal source, he had to put it in the same category with the writers, though the ranking could have been more discriminating. As Planiol pointed out correctly,[330] the opinions of writers have an authority without sanction, but the courts make decisions to be executed. A more serious consequence of this uncritical conception by Gény was that he pitted the writers and the courts against each other, instead of considering both of them and the legislature as partners—with different degrees of effectiveness at different times—in the continuous process of protecting the established social-political order and handling new conflicts of interest in a just, legal manner.[XVIII]

Another slip from Gény's sophistication was his equivocal reaction to the contemporary suggestions about the hunch element in judicial decision, a fact of life even his much more conservative mentor Saleilles accepted without protest. In the original text of the *Méthode*, Gény in fact appeals "to the experience of all those who have reflected on the problems of positive law to confirm that the just decision . . . is [often] reached through instinctive feeling rather than by reasoning," and he defends this procedure against the derogatory epithet "cerebral equity."[158] But in the 1919 epilog[158]—and despite the intervening wholehearted reception of Bergson's intuitionism in *Science*—Gény cites all the published and unpublished evidence in favor, but remains uncommitted and aloof.[XIX]

Last among the major targets of criticism is Gény's position in the debate, still continuing, on the perspective in which the legislation, whether in the form of codes or statutes, ought to be interpreted. Gény's position is this: legislated law is the product of a specific legislative authority.[158] The intent and its verbal expression are inexorably tied to this authority as of the time it acted. As a consequence, the text must be interpreted with reference to that point in time, *ex tunc*.

This attitude we may conveniently, though not unequivocally, call the *subjective* conception of legislated law (*i.e.*, one tied to the subject of its maker). Gény rationalizes it by asking, "What rational base can a system of statutory interpretation retain if it uses the text to justify something quite different than what the lawmaker wanted to achieve?"[157]

Let Lambert speak for the other side, the majority of Gény's contemporaries and successors. In their *objective* conception, still accepted today, legislated law is not primarily and irrevocably tied to the subject of the lawmaker, but is an autonomous result of lawmaking and an object. It is conceived as being connected with the legislative authority only during the process of formulation and promulgation. The umbilical cord severed, the statute "is detached from the legislative will, which is its source, and exists independently, adjusting itself as much as possible to environmental changes." It follows that the proper reading and interpretation is *ex nunc*—as of now—not that which "conforms best with the intent of the authors [of the statute], but that which fits best the present needs." By rejecting the objective conception, Gény attempts "to preserve [in his methodology] the dogma of statutory inviolability" and aligns himself "with the very Laurent [the archetype of the exegetic school] on the absolute rigidity of statute law and its ability to remain immobile amidst continuous changes in the socioeconomic environment."[241, xx]

As in other instances, the dialectic of the critics—here Lambert in particular—has obscured rather than clarified the issue. The semantic and classification duel impedes more profound penetration of Gény's system. And a system he had indeed in mind: "The total legal order required by the needs of present life." The primacy *inter pares* of legislation among the parts of this whole comes from the fact that it is "written . . . more precisely and . . . its force is not in doubt." Quoting Percerou ("Law should above all satisfy the present needs of practice"), Gény's criticism is not directed at new solutions to serve present needs. It is directed at the fact that "our courts and recent commentators pretend to have reached [them] through statutory interpretation," but the "legitimate content of the statute . . . [is] only what its authors intended and in fact expressed in their injuction." He explained: "As soon as the intent is derived from the text and is not contradicted by any extraneous element, it dictates the . . . decision. . . . [If] the absence of, or uncertainty about, the legislative intent does not allow a clear interpretation" of the text as a means to reach a decision, then it "should be replaced by another . . . method."[158] This preparation of the ground for the *libre recherche* is the key to Gény's position on the sources. Lambert passes over it lightly; many other critics have completely misunderstood it.

F

I have so far let Gény and his admirers or critics do the talking. My comments have been added, at least in the text, only where it was necessary to clarify or to emphasize and where no adequate direct quotation was available. This effort at authenticity has admittedly not contributed to the liveliness of the account. Although Gény displays an occasional flash or twinkle ("I must say it if for no other reason than to unload my soul," he comments in the midst of a minor anti-Hegelian remonstrance),[159] he has mostly a flat if not laborious style.

But Gény's text offers also a difficulty that must not remain unmentioned in connection with any effort to interpret him. One reads his key passages with a constant feeling—in fact a growing conviction—that he is in fact saying or intends to say something more relevant for today than his convoluted and old-fashioned rhetoric conveys on its face.

In a situation like this, the danger of overreading, of interpolating too much, is an occupational hazard that I am not sure I myself can overcome, even when I will admittedly speak for myself later. Many others have clearly succumbed to this danger, among them such diverse Americans as jurisprude Llewellyn and "institutional" economist Commons.

It seems therefore wise to enter at this point a general plea of probable guilt of committing acts of ambivalence and inconsistency while trying to clarify for today's reader these very characteristics of Gény's writing. As to the danger of reading Gény too much *ex nunc*, the direct quotations in the first part ought to provide some corrective. As to the rest, Gény is after all not a statute. Nor are these essays an exercise in the history of legal doctrine; they are instead an exercise in the discovery of the links between Gény and the progressive environment from which he blossomed and the ongoing task to construct a scientific jurisprudence in the modern sense.[XXI]

Another threshold difficulty that is involved in any effort to evaluate a major figure is to set him or her in the "seamless web" of history and then show what particular merits make him stand out. Gény was very much in the mainstream of his time. Since the jurisprudential dimension is more obvious, let me talk first about how Gény was connected and synchronized with the new currents in the nonlegal fields.

Even on scanning the table of contents of the first volume of *Science et technique*, one becomes aware of how the then-emerging modern empirical-theoretical conception influenced Gény's vocabulary and perspective. New ideas, developing contemporaneously in many countries, spread and interacted apparently as much by intellectual osmosis as by semiconscious association and admitted reception. So, the role Gény ascribes to intuition in the transformation of his *donné* into the rules of law comes admittedly from Bergson's *La philosophie nouvelle*. But the resulting gestalt conception of law is also akin to the ideas of two contemporaries about whom Gény apparently did not know: German philosopher Dilthey's distinction between description (*beschreiben*), the aim of the so-called exact sciences, and understanding (*begreifen*), the aim of the social sciences; and the philosophy of science of Alfred North Whitehead, which was eventually compressed into the injunction that "the final problem [is] to conceive the whole fact." Both ideas are, of course, of cardinal importance also to the new theoretical jurisprudence.[280]

To follow a different set of relations, there are passages in the *Méthode* that read like Holmes of 1881, like Brandeis of 1908, like Korzybski of 1935. Gény's call for sociological sources of legal decision and the "Brandeis brief" owe a common debt to Durkheim. Gény's line between logic and "legal technique . . . the mission of [which is to deal] with complex and dynamic realities of life . . . fluid economic operations"[158]—like Holmes's better epigrammatic formula, "not . . . logic [but] experience"—reacts to comparable extreme positivism, which dominated in the nineteenth century the European continental as well as the common law systems. In a different direction, jurisprude Gény and engineer-semanticist Korzybski,[238] starting from very different doctrinal backgrounds, converge on the need, in Gény's words, to "consider . . . abstract concept[s], which always deform the reality at some point . . . as pure hypotheses . . . to which the exigencies of life can never be sacrificed."[158]

Another example of the parallel development of an idea that owes more than anything to a similar reaction to a similar environment is a comparison of Gény and Ehrlich. Both acted on the same premise: that the idea of the hermeneutic completeness of the codes is a fiction and, as a corollary, that there are gaps in the written law. Although differently shaded and proportioned, their triple-pronged responses are similar: the gaps must be filled by the *judge* drawing on the *society* as source and using *experimental-inductive* rather than formal-deductive ("logical") method. And yet, both Gény[158] and Ehrlich[117] made it clear that despite the common lineage and reference this response was independent.[XXII]

Gény was, of course, not only an integral part of this onward rush of ideas that were introducing modernity in all human, social, and natural sciences. He also represented the other perspective on any forward movement in time: the passage from the past through the present into the future. Although we are most interested in the future, to evaluate Gény requires also a look at the past and at that part of his present that the past stifled rather than stimulated.

It is not necessary to criticize or regret, as many did, but merely to state the fact: by being a bridge between the old and the new —a position taken very deliberately and consistently—Gény was not only a progressive but also a conservative.

I am not talking now about how various observers looked at him at various points in time and from changing perspectives. I do not have in mind comparisons with, for instance, the fate of his contemporary Planiol, who was first greeted with "nonunderstanding," and, "when the *Traité élémentaire* was recognized, those who a few years earlier called him too radical, now characterized him as too traditional," or—as Duguit did—labeled his work the "swan song of antiquated capitalism."[354] I refer to intrinsic elements of Gény's conservatism in doctrine, in personal philosophy, in mode of thought: the dogmatic argument in favor of his pragmatic thesis, the occasional hairsplitting scholasticism, the vocabulary and style.

To what extent Gény's intellectual manner and approach were further conditioned and complicated by purely personal psychological factors, including a certain linguistic and general provincialism, is a matter for gentle conjecture. For the fact there is enough evidence in the work even after some of the more ephemeral notes have been edited out of the translation.[158]

Born in Lorraine, Gény was fluent in German and obviously had at least a good working knowledge of Italian. But his *Méthode* and its sequels would have been possibly different books had he had comparable facility in English. (But, if Gény was regrettably parochial with regard to the common law world, what about the great internationalist Lambert, who cites Gény as reference for the proposition that "England and the United States are universally considered as typical examples of great nations living principally under a system of customary law" [*sic*]?[241, 369] Oddly enough, there is no record of Gény being involved in the great comparative law upsurge around the turn of the century or of the reasons why he was on the outside. His conservative insistence on legitimacy might be contrasted with the lack of qualms of a Lambert, a Planiol, or a Capitant.

It would be out of proportion, if not gratuitous, to dwell on this critique beyond the duty to record it. The greatness of Gény's contribution is unaffected, though his impact might have been. Moreover, it is obvious, although not quantifiable, that Gény's conservatism was to some extent a function of a formidable Establishment in the face of which he wrote. He himself speaks early in the *Méthode*[158] of "oppressive professional inheritance" and characteristically prefaces it by "if I may say so." The reference of a later commentator to an "adverse doctrinal climate"[63] sounds like an understatement.[XXIII]

Gény had a small, distinguished group of predecessors in France: Labbé, Bartin, Thaller, early Lambert, Saleilles. But the real winds of change were only in the making when Gény wrote his *Méthode* in Dijon (for instance, Planiol) or were stimulated on the appearance of the *Méthode* (Capitant, mature Lambert, late Saleilles).

So Gény was alone and insecure. His quite obvious strategy was to have the greatest practical impact. The tactic he chose was to make it appear that he was on the whole merely correcting some aberrations in the traditional system rather than discarding the system itself. In this frame of reference it was almost inevitable that some superfluous and confusing *ifs* and *buts* would be interpolated. The certainty of the law, anchored in the codes, had to be constantly stressed, since the instinctive human quest for certainty was then (as now) the source of the conservatism of the legal Establishment and the perspective in which any new method or technique was judged.

The idea of "free search" cut the historical legislator down to size and legitimated in fact a new source of judicial decision making, which he did not create expressly. This was an almost subversive position. So Gény found himself preparing the way by saying, "Let us have the courage to confess our faithfulness to tradition and our attachment to authorities,"[157] and by taking the perhaps compensatory regressive position on the formal status of decisional law. His equation of the decisional law with the obviously much less authoritative *doctrine*, the opinions of private scholars, looks in this perspective very much like an act of good manners toward the club whose members he was often taking to task on merits.

In such a more complete perspective, Ripert's quip—"They [the free-search group] are more conservative than it would seem because it is the nature of lawyers and because they were all schooled by the same teachers and positive method"[353]—appears more entertaining than profound despite the fact that the ritualism of *le texte* left some indelible traces even on Gény. Villey's judgment is probably closer to the mark: "Gény's manner is not to lead the attack. With a perfectly legal prudence, which recalls the prudence of Roman jurists, he prefers to think corporatively, or at least with a portion of the guild."[406, xxiv]

To say all this, even when it might sound critical, adds to rather than diminishes the greatness of Gény's work. If he was basically a conservative, firmly anchored in the past, so much bigger the merit of his own *au délà*. Comparisons with the American jurisprudential prophet Holmes impose themselves at this point. Like Holmes, Gény was not only a prolog, but also an epilog. A universal thesis of such grandiose proportions as Gény's is perhaps inevitably subject to the quip, ascribed incidentally to Holmes, that consistency is the quality of narrow minds. Most important, like Holmes's thought and despite the apparent ideological difference, Gény's doctrine has not only survived but in fact has gained in relevance and applicability as time has gone by.

G

The measure of any work on jurisprudence is the impact it has on future problem analysis and solving. The indicators are in Gény's case (*a*) the subsequent scholarly literature, (*b*) the practical application of the free-search method, (*c*) the validity of his work for the purpose of the continuing analysis of the legal process, especially of lawmaking through decision. I shall discuss the scholarly literature in this portion of the first essay, the practical test of the free-search formula in the second essay, and Gény as a point of departure for contemporary jurisprudence in the last essay.

In evaluating the follow-up on Gény, one must try to balance judgments about substance and form. On both accounts Gény made the real follow-up (rather than only praiseful or critical evaluations) somewhat more difficult than was necessary. This I will illustrate when I discuss a little later the various "variations on a theme by Gény."

Before that I must point out that a substantial group of writers, even sympathizers, were a priori disqualified or at least handicapped as effective continuators because they suffered from various degrees of intellectual immunity to Gény. By immunity I mean here an aprioristic conceptual framework, too rigid to permit critical investigation and understanding of fresh ideas that can become effective analytical tools. One thinks inevitably of scientists without microscopes or physicians without X rays. This lack of penetration of the deep structure of Gény was shown to a surprising extent still in the volume commemorating the hundredth anniversary of his birth and published in 1962.[308,XXV] The most striking example has been the massive misunderstanding of Gény's subtle subterfuge in connection with his apparently dogmatic insistence on the subjective *ex tunc* interpretation of statutes.

Besides conceptual and even national provincialism, there was also a linguistic barrier to understanding. The difficulty of reading Gény in the original and the inferior quality of most partial and total translations have been obstacles to the transmission of the precious subtleties in, and implications of, his thought.[XXVI]

As to specific ideas or intellectual fibers that have been woven into later literature, one might in a more voluminous essay try to trace and systematize them. I doubt that such a quantification would add anything to knowledge except volume in a branch of literature that already, with important exceptions, commands attention only by its volume. Apparently also a good deal of osmosis has taken place. However, a selective listing may be useful.

The first group of variations on a theme by Gény deals with formalism and conceptualism in the legal process and doctrine, combined with the thesis of the superiority of legislative lawmaking. One would like to feel that much of this critical follow-up on Gény actually tears down straw men. Literature and case reports are, however, full of evidence that this topic addresses itself to a latent phenomenon in law and that "every generation must rediscover [the] truth for itself."[72,XXVII]

The second, closely related theme is the scope and legitimate projection of legislated law and the corollaries of any doctrine other than absolute "logically necessary completeness of the legislated [code] system."[XXVIII] These corollaries are the recognition and delimitation of gaps, and the freedom of the judge to fill them, that is to "make law." Gény cut here as sharp an edge as he was capable of. His purpose and tactics were not always understood.[XXIX] The largely parallel rather than derivative German free-law movement was abortive, and Gény rejected it.[158] There is no other "beyond" in the literature on this point.[XXX]

The third and logically next theme is the source of the decision that must be made outside the existing normative apparatus (though within the existing legal system). The issue here is not the classification and method of the free search, but its value content. This aspect of the doctrine Gény only barely outlined in the *Méthode*. Even when the whole axiological apparatus of *Science* is taken into account—the hierarchy of the *données*—it is probably correct to say with Stone[385] that, despite "frank and brave effort," Gény made little progress toward "making explicit his theory of justice."[XXXI]

With some extrapolation and translated into simple language, Gény seems to say nothing else than that law consists of policy and norm, in that order. "Policy" corresponds to Gény's "science" and includes the *data*, the nature of things, and the *value judgment*, which determines the selection of the *specific principle of justice*. "Norm" corresponds to "technique," the articulation, on the basis of "science," of the legislative or decisional rule.

The formula must be combined with the thesis of the *Méthode*. Thus completed it would read: law consists, in all its phases, of policy and norm. Although this sounds axiomatic, it is not implemented even today everywhere at all times. There is a continuous stream of mechanical jurisprudence and much evidence of the same state of mind in literature.

Gény himself kept on talking about this simple and organic policy-norm scheme until the very end (note his own summary at the end of *Science*) in a confusing mélange of terms and hierarchical relations between the "scientific elements . . . which should normally prevail over . . . the technical elements of the elaboration of law" and the "conflict between written positive law and natural law . . . [in which] positive law should in principle prevail."[159,XXXII]

The need to infuse social interests and values into the application of law has been one of the most worked over topics in this corner of the doctrine since Gény. The only major exception —Kelsen and his neopositivist followers—helped, in the typically dichotomous fashion, to group all these "opponents" under the sociological banner. Whether the label is correct or not, the new substance in the doctrinal sequel has been meager.

In French literature in particular, there is no important linking of law and values until the contemporary Carbonnier, writing fifty years after Gény. Moreover, the term *sociologie de droit* has been vulgarized to mean everything beyond law in the narrowest sense of positive rules.[308] The capacity of the legal mind to protect itself by macroconcepts against the need for hard extensional thinking is apparently unlimited.[289]

The American realists have drawn in their "sociological" dimension on Gény as well as on the more immediate Pound, both of whom moved from opposite points toward a common mean. An apparently fresh thrust is the "causal series" thesis, by Gény's confirmed disciple Dualde.[109] In contemporary parlance, it might be called *systemic* interpretation and application of law. But it is not developed beyond generalities. This is typical of the unsatisfactory state in this corner of jurisprudence. Sixty years after Gény, legal axiology as a genuine social science still waits for its masters.[XXXIII]

Finally, Gény's gestaltlike conception of the process, whereby the data are transformed into a rule in the course of free search, has been developed not only by the American realists but also, before them and contemporaneously with them, by a number of European writers. Gény developed his intuitionism in *Science* in reference to free search only, not also to decision making based on positive law. Hence the so-called hunch-decision thesis is much more comprehensive. But it is hardly a genuine *au délà*. On this point Gény was left behind by the better doctrine already during his time.

The same is true of the recognition of decisional law as a full-fledged formal source in continental Europe and by some Latin American writers. In retrospect the point seems largely formal. It remains to be seen whether Gény's position is not analytically more correct, although it rests on wrong formal grounds.

H

Can this complex phenomenon that is François Gény and his teaching be summed up in some neat, concise fashion? It must be patently obvious by now that to identify him with some school, even his own (Olgiatti proposed the label Nancy School), is to miss completely the point. Gény was rather one of the first contributors to the sweeping trend that the sociologists later came to call "modernization." The derogatory epithet "eclectic," hurled at him by latter-day Schoolmen, is in fact a badge of honor. It marks the mode of synthesis, the turn from a priori monistic speculation to empirical scientific method. This direction, not some overarching dogmatic "theory," explains the universal nature of Gény's doctrine—the fact that it remains a meaningful, functional reference three generations after him, in a quickly moving world that long ago forgot or set aside the philosophically more pristine but empirically innocent criteria of Gény's contemporaries and critics.

What would be, in the last analysis, the principal features of Gény's doctrinal signature?

First, he was the most articulate and comprehensive of the writers who assigned the judge the central place in the life of law: "There must be some intermediary between the complex, varied, and evasive needs [of the life of law] and the rigid formula of the statute. . . . This intermediary . . . is the judge."[157] Only fifty-five years later would Ripert write, "The birth and death [of the statute] can be decided upon only by the legislator. . . . But during its life it escapes the domination by its creator."[353]

Second, Gény "indicated the foremost problem of the legal order: accurate delimitation of . . . the exercise of judicial discretion,"[306] but recognized that "no matter how broad discretional power we give to the judge, its exercise cannot constitute any interference in the legislative sphere as long as the authority of the judicial decision remains limited to the particular case."[157]

Third, he conceptualized the task of finding the "ought to be" when the "is"—the applicable positive rule of law—is lacking; and he found in "sociology . . . the practical tool," the policy source for the rule of decision, as well as a source of "higher principles that [positive law] cannot violate . . . a more complex system, which, on the one hand, tries to enlarge the formal sources and assign each a place according to its nature; and, on the other hand, recognizes that outside the sphere of these sources, clearly delimited, there is a need for free interpretation [or search] that is subject only to the fact it is supposed to govern and to the requirements of any scientific investigation."[159]

Fourth, Gény introduced (Holmes rather only postulated, though practiced) a modern comprehensive conception of things, "integral experience," under the influence of Bergson. This was first appreciated in America by Cardozo,[60] with reference to, among others, John Dewey's *Human nature and conduct* (1922), but with a strange omission of Gény's key sentence: "What is missing in conceptual analysis must be supplemented by a multiple, diverse, and metaphorical view, which provides us with an integral experience, not only revealing but also informing and creating."[159]

None of the preceding points of criticism, as even as they may be, can reduce the stature of these achievements. It is the essence of a seminal thinker that he does not travel the whole road but that he makes a decisive turn onto it; that his hypotheses stir the imagination of others far in the future; that he shows the method. On all these points, the applied and comparative perspective of the remaining essays will, I believe, only further separate the living figure of François Gény from his many contemporaries and successors who are today mere names in legal history.

ESSAY TWO

The telling test

A. Article 1, Swiss Civil Code: Origins
B. Aplication of Art. 1: The conceptual framework
C. The ups and downs of the pretorian power
D. The paradoxical result
E. Attempt at an explanation: Fictions and realities
F. The doctrine: Contributory responsibility
G. Comparisons and conclusions

This essay is dedicated to the memory of
Walter Yung (1900–1974),
foremost Swiss interpreter of Gény
and a great human being.

A

I trust that, without insisting too much on the point, the analysis of Gény's doctrine as a whole supports the proposition that all that is new in Gény is already stated in the *Méthode*. Even if the doctrinal follow up on this seminal work were more substantial, it would still befit Gény's empirical orientation to look to practice as the true testing ground and indicator.

By a historical coincidence, the Swiss Civil Code (ZGB, standing for *Zivilgesetzbuch*) was being drafted at the same time Gény was finishing and publishing his *Méthode*. As a result of ideological affinity, if not osmosis, between Gény and the chief author of the ZGB, Professor Eugen Huber, the central theme of the *Méthode*—the "free objective search" to fill gaps in legislated law—was adopted as one of the methodological pillars of the Swiss code. Since the code was promulgated in 1907 and entered into force in 1912, the free-search method has been subject to practical test under a legislative mandate for over two generations. This is the "telling test" that I propose to discuss here.

Let me briefly restate the methodological situation: (1) it is in the public interest that all legal controversies (that is, all conflicts over interests protected by law or considered as deserving such protection) be decided; (2) the legislator (even when acting as systematic code maker) cannot foresee and regulate all possible cases; (3) this has been solved in modern times, since the Napoleonic Code, by ordering the judge in various grammatical forms to decide the case before him even if there is a gap in the legislated law; (4) the two recognized techniques for filling the gaps are extensive (broad) interpretation and rule making by the judge (some codes have defined the sources other than statute to which he is to look for guidance); (5) the point at which the judge is free to declare that the rule for his case cannot be derived by any mode of interpretation is contested.

Three distinct positions have been taken with regard to this extreme situation: (*a*) insistence on interpretation at any cost, including the use of fictions concerning the legislative intent; (*b*) Gény's free-search method, which stops short of these fictions and declares thenceforth the field free for judicial rule making on the basis of empirical data; (*c*) the German free-law school, which denied to legislated law any other but concretely expressed meaning and declared the judge to be free from there on, a position that a Spanish commentator pithily described as converting the legal system into one big gap.[109]

Common and central to these discrete positions are the questions of the scope of the gap and of the legitimate extent of interpretation by analogy.

All the elements of the problem of judicial responsibility and power—the existence of gaps in law as statutes but not in law as legal order, the subsidiary sources for decision, and the responsibility and freedom of the judge to fashion a necessary new rule—were brought together in a brilliant formula in Article 1, paragraph 2, of the ZGB, which includes this crowning sentence: "[In the absence of any statutory provision or customary law] . . . the judge shall decide . . . according to the rule he would make as legislator." In addition to "established doctrine and decisional law," which the judge is directed to follow in this process (Art. 1, par. 3), he has also available the general standards of good faith (Art. 2) and of important (or just) grounds and equity (Art. 4).[XXXIV]

No wonder that Gény wrote in the epilog of the second edition of the *Méthode*, "not without some satisfaction," that "Article 1 of the Swiss Code . . . could be proposed as the best summary of my arguments." He lauds the "elegant conciseness"; he stresses that "the main merit of the Swiss legislator . . . is ethical. His action is frank, humble and detached, which is an interesting novelty in the history of codification."

The "legislator" is of course Huber, and a preliminary question of great interest arises at once: what influence did Gény have on Huber? What contribution to the history of the genesis of great ideas does this case make?

Impressionist commentators vary in their conclusions. The suggestion by Friedman[141] that Gény "anticipated" the Swiss formula seems generally close to the mark and is born out by recently revealed documentation, especially also correspondence between Gény and Huber.[150,151]

Gény denied "any paternal influence on the genesis of Article 1"[309] and even seemed to defend the independence of his free-search conception from the Swiss formula.[158] Yung comments that "this should be perhaps ascribed to [his] extreme modesty."[432]

A simple chronology is most revealing:

1. In November, 1899, Gény at the suggestion of Saleilles sent a copy of the just issued *Méthode* to Huber. On finishing the reading during the Christmas holidays, Huber immediately wrote to Gény about the pleasure the book gave him and how it "fortified and clarified" his own ideas. A few days later, Huber wrote to Rümelin, "Perhaps I can use something out of [Gény's book] for the introductory paragraphs to the [draft Swiss Civil] Code."[150]

2. Until about that time, Huber had been busy with drafts of the major substantive parts of the code, the last two being "Real

rights" and "Successions." They were ready in the German original in 1898, in French translations in 1899 and 1900.[266,151] Huber also had by that time drafts and notes on "preliminary title."[150]

3. Four months later, in April, 1900, Huber presented his draft of the preliminary title of the ZGB, including the first version of Article 1, to the governmental committee of experts. It was published with the date 15 November 1900.[368] On 10 January 1901, Gény wrote to Huber about "the great satisfaction with which I have noted the liberal and progressive formulae of Arts 1 and 2 which, as you correctly think, I can only applaud without any reserve."[432]

4. The first draft is, however, in fact less similar to Gény's scheme than the final version (agreed upon between 1904 and 1907). It differs principally not in the key formula of quasi legislation, but in the order of the sources. In the first draft, the statute is followed by customary law and by established doctrine and decisional law, in that order, as the sources the judge is to look to. Only "if he cannot derive the rule from any of these sources is he to decide according to the rule he would make as legislator."[368,295]

This chronology tends to correct Meier-Hayoz[296] whose evaluation I had considered "reasonable [and] comprehensive."[283] So does subsequent publication of Huber's papers.[150] But Meier-Hayoz raises the question of the broader environment, an idea that ought not to be overlooked. Gény refers back to Aristotle and Merlin as his inspirations. Huber was philosophically a neo-Kantian. But if he received the Aristotelian idea through Vangerow,[150] it was derived more directly from the Roman formula *ex aequo et bono*. Both Rümelin (who was Huber's colleague at Halle twenty years earlier)[359] and Heck[198] saw in the Swiss Article 1 the legislative expression of their "jurisprudence of interests." Reichel[350] makes the same claim in the name of the "right law" (*das richtige Recht*) conception of his teacher Stammler.[380] And, of course, there is always the need to recall the magisterial formula of Portalis.[XXXV]

For analytical purposes it is not essential to determine exactly to what extent Gény provided a model or inspiration for Huber or the degree to which both formulae represented parallel responses to the same stimuli. The important point is that the final version of Article 1 is identical to Gény's conception, including his hierarchy and classification of sources.

A comparison between the first and the final versions shows a reclassification downward of what Gény calls the authorities, from a position of subordinate primary sources of judicial rule making to mere models to follow. In this final form the article might seem to say the obvious: that there should be a continuity in deciding both with regard to prior decisions and to the existing doctrinal interpretation of the legal system. But the subsequent history, before the drafting committee of the Swiss Department of Justice and Police eventually returned to Huber's original formula, indicates a deeper motive for the change: the fear of judicial arbitrariness.[XXXVI] That point should not be lost in the subsequent analysis of what Swiss practice—which means essentially the Bundesgericht (federal high court), but also the *bar* writing briefs and arguing cases and the *professors* performing jurisprudential autopsy—did with and about Article 1(2), this twentieth-century resurrection of full-bodied pretorian power.[XXXVII]

B

To analyze the uses by the Bundesgericht of Article 1 is not an easy task. First, this is not a place for a commercial, but Switzerland does not have a Shepard citator. Even worse, many Swiss commentators—including recent ones[23] and in contrast to some of their contemporaries writing law review articles—identify cases only by the bare citation, without a name or year. Although this defect can be salvaged by a self-made card file or similar technology, it is much easier for quick orientation if the cue is, for example, the *Suisa* case (1948) or the *Suffragettes* Case (1957), rather than merely BGE 74 II 106 or BGE 83 I 173.[XXXVIII]

Second, the index of the official reports is apparently unreliable. Du Pasquier,[320] who made a study of decisional law related to Article 1 over a period of almost forty years, reported that six decisions he discovered from 1925 to 1934 were not listed in the corresponding decennial index. Since this was a period of what might be called the ascendency of Article 1(2), this omission has probably to do with the compilers rather than with the language of the judges. But that is of little consolation to the researcher.

Third, there is a problem of classification. Du Pasquier speaks of "the impressive abundance of decisions based on Article 1," but reports actually only an average of less than one case a year. The context and my search elsewhere[164] indicate that this smaller number comprises what might be called clear-cut applications of Article 1.

This fact would not be surprising in principle. One might think that, in the first forty years of a code as well drafted as the ZGB (though there are dissenting opinions on its quality),[266] gaps should be found only exceptionally. But these years, and the additional almost two decades since du Pasquier put together his statistics, were really much longer in terms of events and changes than the calendar count would indicate.

In fact there were abundant decisions in gap situations, but these were not explicitly based on the quasi-legislative power of the court. They were close to the "blurred line of division between lawmaking and broad interpretation." They could have been reached by judicial quasi legislation, but were not. The court tended to lean backward either to find no gap or to fill it through "interpretation" by analogy. The Swiss judicial practice has been marked under the new code, first, by an unequivocal adoption of or, rather, a continued adherence to the objective technique of interpretation; second, by a curious reversal at mid-century of the initial tendency to use Article 1(2) with some effect.

Before I illustrate the second conclusion by concrete reference to Swiss cases, it is convenient to clarify and further elaborate the semantic guide to the house of tricks and fictions that is the classical doctrine and method of interpretation.

The Swiss code, as distinguished from several others, does not prescribe specific canons for its interpretation. Swiss writers use the basic categories—subjective/*ex tunc*, objective/*ex nunc*—

which have been already explained with reference to Gény's doctrine. But the Swiss have made this further distinction:[295]

–*The objective-historical method.* (*a*) "The judge must first establish the meaning of the norm at the time it originated." (*b*) "The judge must develop the law when objective grounds command a deviation from the original [*ex tunc*] meaning." This is of course pure Gény (without citation!), except that contingency (*b*) is, for Gény, "free objective search," not interpretation.[xxxix]

–*The objective-contemporary method.* This is the classical *ex nunc* mode, which predominates in the Swiss practice. The objective mode preceded in Switzerland the express pretorian formula of the ZGB. The Bundesgericht had said already in 1896 that "the value of the statute rests much less on the will in which it originates than on its content envisaged by itself."[163,432] Paradoxically, this position may have reflected the strong tradition of local judiciary, but instead of blossoming out under Article 1(2), this pretorian tradition of the *Laienrichter* apparently helped to foster lack of confidence in professional federal judges.

The objective method was strengthened in the *Seethalbahn* case (BGE 34 II 815, 826 [1908]), where legislative history was declared to be "mere means of assistance . . . which lack any decisive weight where it contradicts that what must be derived, as the will of the statute with regard to the point in issue, from the statutory text, from the meaning and spirit of the statute in general, and from the practical purpose it is to serve. This volitive content of the statute exists by itself, objectified and separated from the opinions of individuals, which were expressed during the elaboration of the statute with regard to its future content." The court adds that, though the federal assembly consults on the eventual text of the law, the people give consent tacitly or through referendum only to this text, not also to the legislative record.

This doctrine suffered a temporary *reductio ad absurdum* in the hands of the public law chamber in 1914 in the *Reiser* case (BGE 40 I 559, 564–65). Conviction for violation of the law of explosives was upheld although the statute was explicitly enacted for the purpose of combating anarchism and the incriminated act was not so motivated. The Bundesgericht rejected this argument on the ground that the text alone is binding and that the delict is formulated in general terms, without any circumstantial restriction.

By 1955 (BGE 81 I 282) the formula reads: "As the Bundesgericht has repeatedly declared [one commentator lists thirteen opinions between 1934 and 1956],[163] it is not determinative what the legislative record contains or what was discussed in council by the legislating authority, but what is to be derived from the statute in the light of general principles of law, taking into account contemporary circumstances."[295]

One year later (BGE 82 I 150, 153 [1956]) the court expressly rejected the third principal method in the Swiss inventory, the subjective-historical method, and also by implication Meier-Hayoz' objective-historical compromise:[211] "Holding on rigidly to the concepts of the time when a statute was promulgated would be an obstacle to its adjustment to changed facts, circumstances, and viewpoints, and would lead to quick aging of the legislation."[163,295] But the next year, in the *Suffragettes* case (Quinche et al. c. Vaud, BGE 83 I 173, 179 [1957]), also a public law case to which I shall return later, it merely says that "the court has shown a certain reservation with regard to the historical method of interpretation," but, "if the legislative record permits to establish with perfect clarity the meaning the authors of the statute wanted to give to the terms they used . . . the Bundesgericht is of the opinion that it must conform to the intent of the historical legislator, unless the historically intended meaning . . . is incompatible with the statutory text or is absolutely unacceptable in practice." This doctrine was affirmed the same year in *Pantet c. Ministère public* (BGE 83 IV 121 [1957]), a criminal law case.[163]

The doctrine frankly admits that the objective method can consider the element of "permanent declaration of will"—the presumed constitutional basis of the force of the statute—only as a fiction, not as a "collective-psychological fact," and that it does not aim at ascertaining the "factual conscience-content of certain persons [the legislative body]" but only "a hypothetical conscience-content."[295]

The objective method of interpretation is, as Gény clearly recognized, the antithesis of avowed judicial rule making. No matter what the dicta or doctrinal rationalizations,[XL] the tactics of the objective method is for the *ex nunc* interpreter to read into the legislative text various and sundry norms and/or purposes that are not there. To placate the historical legislator, he uses, at least whenever possible, the words of the statute, which after all are still on the books even if they have little or nothing to do with the concrete case and justice.[XLI]

Closely related to the chosen mode of interpretation is the existence of the so-called gaps in legislated law. The historical, *ex tunc* interpretation is obviously more gap prone than the flexible *ex nunc* mode. The concept of gap in law is normally associated with the absence of words. But the first modern authoritative statement on gaps indicates that this is a too narrow conception. Article 4 of the French Civil Code speaks of "silent, unclear, or incomplete" statute. The words *silent* and *incomplete* refer obviously to a *verbal* gap.[XLII] If they are not tautological, they must mean the difference between the total lack of any normative statement and the absence of a specific word or words to cover the case to be decided.

But the code uses also the word *unclear*. This does not refer to the absence of words but to their meaning per se or in context. Thus we find in Article 4—and in spite of the awkward sequence of words—a clear reference to a second type of gap, a *semantic* one.[XLIII]

Finally, unless the statute in question is read in the narrowest frame of a fixed command, without any reference to legislative purpose or policy, then it may be silent, incomplete, or unclear with reference to this inner dimension, no matter how many words it contains. This is the third possible kind of gap, a *teleological* one.[XLIV]

Another major concept related to interpretation and gap filling is the technique of analogy. Two kinds of analogy are usually distinguished: the narrower one, *analogia legis*, which means a projection or extension of a statutory rule or combination of rules to cover the unprovided-for case; and the broader *analogia juris*, which is a decision with reference to the general principles of the legal system in question, without any specific mandate from the legislator.

But the process can be also inverted. Instead of arguing in favor of applying an existing rule to the unprovided-for case by analogy—that is, on the basis of similarities of fact and/or equity—it is also possible to argue that if the legislator knew or must be presumed to have known the facts or interests at issue but did not include them within his norm, then it must mean that he did not intend to so govern them. This is the so-called *argumentum e contrario*. Thus we have to make this further distinction between analogy, as a positive reference to the legislated law for the purpose of deriving a rule for the unprovided-for case, and the *argumentum e contrario*, as a negative reference—meaning the rejection of a rule that it would seem possible to derive by analogy, in favor of another, discrete rule.

Still another distinction has to do with the uses of analogy and of *argumentum e contrario*. Both can be used not only for the decisional purpose of formulating a new rule, but also for the purpose of interpretation of, and selection between, contrasting legislative rules.

Thus we have four types of analogies in the broad sense of reference to other rules or principles: positive and negative, interpretative and decisional. The need for these techniques is axiomatic. The dispute is not on the point whether analogy should or should not be used, but whether it is within the province of interpretation or whether it already represents, as Gény claimed, a form and technique of free search. If analogy is part of interpretation, then a rule, not intended by the legislator to cover the present case, is given normative power by the fiat of the judge, who pretends that he is in fact using a legislated rule. If analogy is of free search, then the legislated norm not directly applicable may still be more authoritative than other sources, but its essential value is statistical, alongside other policy or technical elements available for the confection of the new rule to fill the gap.[XLV]

All these considerations, including the inherent element of judicial psychology, have a direct bearing on the evaluation of the Swiss practice under Article 1. In fact, the preceding discussion of the various sources and procedures in the search for a rule to decide elaborates and paraphrases a scale that I constructed originally with reference to the Swiss decisional law and doctrine.[283,XLVI]

There is an additional dimension in Article 1 that should be brought out before we analyze its application in practice. This article must be read in the historical context of the nineteenth century dogma about the priority of substantive law over procedure. The resulting "view, firmly held at the time of its origin, [was] that judicial decision [the end result of procedure] represents always a subsumption of a fact situation under a [substantive] legal norm."[295]

This subordination of procedure to substance is patently erroneous in historical comparative terms, whether the reference is to classical Roman law, traditional Germanic law, prerevolutionary French law, or English common law. They all followed essentially the pretorian pattern: the generation of new substantive law through new remedies.

If the Swiss Article 1 is read in this organic context, the order to the judge to *decide* means to entertain proceedings (give remedy in the *procedural* sense) in order to determine whether a claim not covered by positive law ought to be protected by a particular ad hoc ruling (remedy in the *substantive* sense). The reference to the "legislator" in Article 1(2) means that as a particular lawmaker the judge must use the same data and intellectual processes as a legislator would and is bound (Art. 1, par. 3) to follow already available normative or doctrinal conceptualization (something a wise legislator will also follow, without any explicit mandate).

It is not insignificant that this complete and obviously analytically correct meaning of Article 1 has to be pried out by such an extensive comparative interpretation, instead of being semantically facilitated by its own phrasing, for example: The judge shall decide [even in the absence of statutory or customary rule]. In formulating the particular rule for decision, he shall proceed as if he were a legislator. He shall follow established doctrine and decisional law where applicable. In its actual form, Article 1 carries a semantic imprint of the very doctrine of legislative monopoly (with its emphasis on substantive law), which it tries to correct.[XLVII]

C

Despite the less than exceptionally propitious tradition of judicial practice, inclinations, and concepts, Article 1(2), did have an initial impact. It could even be said that "in the first thirty to forty years the decisions exuded confidence in the suppletory mission of the judge."[432] The principal form and indicator of this mission was the substantial broadening of the scope of gap in the teleological direction. The following series of *rationes* and dicta show the rise, direction, ambivalence, and fall of the concept of teleological (or policy) gap to be found by judges and then filled by judicial rule making.

In 1925 (BGE 51 II 412), the Swiss court declared simply that, "where the text is insufficient to resolve a question, the judge should complement it according to his own judgment." This is plainly what, for example, Article 4 in the French Civil Code orders, but the Swiss dictum goes frankly and courageously beyond the text of its own Article 1. The court says in the same case:

> The existence of a gap to be filled judicially must be admitted not only when a given fact situation is not covered by any statutory provision. It must be admitted also when there is such a provision, but its application to the specific case obviously does not correspond to the true *ratio* of the statute according to its meaning, its text and context. In such a case one cannot speak of simple equity lying outside the positive legal system, which could be considered only in the presence of a clearly and categorically expressed legislative will. On the contrary, the true content of the law, which the judge must find and apply, is at issue.

In this case, involving preferred stock in companies with limited liability, the court specifies the equity issue by saying that "justice would seem to require the recognition of [the controverted] subrogation."[320] This doctrine blossomed out fully in a first-impression case almost ten years later (Haus g. Graber, BGE

60 II 178 [1934]), which also involved the question of subrogation in a very complicated mortgage situation.

The *Haus* case involved the right of the creditor to sue the original debtor and the surety for the unpaid remaining portion of the debt. The situation is not specifically regulated in Swiss civil law. In his exposé of motives, Huber expressed the opinion that the solution could be clearly derived from the Code of Obligations. A corresponding provision was then scored out from the draft of the Swiss Civil Code. Huber's opinion, consistent decisional law of the canton of Zurich (where the *Haus* case originated) going back as far as 1856, and the lower decision were all unfavorable to Haus's appeal.

But the Bundesgericht went all the way:

> The Swiss civil legislation is not oriented toward the regulation of all legal relations without any gaps. . . . Rather, in many fact situations the statute provides no complete applicable rule, or at least no sufficient rule. Thus it is the duty of the judge to find or to supplement the law according to Article 1(2 and 3), ZGB. Such a gap to be filled judicially exists not only when a fact situation cannot be decided under any statutory provision at all. It exists also when this would be possible, but the application of the provision to the particular case cannot correspond to the true purpose of the statute according to its wording, content, and context. In such a case one cannot speak of simple considerations of equity outside the legal order, which could, indeed, not be taken into account against a clear and decisive legislative will. At issue is the true content of the law, which the judge is to find and to apply. In this sense it has been already decided [reference to the 1925 case cited above] that the judge must let himself be led by consideration of legislative policy not only when he fills the statutory gap but also when he examines the issue in controversy. In this perspective, trends that can be derived from the legislative record are also relevant.
>
> Thus, on the one hand, the proceedings of the consultation on the law [ZGB] indicate a gap. On the other hand, the upholding of the controverted subrogation is a mandate of justice, as the lower court correctly remarks (*cf.* also the decision of the cantonal court of St. Gallen, cited in the SJZ 1924, p. 29). Moreover, the legislator abstained from a specific subrogation provision under the impression that the existing law [Code of

> Obligations] already provided the judge with a sufficient lever to make a presumption about the transfer of creditor's rights in a case like the present one. And when we keep before our eyes the meaning and scope of the subrogation provisions contained in the law, the completion of the statute that is here in question imposes itself as something that cannot be rejected. [Pp. 185–87]

As a result, the court in fact ignored Huber's opinion of why it was unnecessary to legislate specifically and filled the gap according to equity and policy. It is perhaps not without importance that this particular court, the civil law chamber, was well briefed comparatively and found its model in the French Article 1252 and in § 268, section 3, of the German Civil Code.

At its best, the Bundesgericht filled gaps in a form that was incorporated in subsequent legislative amendments. Thus the court created the category of preferred stock, nonexistent in the Code of Obligations (BGE 59 II 48 [1933]), using as far as possible the analogy with ordinary stock, but with indicated differences. This regime was incorporated into the revision of the Code of Obligations three years later.[319]

Where the legislator did not freeze the decisional law, the court used its policy-making power with flexibility. To give a famous example, the Swiss law originally did not set any time limit on making known valid liens on property garnished in favor of another. The Bundesgericht declared a gap and decreed that the time limit should be ten days. This was a practice for over thirty years and became an integral part of the commercial custom. Then the court reversed itself and recognized the right to file any claim until the distribution, unless the lienholder acted in bad faith for the purpose of interfering with the normal course of the proceedings.[64]

Frequently, the court was more interstitial. It filled the gaps—or at least was able to make it look like it—"in harmony with the solutions derived by interpretation," using reference to "values inherent in the law,"[167] which is not a "heterogeneous mixture [*macédoine*] of separate provisions but a body of rules held together by a spirit."[319] It moved in the gray zone between *intra legem* and *praeter legem*, within and outside the statute. Thus, it filled gaps in the law that protected a critical press against irate members of the federal council (BGE 71 II 192 [1945]), as well as privacy against commercial exploitation (BGE 70 II 130 [1944] —the *Hodler* case, in which the widow of a famous Swiss painter was vindicated in her effort to withdraw from public display the deathbed scene painted for commercial purposes by an alleged student of Holder's).

But this process was not without ambivalence and seeds of destruction. It is notable that two contemporaneous writers—commenting on the peak case in the application of Article 1, paragraph 2, *Haus* v. *Graber*—would stress, on the one hand, that *Haus* stands for the proposition that "the judge must consider even legislative policy [*record*] in order to determine whether the statute has a gap"[432] and, on the other hand, that "only what has been expressed in the statute can be valid as legislative will."[163] The latter statement implies a rejection of the historical method of interpretation with its reference to the legislative record.

Indeed, while the court was conquering the peaks of the teleological and policy gaps, it also simultaneously cultivated the contrary, objective, *ex nunc* method of interpretation. Thus, for example, in the *Walter* case (BGE 50 I 334 [1924]: obligatory smallpox immunization), in a 1937 case involving industrial liability (BGE 63 II 143, esp. syll. 7), and in a 1952 case (BGE 78 I 14, syll. 4: jurisdictional federation-canton conflict about the utilization of navigable waters), the court brought to comparable heights its technique of interpreting a statute as the court reads it now, not as the legislator wrote it in the past.

Eventually the court began to draw back from the power that it generated for itself by developing the doctrine of teleological gaps. Although Article 1 speaks of text or (not *and*) interpretation and the court could have fallen back here on the traditional distinction of "letter or spirit" in the French version, a decision on a teleological gap does go potentially quite far. It has seemed difficult to draw a satisfactory line between a decision *praeter legem* (outside the law) or *juris supplendi gratia* (to supplement the law) and a decision *contra legem* or *juris corrigendi gratia* (to correct the law). The pretorian power of Article 1(2) did not seem sufficient to authorize the second variant. The Bundesgericht found it necessary to buttress such decisions by a fictitious reference to the legislator and his presumed intent. "The terms of the statute are too narrow," the court says in 1933 (BGE 58 II 443). "That cannot correspond to the legislative intent." Or, it states in an earlier decision: "It would be contrary to all sense of justice and therefore cannot conform to the intent of the statute" (BGE 55 II 17 [1929]).

This language is still on the side of Article 1(2). It may represent subtle differences among the various civil law panels of the court.[XLVIII] But by 1958 we read: "The statute does not have a gap unless its interpretation leads to so nonsensical and unjust results that nobody before 1912 [the year the civil code entered into force] could have intended them." This particular zoning and land expropriation case, *Stadt Zürich g. Teno* (BGE 84 II 402) seems to be an effort to interpret into an apparently clear text a policy consideration that was not effectively written into it. That may account for the strong language, though in an almost contemporary case—also a violation of a "clear" statutory rule by the lower court in a bankruptcy case—another public law chamber reached a similar result with merely a reference to "creating serious legal uncertainty" (Giorgetti c. Tribunal cantonal du Valais, BGE 85 I 77, 80 [1959]).

But the trend had been expressed ten years earlier in the *Suisa* case (BGE 74 II 109 [1948]). Here it was argued by the plaintiffs that, since only silent films were known in 1922, the Swiss copyright law of that year had a gap with regard to sound films and that therefore this gap should be either spanned by custom or filled by judicial rule making, in line with technological progress.

The court could have simply rejected the argument in favor of a rule different from the 1922 statute and relied on an intervening law on commercial exploitation and royalties (1940) in which the legislator clearly defined sound film as a work of tonal (phonic) art "performed through cinematography." In fact it decided on this basis. But the actual holding in *Suisa* is only in the nature of an appendage. In the preceding part of the opinion, the court unburdens itself on the subject of gaps and gap filling:

> The existence of a gap must not be assumed lightly. The judicial exercise of the lawmaking power, which is of course provided for in cases of extreme need (Art. 1, ZGB), represents a violation of the principle of separation of powers, a fundamental principle of modern democracy. The judge must therefore proceed with the making of new rules only where there is no doubt that a norm cannot be derived from the statute. If it is possible to solve a new fact situation through analogous use of existing legal prescriptions, the claim of a gap in the statute must be normally denied even if the resulting order is not the most expedient one. For expedience alone is not the factor that determines the existence of a gap.

The court makes then two additional points of jurisprudential interest:

> This retiring attitude is also in order since the judge is not in the position to hear all interested parties as the normal legislator can and must. To this must be added a final consideration. It may be generally assumed that the legislator will not leave without attention for a long time new conditions that require new legal ordering. If, therefore, a new institution, which has been known for decades, exists without the legislator seeing any reason to intervene, this represents generally an important indication that a solution can be in his opinion derived from the existing law, even if only by means of analogy with the basic principles the law contains.

Then follows what I suggested at the beginning as the sufficient, positive *ratio decidendi.*

Two years later, the court added the final touch to its doctrinal edifice by enthroning the concept that the legislator can legislate by not legislating. In this particular case (F.X. g. X. & Co., BGE 76 II 62 [1950]: relative interest of individual shareholders as against the corporation as a unit), the lower, cantonal court apparently tested, in light of the *Suisa* decision, the continued validity of the 1937 model of objective interpretation, which in fact sanctioned corrections of the historical legislator by the present interpreter. With specific reference to two decisions of the Bundesgericht (BGE 63 II 155; BGE 68 II 124), the cantonal court held (to cite from the opinion of the federal court):

> The possibility of a statutory gap was not excluded because according to the decisional law of the Bundesgericht it is allegedly not determinative what the legislator intended, but what is to be derived from the the text through grammatical and logical interpretation in the light of general principles of law. But the lower court fails to consider the opinion of the Bundesgericht that the existence of a gap must not be easily assumed. The mere desirability of a specific ruling is not a decisive factor in assuming that there exists a gap, especially when the legislator had the opportunity in another situation to take a position on the question whether new provisions were necessary.

The last part is a quotation from *Suisa*, so identified. In *Suisa* it was a dictum only, since the legislator had in fact legislated and the court had merely used its opinion as a vehicle for a jurisprudential pronunciamento. In the subsequent case, the legislator had not legislated. The dictum became the doctrine.

D

This has been the state of the law since 1948. The court has apparently not returned to this problem. The writers "have not considered it necessary to dispute the court's position."[195] A potentially big ripple was caused by the famous *Suffragettes* case, from which I have already cited. Antoinette Quinche and about a hundred other women residing in the canton of Vaud (the capital of which is Lausanne, the seat of the Bundesgericht) requested in 1957 that they be inscribed on the electoral list and be issued voting cards. This was rejected on the cantonal level on the grounds that the operative words of the cantonal constitution of 1885—"active citizens are all the Swiss who completed the age of twenty years"—were intended to indicate only men and have "strictly and intentionally" excluded women from the right to vote. Quinche *et al.* carefully attacked not the constitution itself but the concrete act of application as in violation of Article 4 of the federal constitution (equality); they argued in favor of "adaptation to the evolution of ideas" and against the conclusion that "feminine vote can be introduced only through constitutional amendment."

The court reviewed the decisional law, which built the objective interpretation up to the 1952 peak (BGE 78 I 30), but concluded that "an attentive examination of the decisions shows, on the contrary, that the court does not absolutely exclude any method but that it follows interpretation procedures that appear best indicated in the particular case in order to find the true meaning of the rule." It then proceeded to admit "a certain reservation with regard to the historical method," which I have already quoted. Nevertheless, in the instant case, "to deviate from the [absolutely clear] meaning willed by the legislator and confirmed by consistent [administrative] practice would be an act equivalent to the modification of the statute. Although the judge clearly possesses the power to supplement the law when it has a gap, he does not have, in turn, the power to modify it. This right belongs only to the legislative authority." The court disposed of the conflict with the equality clause of the federal constitution by referring to the consistent decisional law that had declared this issue to be not justiciable. The court, in fact, closed a possible loophole—complaint directed not against the constitution but against the administrative decision based on it—by saying that "the tendency of the court in prior cases . . . not to be seized of this question . . . is correct, and it is convenient to declare it as a general rule."

The case provoked considerable comment and critique. As Yung states,[432] it was the first time the court had upheld the subjective-historical method. It did it, indeed, with a big escape valve ("unless . . . absolutely unacceptable in [present] practice"). This formula turns the subjective-historical method potentially into objective-historical, which is a close variation on Gény's formula. But it does not blunt the critique of Hans Huber[211] that, still reaching the same result, the court could have refined and perfected its methodology.

The most important criticism is Germann's:[163] that the court did not adequately elaborate its arguments in favor of the subjective interpretation and that it based itself on dicta of a fifteen-year-old civil law, while ignoring a contrary position taken shortly afterward by another civil law chamber and the consistent decisional law since then, at least six holdings by both chambers.

This critique only confirms the impression that *Quinche* was an aberration, which may have brought some confusion into the doctrine and increased rather than eliminated uncertainty, but which has not changed anything. The court dusted off the subjective-historical interpretation only in function of a particular case in which it did not want to bring about by interpretation changes that it felt were for the legislator, even though corrective interpretation was feasible. In other words, the argument here was not about interpretation, but was the tool of a particular public law policy.[XLIX]

The "pure" objective doctrine, as culminated by *Suisa* and its sequel, reigns unchallenged.[L] The *Quinche* case, no matter the quality of the argument or the sociocultural context, was a classical and plausible separation-of-powers case. It is difficult, however, to agree with the apparently widely held conclusion that in *Suisa* the court did not change the existing practice but only defined more precisely the recognized principles.[195] There is always the question of how far you can go in terms of quantity before you change quality.

Suisa and the subsequent companion case *F.X. g. X. & Co.* appear to me to culminate a doctrinal development that has substantially changed the relation between the legislator and the judge as written into Article 1, ZGB. The court narrows the applicability of Article 1, paragraph 2, to the barest minimum. It insists on analogy. And it rules out explicitly the teleological gap —the most important type of gap in the long run, as the fact and value content of the code becomes more and more different from the original data. The Swiss legislator in fact did not specifically order recourse to analogy—as was the case in one of the ideological predecessors of the ZGB, Article 7 of the Austrian Civil Code of 1811—nor did he stipulate that the "prescription [to] be drawn from the statute" is not to be evaluated in terms of concrete justice. The intention was demonstrably the opposite.[LI]

Thus the *Suisa* doctrine appears to be correcting a "deviation" from the separation-of-powers principle in the direction of sharing powers, which is implicit in Article 1(2). Inasmuch as the purpose of this provision, expressed in the legislative history,[210] was to turn the judge into an ad hoc legislator under well-specified conditions and procedures, the court's doctrine in *F.X. g. X. & Co.* that the judge must abstain from lawmaking where there *is* a gap, although the legislator has had an opportunity to rule, changes for all practical purposes the quality of Article 1.

This is the paradox of these decisions: by deciding, in the name of separation from and subordination to the *regular* legislator, not to fill a positive gap, the court *qua* legislator in fact exceeded its mandate under Article 1 and thereby changed its legal scope and purpose—something it had no power to do. An accompanying paradox is that this philosophy in fact strengthened the objective method of interpretation by means of which the court constantly adjusts the legislator, but does it under guises and fictions.

E

If we consider the mechanics of decision making, which seem to have many common denominators in the various countries, an opinionated decision of the *Suisa* type was probably a combination of a hard case and an articulate majority spokesman in the conference. But another ingredient was also necessary: a sufficient latent uneasiness that suddenly found a focus and an outlet.

This impression is supported by an opinion close to the event, that of du Pasquier. He was professor at Lausanne, where the court sits, and he wrote shortly after the *Suisa* decision. His explanation is political. The reemphasis on the separation of powers might have responded to the rise of the authoritarian regimes after 1933 and to the "vertigo caused by the recognition of where a deviation from respectful deference for the texts might lead."[320]

The reaction that Du Pasquier suggests has been part of a general European experience, expressed also by German[34] and by Italian writers.[32] Germann[166] injects into the argument the "government of law" maxim, but that hardly adds analytical power.

Moreover, one can easily turn the court's own dictum on separation of powers against the judges and suggest that, since the new situation of political danger to democracy existed for fifteen years before *Suisa* and the legislator did not consider it necessary to amend a provision as relevant to the distribution of powers as Article 1(2), he in fact legislated by not legislating. In reality there was no evidence of abuses of this power in civil law, which the legislator would have had to correct by new legislation. Even more important, the Bundesgericht was quite activist in constitutional cases throughout the crucial preceding decades,[305] and the legislator did not see any reason to correct or curtail it.

The political thesis also contrasts strikingly with a widely held other opinion: that it was precisely the subordinated, bureaucratized judiciary that represented no bulwark to such a regime as Hitler's, and that an independent judiciary of the English or American type would have done better. But neither analysis seems satisfactory. To come back to Switzerland, the situation is obviously more complex. It needs comprehensive technical analysis, the kind that does not eliminate a priori any considerations, including psychological, cultural, or political elements. As a preliminary to an outline of this kind of diagnosis, it is necessary to make some distinctions.

First, in the virgin areas where there is no legislation at all—*e.g.*, conflict rules in the field of obligations, revision of contracts because of changed conditions (*rebus sic stantibus*), precontractual responsibility, etc., to mention only some examples from one major field—the federal court has created decisional law out of whole cloth.[432]

Second, where the legislator has spoken, the court has subordinated itself. But as the survey of the court's doctrine indicates, this subordination, even when proclaimed as loudly as in *Suisa*, was in fact more formal than real. The objective interpretation, which has been by far the predominant mode,[295] is a subordination not to the legislator but to legislated words interpreted from the contemporary viewpoint. The oft repeated formula is "taking into account contemporary circumstances and technical development." Since this amounts to filling the verbal shells with a changing content, the proclamation in *Suisa* about all interested parties having the opportunity to be heard in the legislative process, but not in the court, sounds hollow.

A third point, which must be mentioned preliminary to a technical analysis, is the lack of an important vehicle for judging the arguments and the temper of the court: published opinions that dissent from the majority. The *Suisa* decision is widely known not to have been unanimous. The fact that alternatives to a majority decision, whether concurrent or dissident, are not available outside the chamber also tends to dampen the generation (and stimulation) of new ideas in the natural growth process of the decisional law. Even the best corps of doctrinal writers cannot quite make up for this organic dimension, as the *Ecole-Palais* dichotomy has shown.

At any rate, these observations tend to temper any quick first impression that the Swiss judiciary has become too conservative to do at all the kind of work that Article 1 invited it to. The Bundesgericht has created a great deal of new law. It has developed mechanisms that have allowed it to be flexible. Article 1 offers a perfect example. Paragraph 3 does not list decisional law as one of the sources; it establishes an obligatory *stare decisis.*[432] The court has reacted sensibly: the committee of judges that selects cases for publication often omits "first" cases. This makes a subsequent reversal easier.[305,163,166]

But the fact remains that although authorized by the legislator the judges have, in Yung's words, "frequently dissimulated their quasi legislation under the cover of interpretative artifices. [Esser speaks of 'interpretative disguise'[125]] thus succumbing to a tendency that Gény so resolutely and correctly denounced."[432] Yung raises the crucial question of whether Article 1 has made any difference in Swiss practice. Most commentators agree that it has not.[LII]

The practical result appears anti-Gény, but one must be careful not to make comparisons in favor of free search in the same dogmatic spirit in which resistance to it may have been rationalized. Free search for what? Obviously for better total results, on the twin assumption that (*a*) separation of powers must in practice mean balanced sharing and the distribution of powers that Gény postulated and Eugen Huber wrote into Article 1; and (*b*) that contemporary behavioral and social sciences, including jurisprudence, have progressed enough to eliminate the necessity of the "classical" fictions in law.

The extent of the use of fictions as tools in making decisions and rationalizing them can be considered a direct indicator of the state of jurisprudence. The less good the theory that analyzes, explains, and guides the practice, the greater the need for fictions. In an often fumbling and, by definition, *ad hoc casum* fashion, the judges in a developed system do what needs to be done to achieve workable justice, no matter what the words of the law. But in a constitutional system they also have to explain it and make it look legal. The less *technically* sound base they find for this in doctrine, the greater is the *psychological* need for fictions and pretenses, for these are spans and fillers needed to supplement the power and reach of reasoning. Reasoning is limited by the lack of a deep enough understanding of the operational model of the sociolegal system. This understanding has also an important psychological effect: the judges (it applies to any comparable decision makers) become more confident about their place, duties, and powers. This state of mind can only improve their performance.

This is, I believe, one of the keys to the question about the effective atrophy of the Swiss Article 1. The component of judicial psychology has been slightly implied in the literature. Either the suggested answers are too general and facile to have analytical usefulness[38,166] or the writer merely advises that psychological inquiry would be useful.[305] Ehrenzweig, referring to my very tentative remarks in the introduction to the translation of Gény's *Méthode*,[283] suggests an interesting hypothesis in an article on psychoanalytical jurisprudence:[116] that the Swiss experience may illustrate the eternal conflict between ego and superego, reality and ideal. But this begs the question. Why should the ideal be a doctrinaire edifice, which must be adapted to the needs of life by fiction and subterfuge?[LIII]

Closer to the Swiss judicial psychology might be some cultural underpinning of what on the technical level appears to be an excessive subordination of the judges, or at least their feeling that they should so appear. There was a cultural element of mistrust in the very process of drafting Article 1(2). I have already mentioned the suggested changes in Huber's wording, indicating a fear of his liberal formula. One could understand this in reference to revolutionary France of the 1790s, reforming its law against the background of arbitrary legislation by decision in the Parlements. But in Switzerland the judges were, even before the code, traditionally free to "go beyond the text."[126] So, Huber could write to Gény[432] that Article 1 was less a revolutionary innovation than the sanctioning of a legal tradition. Germann stated still in his lectures in Montpellier in 1956 that the formula of Article 1 "was particularly suited to the mentality and psychology of Swiss judges who, in one form or another, have previously participated in establishing such [quasi-]legislative rules in their cantons or communities."[166] Nevertheless, there was a definite resistance to putting it down in writing. This current of opinion did not prevail in the textual formula, which was eventually enacted as Huber proposed it (though with a significant change in the value of decisional law). But these well-known circumstances may have provoked an undercurrent of self-mistrust in the judiciary, which the eventual words of Article 1 could not entirely overcome. This psychological impediment seemed practically glossed over in the first decades of the application of the ZGB. It certainly does not interfere with the current practice of the objective doctrine of interpretation. But this is, significantly, judicial lawmaking *sub rosa*, not open and avowed.

Closely related to the psychological-technical dimension of the problem is Gény's early opinion (1904),[155] later expanded, that a free-search system can function only with "an independent and highly cultured" judiciary; thus, in Switzerland, "the system of [judicial] elections combined with the introduction of non-professional elements into the judiciary has created, at least on the lower jurisdictional levels, a judicial corps which offers only mediocre guarantees of impartiality, high purpose and learning." This opinion has been voiced also by various Swiss writers.[158]

The Bundesgericht, in spite of being an elective corps, is in fact a professional court with practical tenure. As far as quality is concerned—an indicator that inevitably changes with the different constellations of personalities—it is difficult on the basis of the available data to go beyond the inferences that can be drawn from the preceding account. An outsider who has made the most detailed on-the-spot study of the court—though inevitably affected by a political science background and a concentration on public law—concludes generally less favorably on the judges' performance in the perspective that interests us here. He attributes the regression from the appropriate and open participation of the judges in maintaining the law, notable also in the area he studied, precisely to "the change from politically oriented judges to professional judges." He concludes, "Whatever the cause, the positivism of Kelsen has carried the day."[305,LIV]

F

These and other possible circumstances—for instance, the relative conservatism related to political or religious affiliation of the judges—do not seem to offer the whole answer. Some are symptoms rather than causes. A judicial corps of twenty-six, deliberately selected to cover the geographical, political-ideological, and ethnic-linguistic spectrum, must be a microcosm reflecting to a large extent the community as a whole. But it is also a leadership group, entrusted with a specific power mandate, which it has administered in less than complete, faithful (in the sense of the original intent), and consistent fashion.

The psychological and historical-cultural handicaps could have been overcome only by a clear intellectual model built on and around Article 1 (2 and 3)—that is, the pretorian obligation and the sources of the quasi lawmaking based on it. To be useful, such a model must be in a state of constant interplay with the real world. It can never be ahead of the practical data on which it was originally built and which it must continuously follow and adapt to. Otherwise it would be a piece of speculation about what "ought to be," a set of untested hypotheses.

Yet such a model leads practice because it sorts out, articulates, and generalizes data and synthesizes them as operational concepts and relations. Thus it shows practice where it is going, whether it moves in the direction it thinks, and how it could more effectively get where it wants to.

A well-constructed model allows for incorporation and management (orderly even if only pro tem) of new data not originally envisaged and for flexible adjustment of its matrices to important shifts in the data. It reduces improvisation and ad hoc decisions to a minimum. It indicates what the organic, alternative solutions are within the system, or at least provides for orderly patterns of deriving such solutions. Because of its comprehensive conceptual framework, the model also allows the incorporation of examples and concepts from the outside (*e.g.*, through comparative research), which are systematically compatible. It has built-in, self-correcting feedback loops.

The standard metaphor that illustrates the relation between daily practice and any degree of theorizing is the one about the trees and the forest. For our purposes, the metaphor needs an additional dimension. The implicit horizontal perspective merely tells us that there is a forest (a system, a gestalt phenomenon) rather than only so many trees standing together. We must add a vertical perspective (a satellite photo, in today's technology) to look inside the forest and see how it could be best charted and "developed."

A supplementary poet's metaphor offers itself at this point. "Improving" on Oscar Wilde a little, we can say that "Life/practice, imitates art, or doctrine"—and can be stymied by it, though never completely blocked. If there is no model to imitate, life goes on but proceeds artlessly.

This seems to be the story of Article 1(2) and of the Bundesgericht in a nutshell. The applied moral of Oscar Wilde's aphorism is that the more responsible party is not the life/court but the art/doctrine. Even on the least ambitious scale—empirical analysis and linear synthesis—the job of attending to jurisprudence is not for the practitioner, but for the theorist. (He may be, of course, an inhabitant of both worlds—a professor turned judge, a judge or practitioner who can stand still and back enough to get a wide field of vision and perspective and who has the talent and stamina to communicate his findings. But these are exceptions.)

The scope and value of my judgment about the Swiss situation is, of course, severely limited. First, it would be unscientific to evaluate the state of national jurisprudence on the basis of only a selection of published literature, no matter how representative it may be considered, rather than of the state of legal and general culture, which may be influential though not reduced to published materials. Second, at the present time, the best published sources are five to ten years old. Third, there were signs in the 1960s of comparative-analytical trends in Switzerland that could indicate an approaching age of jurisprudential maturity and sophistication.[166,295] Fourth, law being one of the social technologies, jurisprudence is worldwide relatively the most backward theoretical component among the major technical or social technologies.[289]

Thus my judgments are not conclusions, but rather in the manner of working hypotheses for what could be a most productive multidisciplinary effort by a team of cultural historians, social psychologists of the small-group variety, legal technicians, quantitative analysts, and theoretical synthesizers. But these impressionistic hypotheses are stated with a considerable confidence in their probability.

Self-evaluations of the state and role of Swiss legal doctrine range from optimistic, almost promotional views about the coordination between the doctrine and the court[433] to self-inflicted limitations—for instance, the view that the "proper purpose of theoretical consideration is to make available substantial *rationes dubitandi*" (nothing more than raising questions?).[180] Meier-Hayoz[295] points out that "doctrine contributes with basic investigation of judicial practice and the establishment of theoretical foundations. . . . the most marked influence . . . is on the principles of methodology. . . . The predominant trend in the jurisprudence has impact—mostly after a certain 'period of incubation' —on the grounds of judicial decisions, for instance . . . the recent doctrinal return from the objective-contemporary method predominant in the first four decades of this century, to greater recognition of the historical roots of legal norms." Germann defines, with respect to the same forty-year period, the "principal task of law professors . . . to overcome the deeply rooted positivist method."[161] Gutzwiller's chosen standard perhaps explains why he feels that Swiss doctrine has "covered an enormous distance" from Gmür's (1919) and Egger's (1930) commentaries on Article 1 to Meier-Hayoz' (1962),[180] and a knowledgeable outside observer finds that, compared with Reichel's summary of the early doctrine in 1915,[349] "the past forty years have added surprisingly little to that position on gaps and the methodology of judicial decision." Esser also points to the provincial "warnings of the doctrine" in spite of which "comparative evaluation of progress in foreign jurisprudence gained increasing respect in Swiss practice."[125]

The doctrinal position on three related problems tends to bear out the more bearish visions. They are (1) the meaning/interpretation of Article 1, (2) the thesis of subsumptions, and (3) the doctrine of *stare decisis.*

With regard to Article 1(2), the proper role of the doctrine would have been to explore the frontier of the legislative mandate and so help the courts to conceptualize their role in carrying it out as straightforward as the mandate is written. It is true that the language of the formula contains a built-in possibility of misunderstanding. It can support the conclusion that Article 1(2) gives the Swiss judge greater power than that intended by Aristotle or Gény: for them "the judge should decide as a legislator would; according to Article 1(2) he is to act as if *he* were the legislator."[432] It can also be characterized as "saying too much."[295] The latter position is probably more correct, but the analytical implications have not been drawn.[LV]

Most Swiss writers tend to posit the problem in a stereotyped or even doctrinaire conceptual framework, or they have a correct insight, only to negate it a few paragraphs later, or they tend to worry about possible abuse of the judicial quasi-legislative power.[LVI]

Article 1 is probably most correctly read as representing a distinct shift from the insistence that the judge always ask himself what *they* (the original legislators and, in Julliot de la Morandière's conception, the contemporary legislators) would think today, rather than what *he* should think under the same conditions of responsibility. Into this clear scheme the Swiss practice has reintroduced limitations alien to the spirit, if not the letter. Instead of exercising a corrective influence, the doctrine has on the whole accepted or even reinforced the trend away from Huber's conception.

The second problem area that I use as an example, the subsumption thesis, is a concrete illustration of how the Swiss doctrine has been generally unable to overcome the positivist tradition to the detriment of practice. (Where the artifice was identified—Germann, Meier-Hayoz, du Pasquier—the implications were neither analyzed nor put together.)

Article 1, despite all its path-blazing language, is a product of the orthodox separation doctrine. In principle, the legislator makes the law, the judge finds and applies it. This has two doctrinal consequences. The first is the subsumption concept. As Meier-Hayoz puts it, "Article 1 is stamped all over by the then unshaken view that the judicial decision is always the subsumption of a real fact situation under a statutory or extrastatutory rule (existent or to be created)."[295] The second consequence is the conception of how the judge acts under Article 1(2). It is expressed in the words of Huber in his exposé of motives:[210] "The only thing [the judge] can be told [when he has to decide without formal sources] is that . . . he must do it in the same manner as if he, acting like a legislator, *would [first] formulate the norm and, then, apply the norm to the case* that requires his decision" (emphasis added).

The resulting two-phase scheme, the *dédoublement*, is formalistic and patently contrary to the actual process of rule making, in which a decision is shaped in the concrete fact context. Yet, it is almost without exception the theme of the Swiss doctrine.[LVII] Instead of overcoming a nineteenth-century dogma, the effect has been to paralyze the understanding of an essential dimension of the decisional process, with fundamental implications for the third problem area, the status of *stare decisis*.

On this point, the simple conclusion must be that, despite tradition, the invitation of Article 1(3) and the clear evidence in the practice of the Bundesgericht, the Swiss doctrine has again failed. Rather than developing an empirical model of the value and the limits of past decisions with regard to future practice, many writers have simply insisted that there is no formal *stare decisis* in Switzerland. The tradition of looking closely at past decisions and considering their value for the present and the future—the decisional positivism of Holmes's "bad man"[204]—was decried by Swiss commentators early in this century as *Präjudizienkultus*, the cult of the precedent, thus revealing how much it was in fact part of the life of the law.

Gmür worried shortly after the promulgation of the Swiss Civil Code about "the danger that [Article 1] paragraph 3, could be considered as a sanction of this . . . wrong and dangerous . . . tendency,"[170] which another commentator on Article 1 called "mindless parroting of past decisions."[295]

This "theory" Meier-Hayoz could describe still in 1962 as "until recently prevailing," and he continues, "The courts and the subjects of law . . . in their majority . . . must be described as feeling obligated to follow precedents, even if with certain limitations."[295]

Huber in fact clearly advocated a de facto *stare decisis*. But the eventual shift of *bewährte Überlieferung* from the position of a third-level authority to a subsidiary position of a model for decision, listed together with but second to doctrine (*Lehre*), seems to indicate that the retrogressive *communis opinio doctorum*, represented by Gmür's dictum, had its influence in the drafting committee.

The better writers, mostly in the 1950–1965 period, have spelled out many elements of an empirical doctrine of *stare decisis*, which must correspond to, and logically put together, realities rather than doctrinaire fancies. So, du Pasquier[320] anticipated what I call the retrospective conception of *stare decisis* when he wrote that "the judge knows better than anybody that the future does not belong to him." Meier-Hayoz[295] cites a German writer on the "Anglosaxon [*sic*] law in the making" conception as distinguished from the mechanistic model of subsumption of specific fact situations under general rules. Germann says that "in the case of a groping formulation of the decision we can speak at most about 'law in the making,' "[165,295] "presumptive reach beyond the particular case."[164]

In sum, although the bricks are there, the house has not yet been built. The Swiss doctrine is far from carrying to all its practical consequences the difference between a single holding as a potential precedent (no matter how narrowly or broadly it is framed or whether it is clad in Article 1 or Article 4 "style") and the eventual decisional doctrine into which it may develop because *future* judges have so used it as precedent, not because the *original* deciders so willed it. Rather, the writers tend to simply contrast the individual decision with the "standing practice"[295] or to draw not necessarily relevant distinctions between approaches under Article 1 (quasi legislation) and Article 4 (decision in equity).[LVIII]

The art of handling precedentlike decisional formulae in the same "activist" or even creative fashion in which a statutory text is handled, by means of objective interpretation, has been also neglected by the doctrine. The most immediate reason is no doubt the fact that not only are there no published concurrences or dissents—essentially different perceptions of the cases, which may stimulate new future reasoning toward solutions—but the court "apparently"[295] publishes only those portions of decisions that it considers of possible value as precedents. The comparative sources of inspiration are also aged or indirect: Goodhart on *ratio decidendi*; Maxwell on interpretation (both very conventional analysts); or Cardozo, at best brilliantly impressionistic, with a twenty-five-year delay.

G

On the basis of the preceding representative evidence and the evaluation methodology available in this frame of reference, the conclusions have to be that:

1. Swiss doctrine has not failed in the critical analysis of the court's work, but has failed on two other accounts: (*a*) systematic elaboration and justification of the *political* doctrine of bal-

ance and sharing of powers, rather than the orthodox separation model; and (*b*) the comprehensive development of an empirical *jurisprudential* doctrine of judicial decision and its uses in the administration of the legal system, which would have buttressed the court's willingness in the first decades to implement the intent of Article 1.

2. Swiss practice, as represented and controlled by the Bundesgericht, has shown consistently the effect of this lack of solid political and legal theory. It slipped backwards from the concept of teleological gap, which was a proper and necessary projection of Article 1; it has practiced mechanical jurisprudence not for lack of social responsibility,[305] but because of orthodox perception of its powers and proper role; and it eventually fell into "virtual methodological bankruptcy" in the Suffragettes case. This is perhaps the weightiest judgment, because it comes from a former federal judge (turned law professor in Bern)[211] and so "is especially significant as an expression of the deepest preoccupation."[163,LIX]

The result is paradoxical but inevitable. A court such as the Bundesgericht does everything to uphold the pretense of faithfulness to legislated law and subordination to the legislature—up to the ultimate fiction that the legislator sanctions decisional law if he does not overrule it. Yet it is still a judiciary that is less predictable and "certain" in its institutional weakness[305] and that is more arbitrary in its ad hoc justifications of realistic and necessary decisions, which must be kept looking faithful to the political dogma.

Allowances must be made for the Swiss practice and doctrine gyrating in the right direction, the practice rather ahead of the doctrine. But the combined record shows a frustrated purpose of Article 1—the frank acknowledgment and stimulation of the role of the judges in the continuous process of adjustment value contents and techniques of the legal system—because of carry-over into the Swiss legal culture of enough of the old ideology attacked by Gény and others. Article 1 looks in retrospect to be the personal achievement of a clairvoyant draftsman who did not quite find the executors and doctrinal heirs to carry on even at home, although he hoped for a European codification along the lines of his Swiss model.[433]

Neither the Swiss doctrine nor the court practice is an exception in the overall picture.[410,278,39] If the Swiss test fell short of Gény's realistic and empirical blueprint, jurisprudence in the broader supranational sense has also largely failed to implement his postulates on his level and with his breadth of knowledge and wisdom.

Legal art has consistently limped far behind life everywhere. Jurisprudence has moved between the Scylla of orthodoxy and the Charybdis of analytical impressionism. Recaséns-Siches, commenting on Swiss Article 1,[404] is the civil law Blackstone two hundred years after. Boulanger, a competent and sympathetic observer of the Swiss experiment, would not go analytically farther than to conclude that "subtle distinctions must be established between an isolated decision and an opinion of the [French] Court of Cassation sitting *en banc*. The authority of precedent is felt rather than evident."[42] No statistics, analytical tables or scales, or decisional flow models were presented. Efforts to modernize and quantify—for example, by the American jurimetrists—were marred by too simple jurisprudential foundations.

Gény, indeed, "remains a teacher," as Yung puts it. What he still can tell contemporary European and American jurisprudence and where the road seems to point "through Gény, but beyond Gény," are the themes of the following essay.

ESSAY THREE

Beyond Gény: The unfinished job

A

After my conclusion in both preceding essays on the superiority of Gény's doctrine over his successors—academics as well as judges, principally European—the final goal of this study remains to be dealt with. It is to connect Gény with modern jurisprudence. By this I mean to examine the extent to which his teaching has a continued relevance for jurisprudential reflection and problem solving today, either directly or as a catalyst. What universal and not geographically or systematically limited contribution can Gény make to the analysis of contemporary legal process as a going concern? I have already stressed that jurisprudence as empirical theory must be universal in its principles, even if their application is subject to cultural and socioeconomic variations.

The title chosen for this introduction to the last essay has been borrowed from the first chapter of Gény's *Science et technique*. It was then and is now a perfect motto. What remains to be done still during the third generation after Gény's path-blazing work? The answer depends on what we list as not having been attained by Gény or his successors. Some elements of the list have already been stated in the form of critique in my first essay. They may be now combined with other points of analysis and simply restated under four headings.

The doctrine of free search and its sequels appear to have left without adequate analysis, or even significant probing, the following crucial aspects of the legal process:

1. *The full scope of the judicial power of interpretation.* This refers principally to the discretion judges have in the preliminary process of fitting together the facts and the law—that is, in selecting and classifying the so-called decisional facts, the facts that will determine the application of the rule and thus the decision. This was brought out by Frank[135] and other American realists as an "unchallengeable" power (short of a gross abuse of discretion)[LX] but had not much impact on comparative jurisprudence. The European literature and rhetoric are full of such terms as the "trier of facts," the "subsumption of facts under law," etc., but the macrology of the general doctrine of interpretation impedes drawing the conclusions that finer analysis would permit.

2. *The gap.* Although Gény touches upon the consideration of values (policy) to determine whether an "unclear and imprecise" statute should or should not apply, his emphasis is on values as a source of filling the verbal gap in positive law.[157] He does not elaborate on the doctrine of teleological gap. This would have possibly led him to a discriminating analysis of the objective versus subjective method of interpretation, perhaps even the recognition of the futility of the argument. Allowing for his stratagem, the fact remains that the historical legislator is in practice always interpreted *ex nunc*. It must be presumed that the legislation expressed the *then* prevailing values. The beginning of teleological gap lies in the practical impossibility of reading a statute *now* without any interpolation of *present* values into the value system of the historical legislator.

3. *The making of decisional law.* I have suggested several *ifs* and *buts* concerning Gény's position on free search, not as a process directed toward the solution of a concrete case, but as the resulting gap-filling rule susceptible to application and further development in the future. Perhaps Gény's position was in fact

less dogmatic than that of his contemporaries and of later European writers, who espoused the doctrine of decisional law as a separate, new source of positive law. Thus I suggested in the first essay that Gény might be closer to a realistic modern theory of judicial lawmaking through, as well as in spite of, the precept of *stare decisis*. I will try to show later that the synthesis of the many correct analytical contributions in this direction is yet to be made.

4. *The unified theory of interpretation and uses of legislated and decisional law*. Because there is no empirical model of the generation and development of decisional law, it has been impossible to attempt to construct a unified "field" model of judicial decision making under the normal conditions—that is, proceeding from both legislated and decisional sources of positive law. The dogmatic conception of the separation of powers and the resulting hierarchy of sources has also been an impediment.

These are obviously the principal components of an operational model of the growth and renewal of law as a system. A fascinating recurring thought is whether Gény would have written a different *Méthode* and sequels—especially dealing with the last item on the list above, a realistic and comprehensive doctrine of the uses of legislated and decisional law—if he had been fluent in English, linguistically as well as jurisprudentially, and thus could have reacted with critical understanding to Bentham, Austin, Holmes, Pound, or Gray. The latter two were contemporary with his work on *Science* and the second edition of *Méthode*.

Judging by his reference apparatus, if Gény lived today he would likely fill himself with literature on jurimetrics and the applicability of electronic data processing to legal practice. He would probably be critical of the inelegant pre-computer-age jurisprudence under which we on the whole still labor. He would no doubt set out to do something about it. But the main perspective would be pretty much the same as it was in his time. The role of the judge has remained the pivot, at least in national systems that function in a political environment of distributed and balanced power rather than of a predominant ideology or military power.

It is now, even in "comparative law," a commonplace to say what Aristotle knew and Ehrlich repeated for us: that judicial decision is the key element in the life of law. But the reference is usually to the ultimate, *cumulative* justice that is the function of *incremental* adaptation of the law through just judging. The real dimensions of this truism have not been systematically explored. Judicial decision is normally in the way of application only. The original lawmaking decision is normally political-legislative. The point is that this basic decision may faithfully respond (though it does not always) to the living infrastructure of the law —social data, values, resources. Its practical meaning is, however, determined by the conceptual superstructure administered by appellate judges. By conceptual superstructure I mean the working thesaurus and rhetoric of the judicial corps (and their educators and doctrinal interpreters), which determine and limit the daily practice of fact classification and of the uses of legislative and decisional rules for deciding cases. *A fortiori*, it also determines and limits the attitudes in a situation that calls for free search.

To appreciate these internal dimensions of the problem—for instance, in the United States' context, which is an example par excellence—requires merely to refer to (*a*) any current authoritative analysis of the relations between the executive and legislative branches, studded with references to judicial determinations;[257,LXI] and (*b*) the changing mixture of conservative and less conservative rhetoric in courts and in the society at large.

Thus, the need "to rationalize the process of judicial decision for the purposes of today" is a continuing one fifty years after Pound wrote this formula.[337] Some dimensions of the need can be gleaned from current writings by academics as well as by judges.[130,LXII] But the full task is broader and more complex than the degree of consciousness of what the judges do and how. The important point (and an answer to the question of relevance raised at the outset of this study) is that, despite the state of the art represented by the current literature,[LXIII] the pragmatic temper of America and of its mixed jurisdictions, such as Louisiana, may well be the environment that will send Gény's themes toward their integration into a rational, modern jurisprudence.

B

Let us start in the best Gény fashion with the *données réelles,* a comparative overview of the relevant data from the legal practice and environment. The overall picture of the continental European practice and literature, as sampled in the first two essays, indicates the state of the practice and the theory to be laboring under serious handicaps, almost as it did before Gény and in spite of him. A great deal of recent additional reference is on hand from France, gathered during a research year in the late 1960s, and from Germany, Italy, Spain, Scandinavia, and central-eastern Europe, to sustain this generalization.

Even more challenging is a fact that comes forth from even a cursory sampling of American and English practice and literature.[LXIV] The mixture is different (but not *that* different); the phenomena are highly comparable; the state of jurisprudence is indistinguishable when judged by the primary criteria of process and structure.

It is a case of the vicious circle. Antiquated doctrine, such as "Goodhart on *stare decisis*"[94] or the jurisprudence on which encyclopedic works of reference are founded, is the working "theory" of academic educators and writers. Gény was among the many who pointed out that, despite the inadequate if not reactionary doctrine, the practitioners of the bar and the bench have moved in an experimental way toward new concepts and solutions. The superiority of jurisprudentially inclined judges and advocates over most academics is a fact that can be documented from the most recent publications.[17,392] But, on the whole, practice (which is essentially ad hoc and instinctive) suffers from the lack of guidance that a modern empirical jurisprudence could provide and, at times, even lacks the tools that a correct doctrine could generate.[LXV]

Apart from these handicaps, the judiciary operates under a constitutional formula of allocation of powers, which it is widely believed must be interpreted rigidly to sustain the existing order. The judges are properly self-conscious members of the polity. But their job to render "reasonably equal justice under law"—to touch up a little the lapidary maxim above the entrance to the United States Supreme Court—requires them to do concrete justice even when the formal law is not just or does not exist. This is the meaning and mandate of both Article 4 of the French Civil Code and Article 1 of the Swiss code. This was the material reason for the rise of English equity to correct and supplement the common law.

Concrete justice is, in a pithy Italian phrase, *giustizia di caso singolo*; in Pound's words, "In a developed system . . . the judge seeks, first, to attain justice in the particular cause and, second, to attain it in accordance with law."[337] This standard clashes with the rigid separation formula when it operates within a crude or mechanical jurisprudential framework.[229] The judges deal with the dilemma rather instinctively and, as the Swiss example shows, even surreptitiously. Doing "justice under law" without a specific text is thought of not as something organic, an integral though exceptional part of the life of law, but as something that should not happen. This may result in conscious judicial self-denial, in bureaucratic administration of mechanical jurisprudence, or in doing what needs to be done but with a feeling of insecurity about compromising doctrinaire precepts. In any of these cases the production of justice must suffer.

The Swiss practice, analyzed in the preceding essay, indicates also how deep the roots of the conflict are. Not even an explicit quasi-constitutional mandate could solve it in an effective, organic fashion. Yet Switzerland represents an interesting symbiosis, if not always a synthesis, of the Romanic (written) and Germanic (customary) historical components, methodological sources, and styles. This should tend to make any system more flexible and open to change.

In other European countries the differences lie more in form and degree than in substance. Moreover, as already suggested by previous reference, the state of the art is highly comparable within the Atlantic sphere, specifically also in this matter of judicial attitudes. Several European and American comparatists have concluded (though only within the last twenty years or so) that the distinction between the "civil" and the "common" law systems lies not in "what the courts in fact do, but what the dominant folklore tells them they do."[299] The truth is being "hidden in two ways."[338] The real difference is not so much between the civilian and the common law approaches, the legislated-versus-decisional points of departure, but between dogmatic and pragmatic methods.[40]

I have already suggested in the Swiss context that the key to improving the crucial judicial dimension of the legal system is not political but psychological: through a deeper understanding of the nature of the power and function of the judge in the scheme of facts and rules. To generate this intelligence is a job for the doctrine, a point that Gény understood but that even sophisticated contemporary critics of the state of affairs seem to overlook.[297,299]

Doctrine is by its nature and mission the principal source of orientation and instrument of ordering. It enjoys the detachment and perspective that enlarge the capacity to analyze, associate, and conceptualize. It is a catalyst and an energizer. It is a systematic source of invention and impulse to overcome the force of inertia, elegantly called the conservative function of law. It is the mechanism for rationalizing and coordinating the inevitable, ongoing, ad hoc changes in law.

In a manner comparable to the judiciary, the jurisprudentially oriented doctrine relevant to our interest has been also widely self-limited. In sum (the detailed evidence is strewn throughout this study), much of the doctrine has been purely descriptive and historically oriented. Even when it is critical, the intellectual energy is often spent on the easier, preliminary part of the job, the arguing away of the old. Efforts to shape better, more exact, and realistic concepts recall more frequently the work of a blacksmith than of a silversmith. Much of this jurisprudence would be a feast for the Oxbridge linguistic school—Wittgenstein and followers[422,423]—who find most of the history of general philosophy to have been an exercise in verbal confusion and an effort to answer wrongly put questions.[351]

In sum, doctrine (in the sense of theory) is at best a mixture of valid insights, conventional analysis, conceptual orthodoxy, and outright mythology. In this environment, even writers who had previously shown a deep understanding and pragmatic handling of the living law had their impact blunted by a quasi-Euclidean conceptual ground plan, when they sat down to elaborate their empirical knowledge into a systematic doctrine. Huber is the classic case.[209,LXVI]

Ascarelli's already quoted observation about "a certain contrast between . . . the doctrine and the practical reality" is still valid thirty years later. The reviewer of a worldwide survey of the state of sociology of law—a discipline to which Gény looked with great expectations—concluded in 1969 that "there is still a good ground to be covered before the workers in the vineyard of the academe truly make their mark upon the pragmatic men for whom their findings ought to be provided."[148]

One must not commit a quasi-positivist error of assuming that the written doctrine is all the doctrine. Nuggets of jurisprudential gold, brilliant and apparently empirically correct insights or hypotheses for theory building, are found in the literature of the principal countries. They indicate something about the living legal thought. A working assumption for a forthcoming study of mine is that there are enough of these empirical bricks in the French literature of the last quarter of a century to construct a plausible operational model of the practice of *stare decisis* in French civil law.[LXVII] But the synthesis appears to have been paralyzed on the conceptual level, first, by the general absence of the skill in and the habit of empirical generalization, as distinguished from speculative-philosophical generalization; and, second, by the still prevailing insistence on doctrinaire historical interpretation of Article 5, the prohibition of *arrêt de réglement*. This in itself represents a conceptual slip: the lack of distinction between, on the one hand, the duty of concrete justice under Article 4 and the subsequent development of the specific rule into a "general" decisional law (frequently ratified as *jurisprudence constante*), if and when it takes place; and, on the other hand, the practice of *arrêt de réglement* as deliberate prospective ruling about possible future cases. I shall return to this distinction.

The preceding critique of the doctrine is, in principle, akin to Gény's critique written in 1912–1913[159] and directed at the literature of the preceding thirty years. But there is one perhaps not insignificant difference (certainly significant for my analysis): Gény emphasized "method and sources," not empirically validated concepts. This may be one reason why Gény himself did not make the doctrinal breakthrough that he hoped for in *Science*.

C

It must be assumed that the groping forward of the practice, the bench and the bar, is hampered rather than fostered by a jurisprudence in which several key concepts and their functional relations do not stand even the test of preliminary analysis. Just how much worse the present jurisprudence serves than any other imaginable is not possible to determine with the data available in a study of the present scope and intent. But some random examples will be useful, if for no other reason than further to illustrate the universal comparative character of these problems and of the jurisprudence behind them.

The problems and the illustrations can be conveniently organized into three interlocking categories: (1) the relations between the legislator and the judge (separation or sharing of power), (2) judicial decision making (beyond routine adjudication), and (3) the nature and force of judicial decision (*stare decisis* and precedent).

The following chain of references, added to the various Swiss and French examples already mentioned, illustrates the groping for a pragmatic rather than dogmatic relation between the two sources of lawmaking, the legislator and the judge. (Customary *law* is, despite the orthodox classification on which Gény still insisted, a *judicially* sanctioned customary *behavior* in a conflict situation that arose from somebody violating the usual pattern or expectation and causing individual or social damage.)

Thus, Allen[3] quotes Gény against the voices in England who claimed that statutes were commands that the judges were not empowered to fill interstitially, his last example being a 1952 decision of the English Court of Appeals. Lord Justice Denning, one of the better English judges and well known in America, dissented in this case. But in 1959 he came about, declaring "the fundamental principle . . . that the judges have no right to fill gaps which they suppose to exist but must leave it to Parliament to do so." In the same year, a judge of the Supreme Court of Puerto Rico concurred rather than dissented on the same ground in the *Rosado* case, which I will analyze as a whole later. Almost simultaneously, the second highest English Chancery (equity) judge, Lord Evershed, told an American Bar Association audience that courts should have greater freedom in interpreting statutes, while at another session of the same meeting, U.S. Senator Harry F. Byrd declared that the U.S. Supreme Court "usurped power" and was "undermining our system of government."[46,LXVIII]

Evershed's arguments were expressed more completely at about the same time by Boulanger (then the coeditor of Planiol's treatise), who recalled suggesting to Ripert that the title of his 1949 book should read not *Le declin du droit* but "the decline of the art to legislate," and then concluding that "there is a necessity for judicial precedent without which no legal system can manage, no matter what some suspicious legislator may intend to edict."[40] But much of the practice has preferred to go in the other direction, extending the notion of absolute judicial subordination to the absurd doctrine that the legislator can legislate even by not legislating. This turns the fact of statutory gap into legislative mandate. Judicial subordination was criticized in almost identical terms by Germann[163] with regard to the Swiss practice and by Henry Hart[324] with United States reference. (Given the state of comparative law knowledge and sophistication, neither of the two could have known of the other. Professor Hart's comparative dimension in a contemporaneous textbook-treatise[189] of more than 1,400 pages was an 8-page excerpt from vintage Radbruch.)

In the cases I have mentioned above, as well as in the germane *Suffragettes* case, the judges, by misunderstanding their power to decide a specific case *on policy grounds,* turned their backs on parties in the justice of whose cause they probably believed.

This leads us to the second aspect of the composite problem. It is no news any more that much French law is purely judge made. Still, the readers of the various Louisiana translations of

French treatises are likely to be surprised by the number of decisions cited in the text and notes. Although Labbé, the first great *arrêtiste* (commentator on decisional law), lived and worked more than a hundred years ago, the notion of the role of European judges in lawmaking spread in the United States only within the last quarter of a century, without becoming commonplace.

The really interesting and important similarities between the systems are to be found not on the often superficial level of comparison, but on the submacroscopic level. For instance, a time-worn maxim of the common law tradition is that hard cases make ("are apt to introduce" is Baron Wolfe's formula in *Winterbottom*) bad law. Some comparative research beyond the provincial original context and the quaint implications of a counterpoint between law and equity shows that, on the contrary, hard cases are often the product of bad law. If the maxim is accordingly amended—hard cases make law—it applies widely.

One of the more extreme illustrations is *Miranda*, a case that not only made law but also produced the essence of a police interrogation manual. This made up for federal and state executive or legislative negligence, which had created numerous hardships if not also hard cases. On the other side of the ledger, protection of the society against criminal suspects, some quite hard cases were needed to make law. For example, preventive detention was declared legal in New York for the first time in the case of a man suspected of bombing six buildings in Manhattan, among them the Criminal Court Building; and the decision came four days after a Weathermen's cache of dynamite and homemade bombs destroyed a townhouse in Greenwich Village.[69]

But the striking comparative illustration comes from France. It is the doctrine of *astreintes*, a judge-made injunction that imposes a cumulative penalty for each day or other unit of time during which a court order to do or not to do something is violated. Since *astreintes* has no statutory basis, the doctrine took the better part of a century to develop, against great resistance by some judges (including magistrates of the Court of Cassation) and writers. Gény, as one might surmise, approved of the development of *astreintes* and, in fact, anticipated the later course of the decisions.[230] The doctrine was finally consolidated by a decision of the Assemblée plenière in 1966.

The history of *astreintes* resembles a two-steps-forward-one-step-back minuet, the courts removing one after another the limitations on the applicability of the remedy. When I traced the steps backward, I found a consistent pattern: the "locomotive" cases, in which the courts were persuaded to nudge the doctrine forward, were "hard cases" of extremely outrageous public or private behavior—the city of Marseilles failing to pay for ten years compensation adjudicated in an eminent domain proceeding; state customs retaining, without reason, a lot of merchandise four years after a court ordered that it be released to the importer; a former lessee acting in particularly bad faith, not vacating commercial premises.

Another aspect of judicial lawmaking through decision, and of the related free search, is illustrated, for example, by the Louisiana *Minyard* case (1967). The relevant methodological questions are: How should the court justify and conceptualize its gap filling? What sources should it use for its free search and in what order? What is the nature of equity as the standard and source under Article 21, Louisiana Civil Code? These questions can be briefly analyzed in terms of an extensive comment partly critical of the decision.[70]

Minyard consolidated the law against unjust enrichment in Louisiana by adopting "the modern version of the Roman Praetorian *actio de in rem verso*. By thus adopting the general unitary principle of the obligation to restore [unjust] enrichment . . . and by providing an equitable remedy . . . the *Minyard* decision [represents] one of the marks 'which distinguish a civil law from a common law system.' "[70] The commentator then continues to criticize the court legitimately on account of the first two questions of method stated in the preceding paragraph. Since Louisiana has its Article 21, that should have been the explicit first reference in a gap situation. The proffered general moral principle, traced back to classical Roman law, would then fit in as a specific expression of equity, the source of decision "where positive law is silent." But this kind of historical reference outside the system may be more learned, in the manner of a supportive footnote, than technically and analytically necessary, for the comment writer argues persuasively that the new remedy in *Minyard* could be derived by means of analogy from the "social policy" of the code.[70] I would propose here merely the term *analogia codicis*, as something between the broader *analogia juris* (referring to the whole legal system) and the here not applicable, direct, linear *analogia legis.*

This line of argument is in accord with Gény's commandment that gap and free search be openly declared and practiced, as well as with his conception of the method of analogy as policy tool rather than interpretation technique. It also expresses the rational technique of first looking for the sources of free search extensively at home,[391] before borrowing from *any* other system. Beyond this analytically necessary and therefore pragmatic and technically most useful argument in favor of the purity and consistency of any given jurisdictional system, I will now part ways.

First, and a minor point, there is no basis in the present state of knowledge and analytical (as distinguished from impressionistic) comparison to assume that the various "dissimilar legal systems" are significantly different for the purpose of selective reception to fill a gap in one's own system. There may be terminological compatibility or even identity. But the words of the law are being applied within a very complex environment of (*a*) the legal process with all its factual, institutional, technical, and cultural-psychological components and (*b*) the social structure and process in the broadest sense. These factors explain why, to give one recent example, two identical statutes—the family law codes of Czechoslovakia and Poland, enacted in 1952—administered in essentially similar socioeconomic systems, could produce within a decade such different decisional law.[233] Although the comment on *Minyard* implies the problem of such differences between France and Louisiana, neither the comment nor the decision recognizes that the compatibility of selective receptions from other systems—"common," "civil," or other—must be measured not at the point of origin, but at the point of application.

Second, there is the continued methodologically damaging and substantively unwarranted controversy about the nature of equity in the various systems. The "methodological premises of the historic English or Praetorian system of equity" are being contrasted to the equity concept in the Louisiana Article 21.[70] There is no basis for such distinctions—current also in other "mixed" jurisdictions—or, apparently, any utility to be derived therefrom.

Article 21, as well as comparable articles in other codes, refers to two kinds of equity. One is *procedural*, the explicit or implicit order to the judge to give remedy although there is no clearly applicable positive norm. The other one is *substantive*. In more or less artful terms, the judge is ordered to fashion his ad hoc equitable remedy with reference to certain general sources. No matter what the specific words are, this equity is simply *policy of justice*, which is so essential to a "rule of law" system that it does not have to be stated. It is not stated, for instance, in the French Civil Code, the Article 4 of which merely contains reference to the procedural equity. But any sampling of the commentators—for example, the last in the series of the Louisiana translations[20]—shows that the doctrine assumes the existence of the substantive equity *and* identifies it with the pretorian tradition, which found a comparable expression also in the practice of the English chancellors. (Gény himself accepted the pretorian pedigree; he merely hesitated about classifying the product among the formal sources of law.)

With the question of the concrete sources of the substantive equity, we return to my first point above. If the result is an "almost hopelessly inconsistent series of cases,"[70] it is usually not the external source that is to be blamed, but a mechanical casuistic reception without sufficient homework on analysis and systemic integration.

This integration of the new gap-filling decisional law, to make it form a coherent unit with the body (words and values) of the legal system, is a function of the structure of the system but also, and more, of the quality and pragmatic rigor of the methodology, with the help of which law is daily applied. A cardinal aspect of this methodology is the third rubric I proposed at the beginning of this section: the nature and force of the judicial decision or in other, more current terms, the doctrine of *stare decisis*. I will return to it specifically later.

Here, to round out the discussion of the concepts illustrated by the *Minyard* opinion, let me merely point out that (*a*) the methodology of development and integration is fostered by the codal ("civilian") nature of the system, which is more general in terms of provisions and better integrated in terms of structure and philosophy/policy; (*b*) due to the proliferation of special legislation and regulatory norms, there is no purely or even predominantly codal system in the world. Consequently, the theoretical and practical tasks of methodology are not to emulate one historical model or another, but to move to a higher order of analysis and synthesis to serve present and future needs.[LXIX]

This goal is simply an application of current scientific methodology to law. The first task of science is to understand in real terms what is going on. The second task is to apply this knowledge to social needs in the form of new or better technology. Law as a process is a social technology for the purposes of maintaining order and solving conflicts in a widely approved manner. In the remaining part of this essay I shall address myself to the principal conceptual bases for a better *science* for this social *technology*.

D

In its development toward modernity as a qualitative change, jurisprudence as the "science" of law is even chronologically not so far behind. In the physical sciences, the historical horizon was crossed only in the first decades of the twentieth century. In the biological sciences, vitalism was abandoned in favor of a consistently empirical philosophy and methodology only in the early 1940s; the breakthroughs began in the 1950s. In contemporary mathematics, the avant-garde is calling for a turn from emphasis on theorems—the dominant dimension since Euclid—to problems and synthesis.[401] Ecology as a study of large systems, including the human ecosystems, is coming of age before our eyes.[LXX]

But jurisprudence is maturing under more difficult circumstances. Law is part of the human condition and of the political process that reflects it. Our field is inherently more complex and "messy" than the laboratory sciences. Society and its jurisprudence are penetrated by fictions and mythologies. The world runs on, at best, a set of reasonable probabilities; but law is supposed to be certain and completely predictable. Social thinking is the last sector to begin to overcome the either/or mode of thinking, still current in public rhetoric. The resulting philosophical exclusivity and claims of self-righteousness are compounded by national fragmentation and ethnic-cultural complexes. In the social realm, Gregor Mendel is not equally right in Moscow, Idaho, and in Moscow, U.S.S.R. Social sciences, the source of data and methodology for jurisprudence, are weak. The "scientification" in the form of sociometrics, econometrics, and jurimetrics merely pushed positivism into ever finer system analysis—if not hairsplitting—without the corresponding *system synthesis*.[286,282] This trend has been among the major examples of the narrow twentieth-century technoculture.

Set in this chasm between "theory" and reality, contemporary conventional jurisprudence is methodologically an admixture of applied Euclidean geometry, Cartesian logic, and linear thinking; the substance it is supposed to interpret and order is a complex, multilevel social process, typified by tensions between dynamic changes in values and perceptions, the incremental nature of sociopolitical reform, and a strong force of historical-cultural inertia—as numerous revolutions have taught us.

The indicated thrust in the building of modern jurisprudence can be perhaps best expressed metaphorically. Needed is a kind of Einsteinian shift from mass to energy; from simplified, isolated, fractured views to a systemic field perspective, a conception of the legal process within the social dynamics, which keeps both moving forward and within tolerable limits of disorder.

The theses that follow attempt to identify some of the components and directions that I believe must animate the progress toward a jurisprudence for our times. I will cluster them together following the organic and logical order of Gény's doctrine, the same order in which I discussed some examples in the previous section: (1) the formal and functional relations between legislator and judge; (2) the nature of the decisional power of the judges and the scope and effect of their decisions and opinions; (3) the doctrine of the uses of the legislated and the decisional law.

No matter what the grammatical form of these "theses," they are, by turns, axioms, working hypotheses, perceptions, intuitive propositions. Most of the themes are familiar, and to some readers they will appear obvious, if not trite, as they appear to me. The point is that they all need to be inventoried, reexamined, reinterpreted, revised, and then put together using the best available empirical, analytical, and comparative methodology. The models for the method must come, as Gény already postulated, from the science at large at its present stage of development: experimental philosophy, empirical, social, and behavioral sciences, analytic linguistics, experimental and symbolic logic, and a substantially refined comparative law serving its ultimate jurisprudential mission.[289]

The whole process must be projected as soon and as effectively as possible into primary and continuing legal education, which at this moment rather reflects Welbourne's critical definition of education in general as the filling of the mind with wrong notions before the opportunity comes to see the facts. The present literature on comparative law is full of examples of products of one educational system who, even after an tour of study in another system, could not get rid of their prefabricated conceptual baggage.

The various examples already cited in the first two essays and the additional references in this essay should be sufficient prima facie evidence that what follows is not an exercise in tearing down one set of straw men and setting up a new one.

E

The following are, in the form of theses, some of the most crucial issues that must be addressed in a continuing effort to construct an operational model of empirical jurisprudence—that is, one that proceeds from the life of law, leads and shapes it toward rationality, and constantly returns to it through monitoring and feedback. Most of these theses represent, individually or in clusters, discrete areas of, and targets for, systematic future research.

I. *The principle of separation of powers needs to be aligned with practice as much as it agrees with the requirements of contemporary society.*

As the problems facing modern government are becoming ever more complex, formal insistence on the strict tripartite hierarchy is unrealistic, except as the ultimate reference in a conflict. The classical doctrine reflects a primitive view of the structure and purposes of society as body politic, maintained in a balance by institutions and processes modeled on eighteenth-century mechanics. Post-Vietnam and post-Watergate developments in the United States—to refer to current examples—show how much more complex is the sociopolitical feedback system, which corrects improper uses of power (war, foreign policy, information and communication control, etc.) even between only two branches, the executive and the legislative, both subject to "popular" control through periodic elections and majority principle.

This point must be made because strict separation of powers has been often defended on the grounds of possible abuse of power by those *not* directly subject to such a control, the judiciary. But there is a question about the real extent of the "popular" control, given the steadily decreasing percentage of people who vote, thus turning the majority principle into only more or less substantial pluralities, and given the other realities of accumulated economic power, special interests, and other distorting factors. This has been for some time the working model. It certainly does not warrant the continued lingering of the mythology that "the government consists of three branches, etc."

It is necessary to carry the critical analysis farther. Let us view the problem of separation of governmental powers in the perspective of the notorious incident of the 1930s: the resistance of the United States Supreme Court to the combined efforts of the president and the Congress to enact social legislation. Such a perception goes beyond the rationing and balancing of power among the power holders to the very essence and purpose of a politically organized society: to respond continuously to changing social needs in terms of the constant ideal and standard of concrete (that is, implemented or enforced) individual and social justice. This perspective on the legal process in its social frame of reference cannot be accommodated to the rigid either/or separation model. It calls for a doctrine based on the organic links between law and justice and social values and on a corresponding model of sharing or flexible distribution of power.

This reinterpretation of the doctrine by political and constitutional theorists must be so authoritative as to impose itself on the consciousness of the polity, to help it rid itself of the remaining fictions, and to change the rhetoric of popular political discourse. The task may call for a new disciplinary synthesis, *political jurisprudence.* Only thus can we bring about a sufficiently drastic change in the conceptual and psychological environment in which the legal profession operates. The judges (and the public and private bar, always sensitive to judicial style and temper) can then function in a climate of sanity- and efficiency-promoting correspondence between reality and doctrine.[238,LXXI]

II. *Within the realistic sharing/distribution-of-powers model, it is necessary to reconceptualize the working relations between the legislator and the judge along the actual and legitimate operational lines.*

The empirical basis for this part of the adjustment of doctrine is the perception and classification of the various tasks.

1. The principal *common* tasks of the legislator (including administrative rule makers acting by his mandate) and of the judge are:

to maintain social order within established constitutional principles;

to channel conflicts toward orderly and just legal solutions;

to act in accord with the principle of democratic consent.

2. The *discrete and sequential* tasks are these:

the proper and principal task of the legislator is to formulate general policies and to promulgate legal norms that clearly express them and that allow for their implementation and enforcement;

the proper and principal task of the judge (including all adjudicative agents and institutions) is to be responsible for concrete individual and social justice.

3. The usual sequence is: (1) the promulgation of general norms, the verbal form of which is compatible with their policy purpose and allows for the determination of controversies within the intended scope; (2) the most effective use of the legislated law for the purpose of concrete adjudicative decision; and, exceptionally, (3) adjustment or supplementing of the legislative law by the judge. In analytical terms, this means that where the usual order of discrete sequential missions does not allow a concrete adjudication at all, or does not lead to a just result, the judge must refer back to the shared common tasks and powers.

4. The extreme form of supplementing positive law is to grant a new remedy, that is, to determine that there should be a cause of action—that an interest in conflict should be protected in principle—although positive law (legislated or decisional) is silent. Historically this task was performed by officers, such as the Roman pretor or the English chancellor, who would today fall within the executive branch of the government. In modern times, the task of generating new remedies is shared by legislators and judges. This is the essence of gap and gap filling, no matter how it is conceptualized and whether it is made explicit in the written law, such as in the various codes, or whether it is taken care of in the common law tradition.[LXXII]

III. *The apparent operational paradigm outlined in the preceding thesis needs to be completed and refined in several directions with reference to real examples of the decisional process.*

With specific reference to the United States practice—but with comparative illustrations to be found, *mutatis mutandis,* in all major national jurisdictions—the empirical confirmation and elaboration would likely move in at least the following directions:

(*a*) Inventory and classification of the so-called law-making decisions, to separate the merely apparent ones from the gap-filling and the quasi-legislative ones; (*b*) documented definition (as contrasted to impressionistic descriptions) of the real scope as well as proper limitations of judicial power of decision; and (*c*) a much improved analysis and understanding of the working counterpoint between the crucial limitation of the extraordinary judicial power of decision to only the particular case being decided and the potential of the particular decision to become a model for future decisions or even to develop into an autonomous decisional doctrine. I will now discuss each of these directions in turn.

Examples of the three basic categories of lawmaking decisions are, respectively, the School Segregation Cases (*Brown* et al.), *Miranda*, and the Abortion Cases of 1973.

In spite of their fame and importance, *Brown* and the other segregation cases were in fact cases of literal judicial application of the legislative mandate, using the equal protection clause of the Fourteenth Amendment to the Constitution. As such, these cases were strictly within the basic sequence defined above in Thesis II. The problem here lay not with the text but with the policy that previous Courts (especially in *Plessy*, the landmark case of 1896) had interpreted with reference to the social values as argued before them and perceived by them "separate but equal." There was no basis for this policy interpretation in the Fourteenth Amendment or in the contemporary congressional legislation, nor was this interpretation in clear violation of the formal policy, though it resulted in material violation of the equality principle. This is the rationale of the sociopsychological arguments in *Brown* et al. in favor of the policy reinterpretation in the sense of "separate (or segregated) is *inherently unequal*." In technical-legal terms—the proposition with which I have started above—the sociological argument was unnecessary[LXXIII] or even specious; in terms of social cost-benefit calculation, the total result may be even negative, given the effects on the whole society of such forced corollaries as mandatory busing over long distances and against the wishes of the communities involved,[259] compared with selective busing and local-ethnic control over the school systems.

Even a cursory survey illustrates the complexity of the data and their interdependent nature, which need to be brought to bear on practically useful jurisprudential analysis. The other two categories I suggest (a further, finer breakdown may be necessary when the empirical work is done) illustrate two rather different instances of gap filling.

The *Miranda* decision is quasi-legislative, but the gap it fills should have been routinely filled before by other rule makers, principally state legislatures or state and local police departments, in the form of instructions to police officers about minimum guarantees to arrested persons under existing positive constitutional norms. One could say that *Miranda* is gap-filling without free search.

The *Abortion Cases*, on the other hand, represent a classical instance of quasi legislation in the style of Gény or of Article 1(2) of the Swiss Civil Code. In the presence of serious social problems (*e.g.*, the cost to society of unwanted and uncared-for children, the high health and life risks resulting from surreptitious abortion practices, the disproportionate burden carried in both instances by the underprivileged socioeconomic groups), the Court finds a teleological gap (created partly by existing legislation). It fills it with reference to the best available medical information about the viability of the fetus as an independent unit of life. And it rules accordingly about the mother's right of decision. The underlying social consensus (see Thesis II) is reflected in contemporaneous public opinion polls, as well as in the Congress. It apparently continues to represent the majority view despite pressure-group activities and publicity.

The inquiry into the scope of the judicial power of decision would need to focus on, among other points of attention:

1. Classification and interpretation of facts for the purpose of decision. Although this aspect of judicial power was prominently identified by the American realists, the follow-up[268,367] has fallen short on account of various elements of a complete analytical model.

2. The value content of the decisions and the interface between community and judicial-personal values. Legal axiology is under-

developed and needs to be better related to other disciplines and sources of input. But public opinion research, as well as other technologies, is available, and the methodologies can be interrelated. For instance, research in the transfer of scientific knowledge into improved decision making (especially in environment, resources, and technology assessment) must address itself to the question of personal value bias in scientific advice. This problem, as well as efforts toward removing it (that is, improving the consciousness of the bias and assuring that it is communicated together with the respective policy recommendations), is conceptually and methodologically akin to the problem of value bias in judicial decision.

3. Judicial power with respect to the *determination* of a gap. I separate this phase for analytical purposes from the *filling* of gaps (that is, free search for a rule on the basis of the determination of facts; the identification of the interest in need of protection; the collection of data, including value data; and the formulation of policy and decision, much of it following the basic lawmaking formula of "facts, policy, rule"). I also separate the determination of a gap from the distinction between verbal and teleological gap. All these points have been already sufficiently discussed. The following propositions, concerning the determination that there is a gap, need to be empirically tested and documented. (*a*) Gap is not a phenomenon a priori. Gap is a function of the absence of enough decisional factors (operational facts as selected by the judge, set in the context of policy values, normally determined by the legislator) to reach a just concrete decision. (*b*) Gap is only exceptionally a deliberate act of the legislator. This happens principally in three situations: the legislator orders the judge to use his discretion following general principle(s), such as in the case of the so-called general clauses contained in many codes; or the specific fact situation is not yet ready for legislation, because of technological flux or lack of sufficient data for broad policy determination; or the legislator does not act because of political divisions or paralysis. (*c*) Gap is normally determined a posteriori, by the judge in function of specific facts and equities in the concrete case. This may make the distinction be-

tween the genuine and the teleological (nongenuine) gap merely analytical, *ex post*, if not spurious. The inner working relationship, except in cases of a clear verbal gap, may well be this: the judge finds a verbal gap by interpretation of the facts or of the legislative matrix because he had previously determined, intuitively or otherwise, that the concrete case lies within a teleological gap, meaning that it cannot be justly resolved within the existing normative reference.

We now turn to the third direction.

The limitation of the extraordinary judicial power of decision to only the particular case being decided is a logical corollary of the normal division of labor between the legislator and the judge (see Thesis II) but is operative also when the judge fills a gap. The only difference is that the gap decision has a higher normative potential for the future. An analytical distinction must be made between decisions that fill genuine verbal gaps and those that fill teleological gaps. The elaboration of these concepts belongs in a separate category, the doctrine of *stare decisis*, which I will discuss presently.

> IV. *The analysis/synthesis along the lines of the preceding theses must be focused on the crucial component of the process: the power to determine policy and the various uses of this power.*[LXXIV]

There is an analytical analogy between making law and buying a house. Like a house, the legal rule is a superstructure that dominates the landscape. This dominance obscures the fact that both the house and the rule stand on something more fundamental. The power to make law is primarily the power to decide what the law or rule ought to be—in current parlance, "to make policy." I have made numerous references throughout the preceding text and notes to policy as a concept and function. I have suggested the obvious points of contact with Gény's *données*. Only some semantic and functional clarifications and analytical implications need to be added here.

Generally, policy is the complex of data on which a decision is made. This definition applies to legal process as well as to other areas. It puts in doubt the semantic accuracy of the common terminology of policy maker or policy making, since the effective act of authority is—in spite of the distinction above between the base and the superstructure—the decision, that is, the selection of a particular policy alternative. Thus the authoritative act is not the *policy* making (research, formulation, objective assessment), but the *decision* making. That does not change the crucial importance of policy; it reminds us only that the best policy, on which no decision was made, is an academic event. In this context, the term "determine policy," which I use above, is neutral, covering both the policy and the decision phases. Further distinctions, though important in another frame of reference—for example, in transforming scientific and technological data into effective societal decisions[282]—are not necessary here.

The focus on policy determination puts the doctrinaire conception of separation of powers into a still different angle. One of the first policy data is certainly the determination that there ought to be a policy. If this initiative toward lawmaking is combined with the statistical proportion of laws that are in fact drafted by the executive and administrative branches of the governments, the fiction of legislative monopoly in lawmaking (distinguished from approval of somebody else's draft, which will in such a system as the American still need a nonlegislative presidential signature or a qualified second legislative vote to become the law) acquires even in formal terms an additional touch of unreality.

Our interest is, however, in the distinction between *lawmaking*, by whatever agent or combination of agents, and *ruling*, adjudication. We understand that lawmaking is ruling in general terms and that adjudication is ruling between specific parties. The task of lawmaker—let us identify him for the sake of simplicity completely with the legislature—is to formulate and promulgate generally applicable norms (various special and ceremonial bills notwithstanding). The task, the only proper task, of a judge is to decide the case before him in terms of concrete justice.

To perform his task, a competent legislator will collect the policy data to determine the purpose and outer limits of the legislation—that is, the degree to which and the form in which defined interests should and can be protected by law and their conflict with other interests averted or solved.

The task of the judge is comparable, though the level and format are different. The object of judicial ruling is the interest claimed by one party and its conflict with the interest of another party, be it individual, class, or the legal and social order represented by the government. This process requires properly a reference beyond the positive verbal formula of the law. Decision, even if ostensibly arrived at on the basis of positive law, must amount to an active determination (or passive acceptance) that the explicit or construable policy of the law makes it possible to reach a just decision in the concrete case. The opposite of this procedure is the so-called mechanical jurisprudence, the application of a positive verbal formula without an inquiry into the policy or without concern about the quality of the decision.[LXXV]

A fortiori, the judge must consider policy if he finds that the positive law covers the case only on the verbal, normative level (a teleological gap) or that there is no positive law available (a full gap). He then formulates his rule for the specific decision by one of two modes: liberal interpretation, when the positive law can be made to serve within the legitimate limits of broadening or narrowing its meaning; or by one of the forms of free search or quasi legislation—analogy or a completely independent formulation of a new rule.[LXXVI]

This operational analysis must be related to two previous points: the usual and the exceptional modes of the relation between the legislative and the judicial powers and the postulated superiority of the judicial power in determining the gaps in law. If the participation of the various agents in the legal process is perceived in these terms—on the one hand, the distinction between the primary lawmaking and adjudicative functions; on the other hand, the necessary overlapping and limited substitution—a number of still current concepts become questionable or even analytically useless:

1. Does the judge ever make policy as the legislator does? The answer causes no problem in the routine case; there the judge

simply considers legislative policy and, by definition, upholds it. But even in a free-search situation I propose that the answer is negative. Despite the similarities in the task and the method of determining what the decision/rule ought to be, the judge has merely the mission of taking into account the same policy data (teleological and axiological) as "if he were a legislator," that is, to decide on policy.[LXXVII]

2. Despite the clear difference between legislation and the judicial quasi legislation (the judge acting qua legislator by "making policy" for the specific unprovided case), the rhetoric about "judicial policy making" dominates the discourse.[LXXVIII] In practice, the price we pay for this analytical crudeness is a decisional repertory unbalanced at both ends. The United States Supreme Court provides an illustration. The Court either takes itself too seriously as policy maker—even the least "activist" members have succumbed to the myth and temptation at times, illustrated by the critique of Justice Frankfurter for acting in *Guaranty Trust* as a legislator, "undertaking to decide at the same time all the different cases that would be present under all the various states of fact that the question suggests"; or, it has shown "diffidence in fashioning just [policy] grounds of decisions"[190] in a baseless concern about poaching in the legislative policy-making preserve.

3. The conventional doctrinal web spun around the conception of, as well as the wide acquiescence in the loose notion of, judicial policy making is comparable with the doctrines surrounding interpretation in the extent of confusion about premise and inference. In terms of distorting what seems to be a balanced functional system, which follows from the organic structure and rhythm of the legal process, the prevailing policy "doctrine" is, indeed, a symmetrical counterpart of the doctrine about interpretation. To this I shall return in the last thesis.

4. The reclassification of judicial policy activity to merely "deciding on policy" is not the same thing as the various current reactions to "judicial activism."[LXXIX] But both the reduced policy status and the antiactivist stance coincide in defining out of the proper judicial function *conscious* lawmaking beyond the con-

crete case. The more detailed discussion of this proposition belongs under the heading *stare decisis*. Here it is appropriate to point out how the preceding analysis is likely to affect the rationale, if not also the meaning, of such fashionable rhetoric as the classification of appellate judges as "activists" (or "creative" judges) in contrast to "strict constructionists." To justify this nomenclature, which has served in recent years as a yardstick for selecting candidates for the U.S. Supreme Court, two questions should be tested. First, quantitatively, it should be established for a reasonable sample period how much decision making by the Supreme Court involved gap filling and of what kind. What would have been the decisions and the results had the Court practiced "mechanical jurisprudence" rather than to "decide on policy" where indicated? The second, qualitative question might then turn out to be not whether the decisions were activist or nonactivist, but (*a*) whether they were justified in terms of the preceding theses on the judicial duties and powers and whether they were adequately reasoned out in technical and intellectual terms; (*b*) whether the term "activism" (or some other, more fitting term) should not be reserved only for decision making that does not correspond to the standards of the judicial task; and (*c*) whether such "activism" (as loose constructionism) and "strict constructionism" (as literal, mechanical ruling that neglects the ultimate judicial duty to do concrete justice) are not comparable instances of arbitrary conduct that violates the nature and purpose of the legal process.

V. *The present set of fictions, which "explain" the use of prior decisions for the purpose of subsequent ruling, must be replaced by a universal realistic doctrine built on the validated observation that the operation of* stare decisis *is not prospective, but retrospective.*[284]

The conventional doctrine of *stare decisis* reflects the apparently exclusive and conflicting powers at play in the legal process: the authoritative hierarchy, which underlies the separation of powers and is the final term of reference of the conservatives; and the real and necessary power of the judges, which is the reference of the "activists." On closer examination, the practical operation of *stare decisis* appears on the contrary as a functional, even elegant synthesis and culmination of the legal process. It respects the vital difference between policy making, which aims at a general rule of law, and deciding on policy which aims at a specific ruling between the litigants; and it fuses both into an operational continuum.

The internationally dominant doctrine presents *stare decisis*, with various degrees of dogmatic and hierarchical rigor, as an order to future judges to follow past decisions in similar cases. The *ratio decidendi* of the prior decision, the rule of the case, is the precedent. Its force is conceived as beginning at the time the decision in question became a *res judicata* and as acting into the future.[LXXX] This is why I refer to it as a *prospective* conception.

This model can be shown even on first analysis not to correspond to the real life of law. The actual operational model must be built on at least the following minimum elements in the process of decision:

1. Except in rare first-impression cases, the judge is faced with one or more prior decisions that, according to classification by facts and by norm, are potentially applicable. These decisions may form a fairly sizable and stable complex, which we then call decisional law or doctrine.

2. Only seldom—and probably less in the case of a doctrine than a single decision or a small group of decisions—is the rule of the potential precedent stated in a verbal formula comparable to a legislated norm. Normally it must be reconstructed from the prior decision(s). This may happen with varying degrees of awareness that it is in fact being done.

3. This is so because, conceptually at least, the following steps are inevitable. First, the judge selects the decisional factors that he considers (or finds himself limited to considering) to determine his case. Decisional factors are akin to policy data (facts and values), but they differ on closer functional analysis.[LXXXI] Then, he compares the decisional factors in his case with those of the prior case(s). To the extent that he has to determine what

the (composite) *ratio decidendi* of the prior case(s) is, he in fact defines also the decisional factors of the prior case law. Finally, on the basis of this analysis he decides that the prior rule, *as he reads it*, applies in full, in part, or not at all.[LXXXII]

4. The "hunch" decision is different in that the step-by-step process outlined above is *ex post*. The reconstruction of the prior case rule takes place not only in terms of a desirable result, but also after the result. It is thus a completely conscious and deliberate manipulation of the "authoritative" precedents.[LXXXIII] The concrete ruling, instead of being analytically at least the function of the decisional factors, becomes one of them. A potentially fertile hypothesis for investigation is in the apparent correlations between "judicial activism" and the intuitive, "hunch" method on the one hand and "strict constructionism" and the syllogistic method on the other.

The inescapable conclusion to be drawn, if the preceding analysis is correct, is this: the prior case rule is nothing more than a potential precedent, total or partial. It is interpreted *ex nunc*, not valid *ex tunc* as legislation is. *Stare decisis* operates not into the future, but into the past, *retrospectively*.

In other words, no matter how pretentiously a decision is formulated (or what the traditional doctrine insists on), it is always and primarily only a decision of the concrete case. Its future uses[LXXXIV] are not within the control of the deciding court, including national supreme courts. Even at the highest level, any decision may be a totally isolated, unique ruling, which becomes history in the moment it is executed.

But the quasi-legislative nature of gap filling, from the interstitial in the common law to that mandated in Article 1 of the Swiss code, makes a difference. If the concrete decision involves a fact situation susceptible to repetition or even class application and if it is centered on policy, this ruling is likely to determine other rulings in the future. Thus, the original single ruling becomes gradually a more generalized rule, or decisional law. A "decision on policy" has grown into "lawmaking." If the process continues long enough to create a decisional doctrine, the result is a source of law that is, for all practical purposes, identical with legislated law, though the legislator retains his position of *primus inter pares* in that he can always revoke or correct this judicial law.

In conclusion, if judges make law, it is a process substantially different from legislation. It is not lawmaking by one decision, but by a substantial group of judges, lawyers on both sides, and approving and disapproving law review writers. It is a collective work like legislation is; but it is different in that it does not occur within a group of actors identifiable a priori or in a predictable context of time and space. Nor does it receive its power from one fiat, as a legislative or regulatory promulgation does.[LXXXV]

Several important implications of this analysis for practice can be stated with reasonable assurance even before all the necessary empirical work has been done.

1. The conventional fiction-ridden doctrine abounds in paradoxes and false leads. Three examples must suffice here. First, on the one hand, the judge is cast on both sides of the Atlantic in a subordinate role; on the other hand, the doctrine ascribes to him the power to make law by a single decision.[LXXXVI] Second, although the judge can "make" or, more properly, "find" the law (according to the English Blackstone in the eighteenth century, the French Blondeau in the nineteenth and the Spanish-Mexican Recaséns-Siches in the twentieth),[404] the doctrine from *Beamish* to Boulanger prohibits him from changing his own product.[LXXXVII] Third, even the best writers labor under obviously incorrect assumptions. On the one hand, to quote Llewellyn, "the case-law judge . . . is [assumed to be] distinct from the judge on the European continent . . . in that his responsibility is to the law of the future."[LXXXVIII] On the other hand, according to Lloyd and Carbonnier, the French judge is considered "freer" because of the absence of binding *stare decisis*. Untouched by these generalizations are the following practical aspects of the process. The prior decision functions in the mechanics and time economy of the decisional process, and these factors affect the quality of judicial work. A mediocre judge does well if he interprets accept-

ably the legislated or decisional law; a good and *just* judge focuses on the facts and values and uses available law as a function of the concrete justice of the result. Consequently, even the same judge may use prior law in a different manner in different cases. The style also changes with time. Llewellyn's "grand style" contrasts with periods of "mechanical" or "slot-machine" practice. Even in the grandest style, the judge cannot assume more responsibility for the future than any of us in our sphere of activity. He cannot control it substantially more than any other responsible professional or public agent or even that legal standard of attainable foresight, the *diligens paterfamilias.*

2. A number of other fictions or artificial distinctions are clarified or removed by the retrospective doctrine of *stare decisis.*[LXXXIX] Overruling prior case law and distinguishing prior case law appear to be essentially the same operations. Both leave the precedent in its limbo of potentiality.[XC] The much speculated about technique of prospective overruling only to salvage the fiction of certainty in law (it occupied such minds as Wigmore's,[418] Cardozo's,[59] and Frank's[133]) was supposed to cure the hardship of changes in decisional law on which at least one of the parties relied. It loses much of its substance, if not also urgency, under the retrospective doctrine.[XCI] This model incorporates perforce a conception of predictability (not certainty, of course, but reasonable probability that a given decision can be expected), based on a complete set of decisional factors and measured on a sophisticated empirical scale, rather than resting on mechanistic criteria of verbal consistency. The term "bad precedent" loses its meaning. If it is a single decision, it will be easier to leave aside than if it is a decisional doctrine. But the criteria for use or nonuse are the same as outlined above.

3. The clarification of the genuine elements, structure, and method of the decisional process, introduced as an integral dimension into the first and the continuing legal education, will have fundamental impact on judicial psychology in the sense of "the sum of mental processes determining action."[344]

F

Beyond the specific practical implication, only some of which I have partly illustrated, the jurisprudential concepts proposed in the theses have a more sweeping philosophical significance.

The nature of the traditional doctrine is typically prescientific. Not only are its sources impressionistic rather than consistently empirical, but the already shaky conceptions that result are framed in a mode of dichotomy, an either/or form, which leads to analysis without synthesis. The doctrine faithfully reflects on the technical plane the reductionism of the various philosophies of law. The "eternal name calling" between the naturalists and the positivists[115] appears in practice in the form of sharp and exclusive differentiation of roles and functions, principally those of the legislator and the judge.

The life of law is not served by such useless games. Practice indicates the need for common denominators, continuity, flexible substitution, pragmatic rather than dogmatic stance. The essential elements of the effective operation of a legal system are not the formal sources, but the determination of *what ought to be* (the fact-value-policy level) and a coherent *conceptual system* to put the policies of the law (focused on the ultimate purpose of concrete justice) into effect and to serve as a framework for their continuous adjustment. *Historical continuity* is also an essential element, but only to the extent that it fosters the systemic nature of policies and concepts. This role requires a much more sophisticated empirical analysis than that available in most of the literature about the "great systems."

These points translate themselves into the ultimate practical question for jurisprudence: who makes what law how, when, and why? We want to understand this real process so we can better control and improve it. For this purpose we need to substitute events and relativity for the philosophical "substances" and historical fictions that have dominated jurisprudence. Not unlike modern physics, jurisprudence must move from a mechanistic model of separate particles and forces to a field concept. The crux of the legal field conception will be the unified theory of the uses and development of legislated and decisional law.

The theses not only invite this conception but also appear to prepare the ground for it. They suggest common denominators and operational relations between various lawmakers, as well as observations and hypotheses on basis of which the unified field might be developed and modeled:

1. Lawmaking is a legislative as well as a judicial task.
2. The judge at the application end of the line, not the legislator, is the member of this functional partnership who determines the ultimate concrete shape of the law.[XCII]
3. The judge, when acting as legislator, is subject to a similar limitation of his control over future application. Law, whether legislated or decisional, is always applied *ex nunc*. (*A fortiori*, the judge decides perforce *ex nunc* that there is no law to apply —and then practices free search.)
4. Significant parallels appear to exist between the interpretation of legislated law and the uses of prior decisions. These parallels rest on the common purpose of the need to determine in a concrete case the applicability of positive law (legislated *and* decisional, if both are available) to the decisional factors as the judge had found and defined them.
5. There is a structural similarity between the doctrinaire conception of judicial quasi legislation under Article 1 of the Swiss Civil Code and the attitude toward teleological interpretation (the reading of the legislative text to determine policy) in the United States. Both events are presented in terms of juxtaposition rather than of an integrated process. In Switzerland it is the *dédoublement*. The judge, acting under the mandate of Article 1(2) is supposed to first formulate in the abstract the new rule, then apply it to decide the case—although the facts and policy evaluation of this case determined in fact the need to quasi legislate! In America, to use as an example nothing less than an opinion by Judge Learned Hand (in *Harris*), the straight reading or "logical" interpretation of the text—the French would say *le texte*—comes first; then come questions about purpose and policy. But how can "the omission from, or corruption of, the text [be]

plain" and thus legitimate the second-phase teleological interpretation, unless the text is read in terms of its purpose (or lack thereof) to decide the concrete case?

6. The principal differences between and among the, for example, French or Swiss civilian method and the so-called common law or case method do not lie in the legislative versus decisional point of departure, but in the dogmatic versus pragmatic approach and methodology.[XCIII]

7. There is obviously a difference between the legislated and the decisional sources of the rule for decision.[XCIV] The legislated text is given; the rule of precedent must be normally construed by the judge. The real practical impact of this difference needs to be established and documented on a much more refined level than has been the case.[375,40,57] The result is likely to de-emphasize dogmatic distinctions and emphasize the operational interplay of the two sources. To give an example, one would not simply report an impressionist plaint that any statute in England is immediately flooded over by decisions, which then become the principal source of reference;[97] rather, one would analyze this process as an organic sequence of references to the text and the cases, which illustrate its use (in whatever order it may happen), and then would judge the results in terms of the policy of the statute and the concrete justice of the results.

8. Inquiry into the relative skills of statutory interpretation of the civilian and the common law judges could help to justify the hunch that the so-called mixed jurisdictions probably have the best prospects of integrating their method[390] into a unified field theory, provided they proceed empirically rather than from a priori, historical-dogmatic premises.

The preceding theses and associated propositions imply and to some extent define a large-order, long-term, multifarious research effort. Given the scope and number of variables, the precise route and result can only be guessed. But four characteristics of the outcome are clear in advance: (*a*) it will be a jurisprudence that will help to lead practice rather than mislead it or be simply irrelevant to it; (*b*) one of the principal directions in which it will help will be to establish much more clearly the powers and relations of the various agents engaged in decision making with legal consequences; (*c*) the basic models will not only be "comparative" but, built on empirical data provided by "comparative law," will apply to all closed legal systems on a level of development comparable with that of the Atlantic world; and (*d*) it will be a rational system in the first dictionary meaning of the word *rational*, "according to reason." This indicates the perception and optimal balanced analysis of the whole and changing reality that is society and its law.

G

If my discussion of the dominant jurisprudence has been critical from the first note to the last thesis, it is a stance similar to Gény's attitude toward his doctrinal environment around the turn of the century. Seventy-five years after Gény, the chasm between reality and doctrine is still open. Gény achieved more than enough within the limits of his first concern with method and sources. Advanced practice has overcome much of the doctrinaire, mechanistic image of the legal process, which was never true—Portalis was one of the first moderns to know better—but this was never integrated with Gény's and other germinal thought into an empirical, coherent system of jurisprudence, nor was it popularized through legal education.

So even the rudimentary specifications for a prolegomenon and a research prospectus, as I have sketched them out, go jurisprudentially well beyond Gény and sequels. But the common ground of goal and method they share with him is very substantial.

There could hardly be a greater tribute to a work of jurisprudence than to conclude that it is more directly applicable so long after its prime, and in a so much broader geographical and systemic framework, than that for which it was directly intended. This was foreseen by Lambert[347] as editor of the *Recueil*, which honored Gény on his retirement. Unfortunately, it remained wishful thinking for several subsequent decades. Franklin's suggestion (in an otherwise very young contribution to the same volume),[137] that Gény "will have to be the point of departure" for a revaluation in the United States of the relation between the "law-maker and adjudicator" and of associated methodological problems, appears hopefully prophetic four decades later.

The challenge and stimulus of François Gény are with us. I am proud of having had the opportunity to pay homage to him in my translation of the *Méthode*, in the original Bailey lectures, and in this more comprehensive study.

*Notes**

I

In spite of its length, this note is only a sketchy abstract of some material gathered for later elaboration under the working title "Jurisprudence and modernization." The conception and scope of this note are determined by its purpose: to give the reader interested in going beyond the text of the essay an introductory trend perspective on the conceptual and ideological maze out of which Gény made a conscious and largely successful attempt to escape. In line with the stated purpose, I shall first survey the basic concepts and definitions as they reveal the "deep structure" of jurisprudence from Gény's time to ours. Second, I shall compare Gény's terminology and insights on the same level. (Other terminological and semantic problems are discussed in Note VII.)

As distinguished from these terminological comments and comparisons, the substantive and methodological analysis of the doctrinal performance and of the yet unfinished tasks is the main topic of Essay Three.

Lack of clarity and consistency in the terms that denote the study of, or thought about, law at the various conceptual levels is typical of the period of transition from the speculative-philosophical stance to the scientific-empirical one. The initial stage of development toward a theory in the latter sense—the only proper one—is typically a critique of the philosophical past and a terminological housecleaning. Comparable developments have taken place in neighboring fields such as axiology, the science of values (193), and sociology. A typical evaluation of the existing state of the art in social sciences came from a sociologist a generation ago: "A considerable part of the present [conceptual] content of the social sciences will turn out to be pure phlogiston [a fictitious substance by which physicists explained combustion until the late eighteenth century]. That fact will be discovered as

*The system of reference and symbols is explained in the Preface.

soon as someone attempts operational definitions of the vocabulary which at present confound these sciences" (274)13. Natural sciences faced the problem one generation earlier: "Time, space, matter, material, ether, electricity, mechanism, organism, configuration, structure, pattern, function, all [required] reinterpretation" (415)23. The task has been an unceasing one in the new world of atomic particles, cybernetics, and space exploration.

In law, the process toward empirical theory has been particularly slow. The philosophical past in law is one of divorce between what the philosophers had talked about and what the lawyers and judges were doing—"instinctively, without a clear awareness or [generalized] justification," as Gény observed in the introduction to *Science* (159)3. This condition has been stimulated by at least four factors: (*a*) the jurisdictional and cultural walls around the various legal systems; (*b*) the sophisticated skill of the practitioners in confecting and updating "theories" for the day-by-day administration of positive law, occasionally effectively generalized (268); (*c*) the continued strength of the "analytical jurisprudence," which has supplied the practitioners with a superficially satisfactory sense of philosophical security and a logic that must lead to the denial of any possibility of "general jurisprudence" (49)—which means one going beyond national or systemic jurisdictional limits, *e.g.*, "common law"; and (*d*) the failure of comparative law, also essentially positivist—*cf.* the survey article by René David in the *Encyclopaedia britannica* (1974)—to overcome this limitation and to prepare solid conceptual groundwork for a universal theory, or even to recognize the need for it (289).

Our concern here is not with the substance of jurisprudence or even with a common thesaurus of jurisprudential concepts. We are concerned with the clear meaning of the term. This concern is justified by qualitative changes in conception and method, the need to align the terminology with the operational structure of the field it denotes, and the decisive influence of precise and uniform terminology on our cognition and thought (312,416,422).

Law is not excluded from the generally accepted principles that words are not only elements of communication but also, and more important, vehicles of the articulate mental processes; that nonmathematical questions are expressed and solved in verbal and conceptual terms; and that the relevance and quality of the answer are determined by the form and content of problem formulation. Only "simple-hearted people believe that the names we give to things do not matter," Cohen wrote with specific reference to jurisprudence some forty-five years ago (75)131.

In our field of inquiry, the prevailing terminology is characterized by indiscriminate use and interchange of various terms. It is not difficult to collect numerous examples. Just a small sample from well-known American writers must suffice here: (*a*) the "jurisprudence of codification" obviously refers merely to principles and practice (430); (*b*) "theory of legal science" is a curiously circular title of an early work on the elements of a scientific-theoretical jurisprudence (54); (*c*) the title of the book *Philosophy as jurisprudence* is a classic example of the *pars pro toto* fallacy, for it should read "the role of philosophy in jurisprudence" (53); (*d*) in saying "evaluation must turn on one's jurisprudence," the writers must mean value system, personal "philosophy," or "theory" in the colloquial sense (227)499; (*e*) the expression "theory of law" (291) is used to denote policy, goals, assumptions, rationalizations, etc. (More on this term "theory of law, and its counterpart "theory about law" below on pp. 113–14.); (vi) if "jurisprudence" is used as a sum of "legal theory and legal philosophy" (55)1, then the term "theory" is inevitably reduced to the meaning "empirical data"; but (vii) an almost contemporary prospectus for a new "multi-disciplinary" legal journal promises "in addition to articles . . . *theoretical* in nature" also "articles of an *empirical* nature;" neither of these explicitly counterdistinguished groups seem to be in the nature of jurisprudence in the proper sense of (empirical) theory of law, although the journal allegedly responds to "the revival of interest in the legal system as an object of *scientific* study" (331; emphasis added); (vii) "legal theories of various branches of law" mean obviously operational concepts and doctrines (186)7; also (177)16; and although jurisprudence is termed "master science" it is not considered identical with "legal theory;" moreover, 14 years later, the same author postulates "more adequate philosophy of law [distinguished from 'theory'] than is provided by the presently prominent *types of jurisprudence*" [not any more a unitary 'master science'?] (182)v, (186)8; one year later it is "theory of all law . . . preferably . . . called "jurisprudence'" (183)154; (ix) in a pretentious special issue on "Frontiers of legal research" (1963), "various scholars . . . mentioned . . . jurisprudence" [in the fourth place among theoretical problems considered worthy of attention] and "variously described [jurisprudence] as systematic, scientific, analogic, experimental and philosophical . . . ;" "science of law" is tacked on in the next column for good measure without definition or distinction (8)52; (x) even an innovative writer will start by saying that "Jurisprudence is . . . the sum [synthesis? model?] of all philosophical and scientific [note the sequence as well as the lack of semantic precision: 'scientific' properly *includes* 'philosophical' in the stages of the definition of the problems and formulation of hypotheses] efforts [does this include both method and result?] to create legal theory" (83)1; and ends (Id.) 26, by talking about "jurisprudential theories [plural] . . . for it is precisely jurisprudential theory [singular] that has always emphasized the importance of general legal conceptions [rather than: which consists of empirically arrived at generalizations!?]."

For a summary comparison with Europe, a recent colloquium on "philosophy of comparative law" (239) displays a similar mixing of tongues, or is the clinical term paraphasia (voluble speech but misuse of words) better indicated? Dabin, Gény's contemporary and quasi rival, complained after a lifetime in the arena of "philosophy and general theory of law [jurisprudence] that "the discussion is often based on misunderstanding . . . the concepts are frequently poorly defined, the reasoning is elusive [*fuyant*], vague" (308)15.

The situation is quite comparable with the state of the art, for example, in a geometry in which *r* would mean radius in New Haven, diameter in Chicago, and the center point in Bloomington; *pi* would represent different numerical values for different scholars; and there would be no agreement either on the definition of the problem (calculate the circumference? the area? square the circle?) or on the method.

The critique implicit in the preceding set of quotations—the names are listed only in the bibliography because they matter only as representative samples of the legal-philosophical establishment—is not an exercise in logomachy or an indulgence in fastidious semantic esthetics. In a neighboring field it was concluded a generation ago that "a slight sophistication in the nature and functions of language [using the right words to ask the right questions] would render obsolete the major controversies of the day [1939] in sociological theory" (274)31.

In law, semantic promiscuity and lack of uniform definition not only indicate that the structure, function, and relationships of the concepts are not understood, but also impede such an operational understanding. A writer, who defines his terms of reference by saying that the "stages of legal thought are represented . . . in the work of lawyers and judges, the theories of the particular fields of law, philosophies of law and finally, the interrelation of the legal philosophies in a coherent jurisprudence" (183)153, has neither the complete data nor the conceptual and methodological tools to contribute to jurisprudence as it is discussed here.

A further terminological complication exists in various European languages, as well as in the English usage in Louisiana, where the idiom is strongly affected by French legal terminology and culture (289)n16,n69, n70. It is quite paradoxical that the term jurisprudence should have retained in the English and the general American usage the original Roman meaning of *juris prudentia*—generalized knowledge of, or thought about, law—yet in the so-called romanized legal systems and in such mixed systems as Louisiana, Puerto Rico, and Quebec, jurisprudence means primarily decisional law. (Inasmuch as common law is historically identical with decisional law, the term jurisprudence in the title of the encyclopedic serial *American jurisprudence* has indeed essentially the same meaning as in the Romanic legal systems!)

Although the meaning of *jurisprudence* as a synonym of judicial decisions is deeply ingrained (and is, in this sense, italicized throughout this note), it is nevertheless historically as well as conceptually a terminological aberration, if not a bastard. The reaction against it and in favor of restoring to jurisprudence its original meaning has been afoot principally in France and Italy at least since Gény, that is, since the end of the nineteenth century. Gény writes at the outset of his *Méthode* (157)2—*cf.* also Section 85 (without any reference, which in the broader context of his modesty and consistent search for doctrinal support, means that the idea is his)—about "judicial decisions . . . that we call somewhat technically 'la jurisprudence.'" Two paragraphs later he supports this careful critique of an established term by speaking of "the mission of *jurisprudence* in the positive order." Later in the same first edition of his work, Section 169, he calls decisional law *jurisprudence positive* as distinguished from jurisprudence proper ("*lato sensu*"—here Gény refers to Gierke's brief linking of jurisprudence and sociology, probably around the time, 1895–1896, when Gény began to work on the

Méthode); and he repeats it twenty years later in the second edition (158) *210*n438. To this broader jurisprudence Gény already assigns an empirical society-oriented, and value-conscious meaning (158)*3*, etc. Though the phrasing is awkward, the distinction between a generalized jurisprudence ("science of action") and its application in the form of concrete decisions is clear. In so many words Gény is saying that the judge engaged in free search for a rule (*libre recherche scientifique*) must have a solid empirical-theoretical base ("general framework . . . certain [sociological] categories . . . classification of purpose . . . higher order of things which can be discovered [*sic*, constructed?] only intellectually"), a body of data he calls in his definition of free search global "science" (157)*156*.

At the end of the first edition of the *Méthode* (*186*, in fine), as well as fifteen years later in *Science* (159) II *143*, Gény uses "jurisprudence" clearly as theory, though the context shows that the various terms are not yet crystallized in the sense I postulate. He writes: "Cathrein [a natural-law writer] has no difficulty in showing that lawyers need a strong *philosophy of law*. Considering the contemporary poverty of *science* relative to the basic concepts of *jurisprudence*, he explains it by the general decadence of philosophy and the disgust that the metaphysical fantasies about law [Schelling, Hegel] provoked among lawyers" (emphasis added). But Gény's usage is not consistent. Several pages later in Section 145, it is "*doctrine générale de droit*," a literal translation of the German *allgemeine Rechtslehre*.

Since then, but mostly with a lead time of several decades, various French and Italian writers have spoken of "*jurisprudence* in the French sense of the word" (124) or have used *guirisprudenza* in the common local sense, but with an explanation (12)135, or have used instead the term *droit judiciaire* (10, 399). This is of course a correct projection of Gény's "*decisions judiciaires*" as quoted in the full context above. It counters the contemporary, etymologically and technically less fortunate use in France of *droit judiciaire* in the sense of procedural law (Solus, Paris, since the mid-1950s), since *judicial* has, in French as in English, the primary connotation of something related to the authority of the judge to decide and to order, not to the formal rules of procedure within which this authority must be exercised. Sociologist Lévy-Bruhl has tried to get around the common usage by coining the term "*jurisprudence théorique*" or "*juristique*" (258); Boulanger used "*droit de la jurisprudence*" for decisional law (38); Carry fell back on the simpler but still compromised term "*droit jurisprudentiel*" (64). But for Carbonnier (57)111, jurisprudence is still "technically" decisions; as "science of law," the term is for him "vague and somewhat antiquated."

After this special terminological detour we can turn to the contemporary categories of study of the phenomenon law, contrasted with jurisprudence as an autonomous empirical-theoretical discipline. The various current definitions and the conceptions underlying them can be roughly classified into three groups: conventional-philosophical, transitional-philosophical, and transitional-empirical.

The *conventional-philosophical* group equates jurisprudence with philosophy or with science in the old sense of a composite of a systematic scholarly study and synthesis of positive law and a philosophical speculation about law. A few illustrative examples follow: (*a*) Pound speaks of "jurisprudence . . . as a philosophical discipline" (335); (*b*) Fuller considers it "roughly equivalent to legal philosophy . . . like other branches of philosophy, jurisprudence has its 'schools' " (146); (*c*) another encyclopedist, Dias states that "the various theories of law [reflect] the trends and requirements of each age" and correctly concludes that "a theory to satisfy the needs of the present is still to be evolved" (106); and (*d*) Bodenheimer equates jurisprudence with "the philosophy and methodology of law" (33).

Even the most recent literature continues this long outdated conception. In the *International encyclopedia of social sciences* (1967), jurisprudence is still identified with "various philosophies of law," although the author has previously quite adequately defined jurisprudence in the comprehensive theoretical sense (83). The article even reflects Buckland's premature defeatism (49) by emphasizing historical, national, and regional differences. The *Encyclopaedia britannica* (15th ed., 1974) simply leaves out "jurisprudence" as a reference word and has a political scientist discuss it *de minimis* in the framework of the "Western philosophy of law."

Complaint about the "failure of philosophy to provide a theory of law" appears in a contemporary American law school symposium without any indication of awareness of the semantic and conceptual non sequitur (7). A trend article in the European review *Rechtstheorie*, dedicated to "logic, methodology, cybernetics, and sociology of law," states that "the technical term 'theory of law' [which is the title of the journal] is here used in its most usual sense, as synonymous with such terms as 'general theory of law,' 'jurisprudence,' 'philosophy of law' " (277). "Theoretical" in this article means analytical-descriptive as distinguished from historical-descriptive (*e.g.*, at 100). This is in line with the continuing identification of theory with analysis by neo-Austinians (191,192), which has received its latest philosophical justification from logical positivism. Although the "ordinary language" critique by Wittgenstein (422) and followers is of primary importance in keeping the approaches to jurisprudence clear, it is not the equivalent of jurisprudence. Nor can it serve even its proper critical function unless the substantive reference is empirical-sociological. Otherwise the claim of being positive—existing, complete—is a fiction.

The *transitional-philosophical* group represents a kind of philosophical scientism. So Allen offered in 1931 this hesitant definition: "Jurisprudence . . . would seem to be the scientific synthesis of the essential principles of law . . . without reference to their goodness or badness" (4)18–19. In 1958, Davitt had this "correction" to offer: "If jurisprudence is defined, as some have done, in terms of 'legal science' as opposed to 'legal philosophy,' it should be kept in mind that according to the root meaning of science, philosophy is a science" (101)vii,n1. Both authors—Allen, writing against the background of English positivism, and Davitt, an American jurisnaturalist—follow a common though not avowed Kantian tradition. They, like the neo-Kantian Kelsen, also violate the fundamental scientific postulate of the complete fact by excluding values from the province of jurisprudence (Davitt: "Comprehensive ethical evaluation of . . . law's content . . . pertains to a separate study, by whatever name it may be designated"). To grant that *scientia* means knowledge does not obviate the need to distinguish between the traditional philosophical method of arriving at knowledge as contrasted to modern science. Nor does it impose any dichotomies in the Aristotelian tradition of natural law. The empirical and the philosophical form a functional continuum in the modern sciences. The same must apply to jurisprudence.

Much more sophisticated is Jerome Hall's call for "integrative" jurisprudence. But the lack of precise empirical definitions, consistent in their operational relations, is still lacking here despite the postulated reduction of "verbal difficulties" regarding the "jurisprudential problem" (185)395. As I have already pointed out, verbal difficulties are merely a symptom. The easy handling of the concepts of jurisprudence and philosophy as if they were interchangeable (184) persists even when, almost twenty years later, Hall defines jurisprudence as "theory of all law." The argument still ends with a multiple verbal as well as conceptual contradiction in terms: "A constant traffic between the practically oriented legal philosophers and the theoretically oriented ones" requires a still higher level where "the legal philosopher surveys all the arguments, theories and legal philosophies . . . to interrelate these types of jurisprudential knowledge" (183)154f. The subsequent relation of the "integrative perspective" to the "perennial . . . human . . . effort to construct a coherent view of experience" shows the essentially philosophical lining of the integrative jurisprudence, qualitatively different from the empirical-theoretical conception I postulate.

Reale has formulated in the context of the European–Latin American tradition, and independently of Hall, a similar conception with his *teoria tridimensional do direito,* a call for an integrated conception of fact, value, and norm (345). This model contrasts with the dogmatic philosophical model of law. But labeling it as theory does not yet get it methodologically over the wall of conventional philosophy.

McDougal and Lasswell's call for a "configurative" jurisprudence (292) is germane to these various trends toward synthesis—there is also a school of "synthetic" jurisprudence (373). But considering the environment of taxonomy, quantification, and more or less sophisticated modeling in the policy sciences, out of which configurative jurisprudence has come, it deserves a separate later comment.

With the exception of the schools already mentioned, common conceptual-semantic difficulties seem to accompany approaches to theoretical jurisprudence from an essentially philosophical background. The attendant software is inadequate in concepts, method, and rigor. This has been demonstrated dramatically, if not brutally, for general philosophy by the Oxbridge logical positivists and philosophical linguists (Wittgenstein, Ayer, Ryle *et al.*) and summarized in a lapidary form by Reichenbach (351)117: "The history of speculative philosophy has been the story of the errors of men who asked questions they were unable to answer." Recent symposia of philosophers about law on both sides of the Atlantic confirm this judgment specifically (239,207).

Even when a conscious effort is made to build bridges, inadvertent slips reveal the internal structural faults. Note the meaningless term "pure science" in this otherwise correct statement: "Law has been a technology in search of pure science" (223)144. Or the patent methodological misunderstanding implicit in the juxtaposition of a correct critique of the misuses of the term jurisprudence and of this conclusion: "Most professors of jurisprudence are law-trained men who probably should have been philosophers" (222)39. The very opposite is obvious: only professional lawyers equipped with the software of scientific methodology can build theoretical jurisprudence because they will observe the empirical working of law as insiders (280)293–94; (281). Gény understood this (159)3. Judging from the results, and indeed inevitably, philosophers have experienced law from the outside and continue to illustrate Ehrlich's dictum about the impossibility of "mastering real things by means of mere words" (117)70. But "the power of words is the most conservative force in our lives." Kant's sarcasm about "the lawyers still seeking a definition of law" was quite misplaced. It was the legal philosophers who did not understand that law is a verb, not a noun. Kant's own separation of ethics and law did not solve the problems of jurisprudence either; nor did it even dissolve them helpfully for later synthesis.

But the magisterial fiction and a false philosophical superiority complex linger on. In the preface to his interesting *Théorie générale de droit* (358), Roubier too modestly explained that he did not want to give his book the more respectable title "philosophy of law," since he was merely a legal theorist, not a professional philosopher. In contrast, professional philosopher Jaspers considered traditional philosophy so discredited that he preferred not to use this term and spoke of "mode of consideration" instead.

It must be emphasized again that philosophical thought continues to play an important role in the postulated jurisprudence, just as it does in other scientific methodologies, including social sciences (43)70. Its proper function is to supply ideal or critical standards for the purpose of formulating problems, concepts, and working hypotheses. This empirical-speculative function does not eliminate entirely the traditional speculative mode of philosophy of law. But it relegates it to the sphere beyond the pale of empirical investigation—that is, into the realm of axiological and ontological thought concerning values that we are not able to analyze and conceptualize empirically. When the magisterial pretenses of legal philosophy are so reduced, it becomes a more concrete, serious, valuable, and indeed indispensable pursuit (289)*VI*.

If the preceding group of reactions to the legal-philosophical past could be covered by the common label philosophical scientism, the *transitional-empirical* group to be surveyed now can be labeled empirical scientism. It is directed not so much against the speculative, metaempirical philosophy of law as it is against the abstract conceptualism of the nineteenth-century legal positivists. Here is one example of this approach: Savigny "regretfully" ruled out negotiable securities as logically and therefore legally impossible because he could not fit them into the Roman law conception of contractual relations. The first reflex was Jhering's insistence that scientific method is one that keeps in touch with social reality (225)64–65. But his related remark, that "jurisprudence is the concentrate of common sense in the field of law" (218)*III* 13, (158)128n343 shows that the source and method are only empiricist. Other early reactions are Ehrlich's search for the "living law" and, more generally, Durkheim's insistence that social fact, including law, must be studied through observation (112). Instead of manipulating verbal abstractions, one must find out how the law concretely works so as to be able to understand, direct, or reform it. The indicated methodology is to gather working data. Good examples are the three most important American efforts in that direction in the last thirty years: the effectiveness of parking signs (303), the relation (or lack of it) between the practice of passing bad checks and the legislation that aims at preventing it (27,28), and the functioning of the jury system (227).

At its worst, mostly in its early stages in the 1920s, this endeavor was the legal-size reproduction of what Hartmann called the "fallacy of philosophical positivism that 'concrete knowledge lies in the most concrete' " (193)13. To use Rutherford's critical word for nineteenth-century physics, it was pure philately. The faith in data could obviously be as metaphysical as the faith in ideas that kept the preexperimental philosophers going.

At the medium level, empirical scientism in law has been a particular verbalization of the commonsense method of inquiry, with more data than necessary to reach sound conclusions (27,68). At its best (227) it still seems to fall within Cavers' stricture aimed at Beutel: that the absorption in quantification may divert scholars from more rewarding inquiries or, to go one step beyond Cavers, from jurisprudential follow-up on the empirical base.

To use the best example, *The American jury* is certainly a work toward jurisprudence, toward "measurement with meaning" and "quantification of behavior . . . in partnership with qualitative emphasis." Contrasted with the seductive impressionism of a Jerome Frank ("jury is an instance of law's irrationality"), it is a classical application of scientific methodology in collecting data, hypothesizing, testing, and confirming or correcting prior assumptions or conclusions. This most honorable mention aside (would the constitutional right to jury trial have been abolished if the result of the study had supported the hypothesis of irrationality?), the work not only lacks but it does not even postulate any systematic generalization that would grow out of, and match, the considerable empirical and methodological sophistication. The "quantitative dimensions" are merely added to the "pre-existing frame-work of significance and expectations" that "the law supplies" (227)492.

A subsequent intellectual inventory by the principal author (226) tends to confirm the verdict: the arduous and brilliant empirical voyage was indeed "intellectualized fact finding" but stopped short of articulate jurisprudential contribution. The pool was built but not jumped into. Even the most rigorous empirical methodology does not automatically yield concepts for theory. An additional dimension is needed, but was apparently unavailable in the intellectual environment of the jury study. Note, for example, Kalven's overevaluation of Patterson, while correctly judging the "small insight" into a concrete situation. The directional signal to "empiricize jurisprudence" (226)57,72 is correct but, when jurisprudence also means "personal set of values" (227)499, the semantics for the purpose of jurisprudential analysis/synthesis does not significantly rise above the loose talk of conventional philosophers.

Although the "shoddy empiricism" of a Roscoe Pound (226)60 has been overcome, shoddy theorizing has not. Cowan's postulates for experimental jurisprudence (84) have not found further elaboration or application. Methodologically interesting quantifications of judicial behavior, from Schubert (367) to Lawlor (249), suffer from weak conceptual foundations as well as structure, which the "jurimetrics" roof cannot turn into a theory of law. "The contemporary need in law is for much wider and deeper understanding of empiric method and its . . . applications." Indeed. But this postulate does not add up to a call for "jurimetrics, not jurisprudence . . . not a lawyer oriented jurisprudence, but socially oriented jurimetrics" (270)550. Jurimetrics, as the "application of statistical and mathematical techniques for the purpose of verifying hypotheses and elaborating theories about law, as well as solving certain concrete problems" (275)3–4, is one methodological component of empirical jurisprudence; it is not the whole thing.

The tendency is still to build exclusive philosophical schools, no matter what the name, rather than inclusive theory. The empiricists have not yet crossed the theoretical Rubicon, despite some prodding from the inside (55)1. But even in this particular context, jurisprudence is related to the "total intellectual environment" in the same sentence in which the integrated concept is undermined by a casual verbal separation of "legal theory and legal philosophy."

Somewhere between the philosophical (second group) and the empirical (third group) is the emerging legal phenomenology. It seems to be limited a priori by Husserl's curiously tentative and contradictory definition: "Science is not naïve learning [*Erkenntnis*] in the interest of theory [*sic*]; from now on its essence includes also a certain type of [principled] critique" (397)214n4. Phenomenology is recognized by its proponents as principally a method toward a theory of law (9), but its philosophical baggage far outweighs its empirical ambitions.

Because of McDougal's unquestioned standing as an innovative analyst in several fields of law or related to law, including the so-called policy sciences—incidentally already postulated as a complement for technical law in the *Méthode* (157)*186*—his effort to define jurisprudence as theory deserves separate attention. Following the tenor of this note, I should at least mention the great amount of loose terminology in the first part of what is planned as a comprehensive jurisprudential statement (292). Despite coauthor Lasswell's taxonomic and analytical strivings (245), we read there in one paragraph about "comprehensive . . . more viable . . . more configurative, hence viable jurisprudence"; elsewhere "our inherited theory about international law" and "our legal philosophy or jurisprudence" are apparently used as synonyms; the postulate of "more comprehensive and deeper oriented" theory, predicates merely quantitative adjustments rather than qualitative reconstruction, which may or may not be the authors' ambition (292)188–189,193,195.

But let us turn rather to the new terminology introduced by McDougal in calling jurisprudence "theory about law." (I shall mention only parenthetically that this term is in fact used in the plural in the title of the article just cited, although I believe that it is not an accidental slip but a conceptual indicator.) McDougal distinguishes theory *about* law from the usual term theory *of* law. To the latter he ascribes the meaning of "the theory actually employed by decision-makers in obtaining and justifying effects within power processes and . . . one of the variables" subject to study by the theorists about law (291)7.

The first question about any neologism must be whether it describes more precisely the existing or postulated fact. The first test in the case of expressions that are not newly constructed is their clarity in terms of ordinary language.

The term theory about law goes against the still prevalent vocabulary meanings of the prepositions *about* and *of* (316). Although they may tend to converge (344; "About," def. 1: of), *about* does not mean primarily "concerned with." It rather connotes a position or motion on the outside of, around. Even the "concerned with" meaning implicit in the McDougal terminology would then imply a concern directed at something from the outside. On the contrary, *of* in our context indicates the subject matter to which thought or action is exercised–*i.e.*, an inside connotation in which the subject of knowledge and the process of arriving at it are one in the sense of epistemological monism.

McDougal's terminology also violates two axiomatic ground rules of scientific vocabulary: (*a*) not to change the established meanings of terms that do not require corrections; and (*b*) not to use, whenever possible, the same term to designate two different meanings. In this particular case, change is unnecessary and therefore confusing, despite the prepositional distinction. McDougal's theory about law is meant to be theory of law. What he proposes to call theory of law is known by established terms such as policy, assumptions, hypotheses, justifications, etc. These are not theories except in a conversational sense. In reality, they are elements or phases of law as a process and as such are proper objects of analysis toward theoretical jurisprudential generalizations. I have criticized earlier the similarly indiscriminate use of the word *theory*–meaning doctrine, assumption, premise, hypothesis–in the conventional European terminology (283)xv.

But McDougal's conception would be short of the organic (as distinguished from verbal) definition of jurisprudence as theory of law even if it were not for the obvious linguistic criticism. The disagreement is not over the phrasing of the primary concern of jurisprudence as the "enlightenment about the whole community process, which includes the relationship between authoritative decision and other processes." This formula can be easily given a meaning in ordinary language.

The point is that the verbal distinction and the meanings ascribed to the two kinds of theory (*about* versus *of* law) still project the old dichotomic mode contrary to the holistic mode fundamental to modern scientific methodology and structure in any field. This mode, intuited already by Gény, seeped down to the textbook level in the neighboring social sciences a generation ago (274)10. In a curious sense the preposition *about* in the key descriptive term of the McDougal-Laswell conception also indicates—although no articulate intent can be ascribed—the continuing outside perspective of the traditional philosophical reflection about law.

To sum up the critique of the various efforts to rise above, or to turn away from, the conventional philosophical modes in jurisprudence, we must conclude that jurisprudence becomes theoretical in the modern scientific sense not only because it is "empiricized" or because it aims at comprehensiveness like Hall or McDougal, but also because it is consistently scientific in the method of "reflective inquiry" (76)194, in the unified field conception of problems and results, and in precise and critical concepts and terminology. There is a not insignificant difference between natural and social sciences in general (and jurisprudence in particular). This difference lies, however, not on the level of these scientific precepts. It lies in the field of methodological variations contingent upon the quantity and composition of data, the number and control of variables, and the like. Concretely, the jurisprudential "complete data," as distinguished from jurimetrics, are likely to be not only empirical, but also intuitive and speculative, "gross" as well as detailed. They include more complex variables less readily susceptible of quantification and modeling, since they consist not primarily of "objective" laboratory data, but rather of human behavior parameters.

A contemporary example, which warns of what happens to a social science when it does not follow these precepts about the data base and methodology, is economics. The reduction of the problems to only data that can be quantified and modeled has seriously affected the claimed predictive powers in real social situations such as economic recessions. The quality of the predictive analysis has not significantly changed through two decades of revolution in computerized data storage and retrieval, *e.g.*, (272)163. The failure to consider all data, not only the market ones, in economic accounts of production and consumption has been a prime contribution to the contemporary crisis in environment resources (301,282,286).

Comparison of the contemporary state of the art with Gény's ideas, which go more than seventy-five years back, shows that he represents a bridge between the old and new conceptions and the corresponding meanings. He continues to use science in the sense of systematic, scholarly study of law. (This is still the conception that underlies, and limits, the top organization in our field, the International Association of Juridical Science/UNESCO, whose working philosophy is hardly further improved by using the plural *sciences* in its French title.) But Gény was among the first to recognize that *scientific* is not synonymous with *logical*. And he moved deliberately toward taking out of the "science" of law the philosophical-deductive element by postulating a shift to the empirical mode at the rate the social and behavioral sciences made the necessary data available. In the first edition of *Méthode* (Section 156), *science* is still only doctrine. But in a note added to the second edition (1919), he suggests in lieu of the meaningless term "*science pure*" the term "*technique juridique*" (157)59. In the translation (158)—as distinguished from my introduction (283)xiv,n20—I integrated Gény's 1919 footnote correction into the text, though the term jurisprudential, which I use for *juridique*, seems in retrospect not discriminating enough. The shift reflects Gény's intervening work on the first volumes of *Science et technique*. Here he postulates at the very beginning the "adaptation to law of a rational theory" (159)1. He corrects his prior view about the fundamental methodological role of philosophy and begins to grope for the modern limited conception of philosophy (159)2. Over the span of twenty-five years (from Section 1 of the *Méthode* to Section 303—last but one—of *Science*), he goes from a dichotomy (*science* as ideal law versus *art* as positive law) to an operational synthesis of both, integrated into the phenomenon of science as a whole. Throughout he gives the word *science* a meaning that includes in a rudimentary form all the elements of modern social sciences: empirical data including values, philosophy as a source of hypotheses, and intuition as a supplement to rational (in the sense of logically structured) reasoning. Elsewhere Gény uses the term *empirical* in the modern sense of relying on systematic social data and building a theory on them (157)*159*.

Gény's vocabulary still shows, as it must, the philosophical and semantic mortmain against which he labored. For instance, he obscures rather than enlightens his concept of the empirical by a reference to the "nature of things." But he is trying to put into the term a new content in a linguistic, cultural environment in which even two generations later *empirical* has still retained the older meaning of ad hoc, without reference to principle, arbitrary (39)433. To give another example, in his key term *libre recherche scientifique*, the word *scientific* means objective. So Gény says interpreting it (157)*156*, and so I translated it, breaking a distinguished line of evasions or literal translations (283)x–xi. But then Gény falls back into semantic ambiguity in this oddly circular definition: "*l'élaboration scientifique* [meaning doctrinal], *pour être vraiment scientifique* [meaning objective, based on empirical hypotheses, well-reasoned], ..."

These apparent slips show the difficult struggle toward the new; they do not diminish the actual progress and insights. The dynamics of Gény's thought runs frequently ahead of his rhetoric. Sometimes the limitations are self-imposed as he professes and tries to show that his doctrine "remains in spirit in the solid tradition of civil law." But all along he works up to the more solid foundation of modern jurisprudence. He takes a stand against "jurisprudence as a kind of social geometry" and in favor of recognizing "relativity, essential to all [scientific] knowledge" and thus "incorporating . . . law in the social sense . . . into the contemporary hierarchy of sciences" (157)*184*, *186*. Gény even anticipates the abuses of empirical scientism when he warns that scientific method in law does not mean the gathering of ever more data, as advocated by some "natural legal scientists" early in the century (157)*220*. Compare also the excerpts from *Science* (Sections

1–6, 303) in the subsequent text. Dickinson set up Gény's doctrine as an object lesson to the "many American legal scholars who think that there is a science of law comparable to physical or biological sciences" (107)523.

It does not seem necessary to multiply the quotations. No matter how scattered, as some are, or how tentatively expressed, they translate in modern idiom as a critique of the conventional philosophy of law and of the valueless social science that sought to replace it. They move clearly toward the conception of the complete fact, which Whitehead later identified as the fountainhead of the modern philosophy of science (415). Comparisons with Holmes are irresistible. Almost simultaneously with Gény but independently of him, Holmes postulated that "theory is the most important part of the dogma of law" (204)478. (Not to make this a circular statement, theory must be given, as Holmes probably intended it, the narrowest meaning and dogma the broadest.) He correctly identified jurisprudence as "simply law in its most generalized form" (*cf.* Jhering's earlier phrase cited previously) and insisted that it "should draw its postulates and . . . justification from science," meaning empirical data (206)67. Contrary to Buckland's provincialism forty-five years later—indeed, not entirely representative of English "theory" of law, *cf.* Holland (201)10, speaking of a "system of generalizations which holds good everywhere"—Holmes already sensed that a valid scientific theory in any field must be consistent with any other relevant scientific theory. And as early as 1898 he listed the many disciplines that must be drawn upon and coordinated with law in its theoretical as well as applied aspects (205). These thoughts go far beyond the usual textbook quotations from Holmes—*e.g.*, "The life of law has not been logic; it has been experience," an idea that incidentally appears also in *Méthode* (158) *158*n219.

II

Aristotle made a number of statements we still consider valid, and he said them much better than successive relays of philosophers about law and politics. Gény could quote him in the same breath as he enunciated the central concept of his *Méthode* (157)*156*. Ehrlich's sentence, "There is no guarantee of justice except the personality of the judge" (117)21, was preceded by Aristotle's aphorism, "Judge is living justice." Llewellyn allegedly ceased to footnote on the grounds that all important reference goes back to Aristotle anyway. Cahn (52) thought he was lifting an idea from Hume until, "as usual," he found the archetype in the *Nichomachean Ethics*. This very fractional sample noted, it is still true that Greek philosophy took the "great turn" approximately a century earlier, when Socrates shifted from speculation about nature to speculation about men, institutions, and law.

There is a striking parallel in the timing and the extent of the break in law and in physical sciences: "It was presupposed that there was only one coherent analysis of the notion of space . . . that any two people talking about space must refer to the same system of relations. . . . We know now that the notion which has triumphed for about two thousand four hundred years as the necessary foundation of any physical science, was a mistake" (414)100.

III

Let me mention at least one predecessor and one successor in the common vineyard who might seem to be prominently missing. The first is Savigny. He is obviously a common ancestor of several of those on the list. Jhering was his pupil. Ehrlich credited Savigny with the term "living law" (370). Holmes's "not logic but experience" has a common cultural referent with Savigny via Jhering's statement that "concepts are to serve life" (218,435). Gény is Savigny's frequent quoter and Jhering's devoted admirer. Yet Savigny's conception of "law as the totality of life seen from a specific viewpoint" gives the impression of a brilliant but accidental insight, too shrouded in the mystique of the *Volksgeist* to lead to scientific quantification rather than to emotional nationalism. To say that Savigny is the "most influential, unless Aristotle rivals him," is a piece of Llewellynish exuberance (269)73, not repeated upon further consideration (268).

The other name some may miss is Kelsen. For all its logical seductivity and consequent wide influence in Europe and Latin America, Kelsen's "theory of law" is metaphysical in its assumptions and antiscientific in its reductionism. It is "pure" by being socially aseptic. Thus, despite a distinguished line of predecessors, Hume and Kant among them, it is the end of an old philosophical road, not the beginning of a new jurisprudential highway.

IV

It is also necessary to understand—and it sets Gény's work better in the broad intellectual framework—that only some of the ideological continuity among these architects of jurisprudence came from direct transmission of ideas. So, Holmes read *Zweck im Recht* in French translation (370); Gény read Jhering's major works in the original German.

The more important similarities came not from transmission or even osmosis, but from the fact that all these men were part of an intellectual process with two related characteristics: first, a sharp reaction against mechanical positivism and the self-propelling exegetic logic that it generated; second, an orientation to life and its environment as the source of data and as an operational model, which was first prominently stated in Riemann's injunction to his fellow mathematicians in the mid-nineteenth century to "study nature, not Euclid!"

The times before and around the turn of the century were marked by a revolution in scientific thinking, which brought forth such innovations as the concept of numbers as functions and the concept of field, which are the foundations of our nuclear, computer, and space technology. The ferment was felt throughout the world of knowledge.

The group shared, perhaps with the exception of Ehrlich, a quite exceptional awareness of contemporary developments in the sciences. Gény's footnotes testify to his wide learning and active interest. To accuse him of an "exacerbated cult of science" (406)48, is a misunderstanding and is provincial, too; the germane contemporaneous stance of Holmes has been already cited.

The cultural similarities in this group, which spans the Atlantic, go as far as circumstantial incidents. For example, Jhering's *Kampf ums Recht* (his first public attack on the conceptual *Begriffsjurisprudenz*) and Holmes's *Common law* (of which the famous dictum about logic versus experience is the opening sentence) were presented, respectively, in 1871 in Vienna and in 1881 in Boston to similarly distinguished audiences that had come to enjoy a professional event and left with their articles of faith shaken.

V

Jhering formulated some of his teleological ideas in his main doctrinal work *Der Geist des römischen Rechts* (3 vols.; 1852–65): rights are legally protected interests; the addressee of all law is man; human purpose must be subordinated to social purpose. In *Zweck* these ideas coalesced into the concept of social interest—the fountain of Pound's sociological school and of the German *Interessenjurisprudenz*, as well as an important dimension in Gény's work.

VI

Gény's appreciation of this literature—including Stammler, Radbruch, Sternberg, Jung, Brütt, Bozi, Kantorowicz, Fuchs—appears in the last two sentences of the 1919 edition of the *Méthode*, just preceding his own summary of the book's theses: "None of this work [has] gone methodically back to the deep foundations of the discipline of law and tried to discover how its constitutive elements originate and develop according to their own nature and purpose. Until this job is done, we shall lack the indispensable basis for a solid positive doctrine of legal method" (157)222.

VII

The immediate need for this note is to elaborate on Gény's crowning concept of *libre recherche scientifique* and the proper meaning of these words. If this particular expression has caused difficulty in understanding and translation, there is a host of other terminology in Gény's writing that also needs interpretation for contemporary readers. There is the inherent difficulty of cutting through Gény's rhetoric to the relevant ideas and meaning, as well as the havoc this difficulty has caused in the transmission of Gény's doctrine outside its immediate frame of time and culture. Hence, this note is more comprehensive than the immediate reference seems to require. It anticipates several other references in subsequent text and notes to the sometimes strained counterpoint between language, meaning, and translation or interpretation of Gény's doctrine. I addressed myself to some of these questions in my introduction to the American translation of the

Méthode (283)viii–xv and *passim* (1963). To the extent that these critical remarks are not repeated here for the purpose of providing a rounded-out statement, they are in fact incorporated by reference.

Gény's key term *libre recherche scientifique* has been largely translated literally—"free scientific research" in English—though with some variations. Bruncken, Gény's first translator into American (48), uses seven different versions on forty-six pages, thus illustrating the insecurity involved in a literalism not based on solving the underlying questions of meaning. Other writers—Pound, Stone, von Mehren, and all the Italians and Spaniards I have consulted, as well as Dawson (102)400, still in 1968!—have used the literal version without apology or hesitation. But they accepted the awkward literalism as a technical term, frequently cited in quotation marks. Cardozo (61) used repeatedly the term "method of free decision," which seems to stradle uneasily the line between Gény's precise and limited conception and the freewheeling German *Freirecht* movement. Cohen's (74)287 "free scientific inquiry" is not a great improvement.

Most Swiss writers have simply used the original French term; others have translated it as *freie Rechtsfindung*, which is substantially correct (though *recherche* would be rather *-forschung*) but which does not sufficiently distinguish Gény from the German "free law." The most sophisticated contemporary German dealing with Gény, Esser (127)195, also prefers the French original. The cross-reference in his index between *libre recherche* and *bewährte Lehre* (established doctrine of the writers) is incorrect, but the error is probably the indexer's, not the author's. Friedman (141)826; (142)212f (1944), 284f (1960) represents both trends, original French term and literal translation, and continues with the awkward literalism long after the American translation of the *Méthode* (*cf.* his 328f [1967]) without any reference. Other variants in the literature are: (*a*) "free investigation by the judge" (225)67, which is better than "research" but leaves out the *scientifique*, although Jones later, at 68, correctly explains it using the word *objective*; (*b*) "free scientific enquiry" (315)456n5; (*c*) "liberal and elastic judicial technique" (*la libre recherche scientifique*), a vague paraphrase without translation (3)27–28; (*d*) Stone's subtitle (385)149, "Criterion of values where the formal sources fail (La libre recherche scientifique)." Elsewhere (383)731n138, Stone uses the term "free finding of law," which is more precise but is inspired in the immediate context by the German *freie Rechtsfindung* rather than by Gény. Compare Morrow (306) 554. Contrast Allen (2)15.

My rendition of Gény's term as "free objective search for a rule" is perhaps the best example of my views about the translator's duty to select or make up a concept-idiom combination that does not force the discriminating reader to try to retranslate word by word into the original language to give a term of art its proper contour and depth. Yet, the French original makes the translation relatively easy. The word *libre* clearly means free of the compulsion to follow any positive authority (statute or custom) because there is none applicable within the bounds of legitimate interpretation as set by Gény. *Scientifique* translated literally was meaningless at the time Gény wrote. It is even more so today. In American legal terminology, "scientific" has the meaning of scholarly, systematic, jurisprudential, theoretical, etc., all contrasted with the practical, applied, day-by-day. In Gény's frame of reference it means objective, "based . . . upon objective elements that scientific jurisprudence [*i.e.*, one informed by empirical social and behavioral sciences] alone can reveal" (157)*156*. Previously, he speaks specifically of "objective rules . . . derived from the common base of the nature of things" (157)*87*. "Research" is only one meaning of *recherche*, with a specific scholarly connotation that Gény did not have in mind. The more basic plain meaning of *recherche* is "search," a fact that can be illustrated by references ranging from Marcel Proust (who was clearly not engaging in research in his *A la recherche du temps perdu*, but rather in a search for times passed or, as the English translation goes, things lost) to INTERPOL (whose 1972 bulletin *Les 12 oeuvres d'art les plus recherchées* has the correct English subtitle *The 12 most wanted* [searched for] *works of art*). This basic meaning is precisely what Gény had in mind: looking for the elements from which to construct *a rule* needed to decide the unprovided case. Cardozo was one of the very few who showed some uneasiness by putting the word *recherche* in parentheses following the literalism "research" (61)119; later, at 163, when he is not shackled by a foreign text, but writing freely in his own sensitive idiom, he speaks correctly of "the judicial process as . . . a process of search." At the other end of the spectrum—and surprisingly so—Kantorowicz never seemed to give the matter a thought (228)700n68, but the English version of his article was in fact by Patterson, comparatively a rather insensitive writer.

The last portion of the term I use to express Gény's *libre recherche*, "a rule," deserves additional separate comment, because it illustrates the lack of success by many who have tried to translate and apply Gény's thought. The terminology in question has two components: the indefinite article and the word *rule*. As to the first, I consider the indefinite article as correctly expressing the a priori indefiniteness of the rule to be created, with the implied leeway, rather than to be found ready, prefabricated, in the Blackstonian fashion. As to the second, *rule* appears preferable to the word *decision*, used by many in this context, including Bruncken (48) and even Cardozo (61)17 and *passim*, in terms of both substance and logic. Semantically as well as analytically there is a clear difference between a rule and a ruling/decision, even though the difference tends to be wiped out by quaint common law rhetoric, such as "rule for the plaintiff." It is the essence of the free-search situation that the positive rule for the purpose of the ruling/decision is missing and that the free search for a rule is set in motion in order to fill the gap.

Though it is necessary to insist on semantically subtle analysis, to replace the sign language and blunt instruments typical of traditional jurisprudence, this must always be only preparatory to operational synthesis. On that plane, the lines cannot be drawn so sharply (as the Swiss have tried to do): the practical process of fashioning a free-search judicial rule and of deciding the concrete case is seamless; and *a* rule that decides the case may become *the* rule through the operation of *stare decisis*, explicit or de facto.

Gény uses constantly the word *interprète*. In the tradition of the commentators, he includes in the term interpretation also doctrine (writers). But in the great majority of instances, when he says interpreter(s) he means judge(s). So, immediately following his own definition of the term *libre recherche* (157)*156*, he distinguishes (*a*) the judge as "the effective and official interpreter of positive law," (*b*) the writer as "the doctrinal or critical interpreter," and (*c*) "the practitioner." With regard to the last two categories, he also uses occasionally a collective term *jurisconsulte*. This follows Portalis' terminology (131)I 476, (241)39, which refers in one sentence to "judge and counsel" and in the next sentence collectively to "the interpreter." Bruncken, on the other hand, uses on three pages (48)2,3,5, interchangeably the terms court, lawyers, judge, administrator (of positive law), with the resulting semantic and, occasionally, even syntactic confusion ("The *Court* . . . renders *his* decision" [emphasis added]).

Gény's analytical rhetoric can be illustrated by his use of the words *notions, conceptions, constructions*. By these terms he describes various levels in the hierarchy of legal abstractions. He uses them so frequently and they give the text such a specific flavor that in the translation of the *Méthode* I decided to follow the closest American approximations: concepts, conceptions, and constructs. The first of these terms is clear and idiomatic. Nevertheless, Bruncken translates it by the redundant and imprecise "abstract notions." Gény does not intend to convey here any sense of vagueness, but rather to distinguish concepts from reality. The intended meaning of Gény's *conceptions* is (general) principles, but at least Pound (333)484–85 and Cardozo have used the term conception in a context similar to Gény's. A better, free translation of the word *constructions* would be doctrine(s) in the dogmatic sense. But construct(s), though less elegant, has a clearer meaning: a complex product of intellectual synthesis (the emphasis is on the process, not on the value of the result), exactly Gény's idea of *édifier des constructions abstraites*. The emphasis here is on the conceptualistic (as distinguished from conceptual) quality. I have therefore on occasion followed Gény's apparent redundance and translated literally as "abstract constructs." There is a parallel between Gény and German or Swiss criticism of the same phenomenon (*cf.* the term *Konstruktionsjurisprudenz* by a radical free-law advocate Fuchs or the also seemingly tautological *begriffliche Konstruktionen* by Germann, referring to mechanical conceptualism contrasted with *wertkritische Methode*, value-conscious jurisprudence). The idiomatic confluence of Gény's *construction* and "doctrine" appears confirmed in Pound's context, cited above. Bruncken's literalism "construction" is less appropriate (and he himself put it in quotation marks), for construction is related in American legal usage rather to interpretation, though it implies here equally a more complex intellectual process (again without any reference to the quality of the result).

The words *jurisprudence, science, théorie*, and *doctrine*, which constitute important ingredients of Gény's vocabulary, deserve a few comments. *Juris-*

prudence has already been extensively discussed. The primary traditional meaning is, of course, decisional law; the more modern and preferred meaning is theory of law. Bruncken's seven different versions are legal science, judge, the law, modern development of law, legal system, law, and courts (48)16,17,18,26,33,34,37—most of them false in the context. In the more authentic, second sense, jurisprudence corresponds to the traditional French words *doctrine* and *science.* Gény still uses them, as well as the term *théorie,* ambivalently; but at the same time he represents a bridge to the modern meaning of science and theory as terms descriptive of empirical research toward experimentally established and testable concepts and models, even in the field of human and social sciences, including jurisprudence as legal science. Gény's eventual conception of *science* in his latter work deserves a separate comment (Note IX). Therein also on *donné* and *construit* and on further semantic implications of these concepts.

Gény uses consistently the generic term *la loi* in the sense of formal norms emanating from the legislature. In the translation of the *Méthode,* I used mostly the literal counterpart statute (law). But Gény's *la loi* includes also codified law (which is technically only a species of statute law) or written law (a term correctly used only with reference to the primitive stage of development of a legal system, when judicial decisions, *i.e.*, decisions about concrete disputes, merely declare and help to form the heretofore not recorded custom). The more precise terminology with which Gény would probably agree today is legislated law, as distinguished from customary law and decisional law.

Gény was very conscious of the role of technical language. *Méthode* contains various references to the language of law. For instance, in Section 81 he goes so far as to coin the term "jurisprudential transcendentalism," referring to the philosophical doctrine that principles of reality can be discovered by mental processes. In *Science* he devotes a whole chapter in Volume III (*254–60*) to "language (words and phrases) as instrument of legal technique." This chapter includes footnotes with long lists of writers on linguistics and semantics, as of about 1920 (*e.g.*, 450n2, 453n1). It contains a great deal of nineteenth-century mechanistic notions (quasi-Comtian, not acknowledged) and unresolved contradictions between the "impotence of the language of law to transmit all the expressions [*représentations*] of the mind [*esprit*]" where "the creation of the rules of law essentially happens" (159)*254,256*, and the unqualified reception of Sumner Maine's "aim to reduce all language in the service of law to the state of algebraic symbols" (159)*257*. ("But," Gény catches himself at once, "this precision must not degenerate into pedantic rigidity.")

Yet, on these same pages there is enough to put Gény among those who were feeling their way to modern linguistic theory and general semantics introduced in the 1920s and 1930s by Ogden, Richards, Whorf, Korzybski, and others. His call for a thesaurus ("common corps of terminology," at 459) has not gotten much farther than Hohfeld's independent, contemporaneous effort (200). Perhaps Gény did not have more in mind then. But his work, and that of his followers and critics, would be a valuable point of departure toward the construction of a much needed comparative jurisprudential thesaurus, using the new technology of semantic analysis and symbolic logic (289)*VI*, which was not available in his time.

Gény's style and general rhetoric, as distinguished from his technical thesaurus, is another matter. Because of my patent admiration for the man and empathy with his work, I felt I could admit in my introduction to the American translation of the *Méthode* that Gény's style and vocabulary are a translator's nightmare. Many other disciples and admirers could not obviate some reference to Gény's literary qualities. So Hernández-Gil (199)222 considers him "ponderous . . . at times"; Pound (332)466; (336)I, 184 speaks of Gény's "complex and somewhat laborious" style; Llewellyn, admitting that one of his own theses "has been hammered . . . until a reader may threaten to rebel," hopes he has been "almost" as successful as Gény with the illustration of Gény's "simple and glorious formula for handling the Code: until the technique moves into the reader's fingers, no longer making a call upon the brain" (268)260–61. Gény's mode is scholastic, compounded by overcomplex structure of sentences and paragraphs. His argumentation often recalls the verbal gyrations of a judge unsure of himself and of the opinion he is expressing.

All this cannot be explained by his modest claim that he wrote *Méthode* originally for his own purpose and only later decided to publish it (still with the subtitle "a critical *essay*"), self-deprecating it to Huber in 1900 as "temerarious, premature." The style of the epilog written for publication twenty years later and of the intervening and subsequent works is not appreciably different. It is not that Gény was unaware. In an early article (155); (160)507, he insists that a statute or code (one should add, *a fortiori,* doctrinal writing) ought to possess all the qualities of a good literary work: "unity, order, precision, clearness." But apparently, for all his human simplicity and charm, Gény was a complex, struggling personality, and his style shows it. The contrapuntal tension between the sweeping universality of the thesis and the simple requirement of clear and consistent exposition calls to mind such a germane spirit as Ortega y Gasset (281).

It is surprising how much shadow in Gény can be separated from substance by simple semantic analysis. But the fact remains that Gény's insights, sharp formulations, and hypotheses are buried in a mass of words that must distract and tire all but the most interested students. Gény, indeed, modernized somewhat his language as his work progressed, and his sophistication grew. In the twenty years between the first and the second editions of the *Méthode*, he substituted for the tradition-bound, philosophically vague term *spirituel* the word he really meant all along, *intélectuel.* Instead of the term *science pure*, with its connotation of an abstract system of concepts, he proposed *technique juridique* (today we would say legal technology). But these and other refinements could not make any perceptible difference in Gény's writing as a whole. He did not even incorporate them into the text of the 1919 edition, which he left deliberately as written twenty years earlier. These shifts in his vocabulary as a symptom of changing dimensions in thought can be traced only through the notes added to this second edition.

VIII

Since *Science* is not available in English, some supplementary extracts will help to round out the account. They are presented under several headings, in a combination of narrative and quotations.

On empirical theory. At the very outset (159)*I*, 3f, Gény notes the "meager harvest that general philosophy offers to lawyers." He turns to the contemporaneous currents in physical and mathematical sciences, especially the critique of method, and to the then beginning modern philosophy of science (Ernest Mach *et al.*) as the models of empirical approach. The philosophy for law will not be the "professional philosophy," but "progressive commonsense philosophy . . . of law in the sense of philosophical critique of the science of law, following the model of [*à l'image de*] critique in the various natural and social sciences" and the lesson that "the critique of each discipline must take place in terms proper to it." Gény finds the idea of the *philosophie du sense comun progressif* as far back as Leibniz' *philosophia perennis.* "By definition it arises spontaneously from attentive reflection and refines itself by means of a continuous integration of elements of collective experience" (at 73–75). The view that "theory is without influence on the actual development of legal practice, [that] method is more a matter of *pouvoir* than of *savoir,*" is "a sheer sophism. . . . The choice is not to sacrifice practice to theory. The question is whether enlightened practice does not reach its goals with greater assurance and more fully than blind [purely pragmatic] practice. . . . When the question is posed in this manner, there can be no doubt about the answer" (at 14f). The philosophical basis as a "philosophy of action"—a conception that has a strong affinity with John Dewey's experimental philosophy, but is in Gény's text supported only by French references and by Cathrein, the Swiss natural-law philosopher!—must also draw from Bergson's *philosophie nouvelle* and "continuously combine intuition with analysis" (at 72–85).

On the course and tasks of jurisprudence. Gény sees an analogy between the reorientation of philosophy of law and the change in the perspective of astronomy when Earth lost its assumed central position in the universe. As a result, "better informed research into the bases of law will put judicial decisions, custom, and even statute in the proper relation to positive law of which they are only partial reflections [since] positive law . . . is an integral part of the social environment . . . and the function of intellectual and moral values" (at 41). The movement in jurisprudence has been from the "formal and passive" to the "critical and active" (Gény contrasts Laurent and Planiol as the opposite prototypes), from "interpretation of sources" to "interpretation of law." This "emancipation" of lawyers appeared to Gény comparable with the development in various other fields from the sixteenth and seventeenth centuries on. Public law has led the way after having been a "long time retarded by certain doctrines (as, for instance, the separation of powers)" (at 26–27). To fulfill their normal functions of *savoir pour prévoir* (capacity of prediction and prevention) and *savoir pour pouvoir* (knowledge for action), lawyers need broad knowledge of neighboring disciplines (at 18–21, 71). Comparisons with Holmes again impose themselves, though Gény was more technical and less Olympian, indeed, apologetic for his vast apparatus of comparative reference (at 20). The result will be "progressive jurisprudence," which will put "each formal source . . . in its place according to its nature" and will "recognize outside of their clearly delimited sphere the necessity of free interpretation subject only to the facts on which it is supposed to rule and to the requirements of all scientific research [*investigation*, not *recherche*]"—an awkward but clear reference to *libre recherche scientifique* (at 40).

On the relation between progressive jurisprudence and modern science in general. Among the many references available, three particularly contribute to the clarification of Gény's perspective: (*a*) the postulate of scientific objectivity in the method of free search; (*b*) the rejection of Durkheim's valueless sociology; and (*c*) the holistic view of science. The specific reference to Durkheim was made in the preface to the last volume of *Science* and was immediately provoked by some indiscriminate lumping of Gény and Durkheim in the literature. It expresses, however, Gény's conception from the beginning, a holistic conception that began to be vindicated beginning sometime in the 1950s as a reaction to the increasing sterility of sociometrics. Gény's holistic viewpoint is specifically expressed at the end of *Science, 303*: "We must see science as a whole and, in this complex, find the proper place for law." It is unfortunate that Gény's simple and obvious thesis, that scientific (meaning complete) jurisprudence must integrate values, was obfuscated by the language of natural law, which so much delayed its proper understanding and application. The theses of *Science* are summarized by Gény in twenty-one paragraphs (159)*IV 302.*

IX

Gény uses two different expressions, *le donné* and *donnée(s).* According to a standard French dictionary (261), *donné* as a masculine noun has only one relevant meaning (of two listed): that which is immediately available to the conscious, even intuitively perceived (Bergson), before any mental elaboration takes place. As such, it is "frequently" opposed to *construit.* Giving it the generic meaning of data, Gény apparently to some extent coined his term. *Donnée* as a feminine noun has, according to a common desk dictionary (262), three definitions: (*a*) an uncontested point; (*b*) in mathematics, known data, quantities, which constitute the base of a problem to be solved; and (*c*) in philosophy, that which is given to the spirit before any mental construction. It is impossible to determine which of the two latter definitions Gény had principally in mind. The first one seems more objectively indicated; the second has some natural-law dimension, but if *spirit* is given the dictionary meaning of "mind, intelligence," it also fits. Gény's use was not entirely consistent; *e.g.*, (159)*IV* 256, he uses *"les données de la vie juridique,"* where the generic singular form would be more in line with his usual distinction. Compare that with *"Le donné . . . est toute la vie sociale"* (159)xv. Some commentators have captured the distinction that *le donné* consists of various categories of *données*, *e.g.*, (427)41; others have paid no attention, *e.g.*, (142)330; (2)15.

As to the genesis of the meanings, Gény's preview quoted from the *Méthode* in the text is from the penultimate section of the 1899 edition. But Gény had the basic distinction in mind at the very outset of the book. In Section 1 he distinguishes, on the one hand, "positive law . . . matter purely for legal interpretation," and, on the other hand, "outside of and above the legal text . . . the broad field of intellectual inquiry . . . the social phenomena and their natural laws . . . sometimes called sociology . . . the only complete and genuine scientific matter [relevant to law]." His reference here is an article by Duguit, published in 1889. Later, he compared his *donné* and *construit* to the Bergsonian distinction between "crude fact" (*fait brut*) and what I would translate as "applied fact," since the original term *fait scientifique* tends to confuse matters: it stands in Gény's scheme for *technique*, not for *science*. The word *technique* (corresponding to *le construit*) is a result of Gény's conceptual refinement. Originally, in the *Méthode*, it was *art* (Taine's terminology), but Gény later found it "equivocal and unsatisfactory"; he also tried to distinguish his terminology from the Germans, relating it rather to Demogue's distinction (1911) between "the bases of law" and "its technique" (159)*I* 95–99.

Just as it happened with *libre recherche*, many writers have simply used the terms *le donné* and *le construit* without any effort to translate them. Others have tried with varying degrees of success. Wilk (419) translated *le donné* (as borrowed by Dabin) as "the given." I called this "meaningless and inelegant" (283)xiv,n24, but this translation does express correctly the participle quality of the term. Patterson, who edited Wilk's translation, propagated "the given" further in his textbook (322)353n83, but used also on the same page the more elegant synonyms: "elements," quoting from Jones; and "factors" (data), referring to Cardozo. *Datum* or *data* is a literal but meaningful translation, *e.g.*, by Legaz (250)68, with direct reference to Gény. Contrast the rendition as *supuesto* (assumption, premise) by a Spanish translator from the French (45)119, which is far off and illustrates the obstacle course to understanding that a casual translation can present. Stone's "social facts" (385)149n1, is correct only with regard to the environmental and social *données*. Pound's "starting points," quoted by O'Toole (315)456, is equally narrow.

Wu (427)40 is among those who preferred to paraphrase on the ground that, though "etymologically 'datum' should be an exact equivalent," the loose usage of datum or data has deprived it of "the ontological connotation of *donné*, that is what is given in nature and in social realities."

The idea of *le donné* as the substratum of positive law has been applied and paraphrased by numerous authors as "preceding legal reality" (Djuvara), "concept of law" (Bonnecasse), "the right law" (Stammler), "the social reality seen through its natural purposes" (Delos, Russo), "the social norm" and "the rule of law" (Duguit), "law in the material sense" (Réglade), "the normative facts" (Gurvitch)—all cited by Dabin (93)126f—and the "pre-normative perspective" used by Esser (127)304.

When Gény's verbal and conceptual structure is taken apart and reassembled in contemporary terms, it appears that the generic labels *le donné* and *données* cover at least the following systems: (*a*) the human and environmental data and their cultural, economic, and political effects (levels 1, 4); (*b*) the values dictated by or resulting from these data/effects and acting upon the actual and the desirable rules of conduct (levels 2, 3, 4); and (*c*) the historically accumulated law, based on normative principles that incorporate the social values (levels 2, 3). The first system is sociological in the broad sense, the second is axiological (including the ultimate ethical value of justice), and the third is legal.

With regard to the kingpin of Gény's scheme, see Allen's comment (2)15: "Practical reason (*donnée rationelle*) . . . like Coke's, is 'not every unlearned man's reason . . . [it is] partly the intuitional [*sic*] understanding derived from Bergson . . . and partly from the frame of mind . . . inculcated and developed by practical technique."

With his *donnée idéale*, formally on top of the pyramid but functionally subordinated to and empirically derived from the other *données*, Gény anticipated the present state of philosophy—also of law—as being merely (but most importantly) the source of ideal standards and creative hypotheses for theoretical jurisprudence. See also (280)293.

Although I consider in another context the extrapolation of Gény's terms and their simplification into the current policy/law distinction to be "permissible," Gény's conception and rhetoric are not without equivocation. The symptom rather than the cause of it seems to be the wordiness of his formulations, *e.g.*, (159)279. Consider this sequence (all references are to *Science*, Volume IV): (*a*) at xvi, Gény denies that he has proclaimed the supremacy of *le construit* (law) over *le donné* (policy); (*b*) at xv, he seems to enunciate the thesis of procedural creation of positive law ("As soon as one leaves the sphere of the great principles [of policy?] and descends to the level of dealing with concrete questions . . . it is impossible to satisfy this need other than by means of . . . legal technique"; (*c*) this emphasis is repeated at the end of the volume, at *303* ("The principal effort of the lawyer turns around technique"); and (*d*) the *donnée rationelle*, policy in the proper sense and the pinnacle of Gény's system of *science*, is surprisingly though realistically subordinated to positive law, at *287*. Obviously, a statute can be against the better policy and even against implicit or explicit moral values! Gény, indeed, does not exclude the extreme case of revolution against "despotic laws," but this is not the "normal," inevitable practical reality of divergence between law and the *donnée idéale*. So Gény must admit an element of relativity here, at 265 (as he did also in *II* 387). But he recoils from such practical effects as divorce or birth control and reaffirms what looks like old natural law in the preface to Volume IV (at xxiii), the chronologically last lines he wrote on the subject in *Science*.

Notes

X

This note presents an additional sampling of the key words from favorable appraisals, mostly but not exclusively addressed to Gény's *Méthode*. The sample shows the range and diversity of Gény's impact and extrapolations.

Allen (2)15 compliments Gény as "moderate among the idealists." Battaglia (19)185,200,211 speaks of the "fine thinker," the "first to move toward a superior solution," whose "work is truly basic" and whose "germinal insight [overcame] the dogmatism of the exegetic school." He includes a list of dicta from Bugnet, Demolombe, Proudhon, Laurent, and Demante, all nineteenth-century treaty writers, to illustrate the ideological identity between the legal and the biblical exegetes. Bonnecasse (35)*210*: "Gény was to revolutionize legal doctrine." Capitant (56)vi: a "lovely, so suggestive book." Cardozo (61)119,138: "boldness and suggestive power . . . brilliant book." Croce (87)328: "a firm conquest in the philosophy [*sic*] of law." Dawson (102)394,480: "devastating attack" on the prevailing method; "French law . . . could not be quite the same" after Gény. Dualde (109)44: "illustrious promoter of modern methodology."

Friedman (142)211,215,216; (141)826: "one of the first and perhaps most important leaders in the fight for a new sociological conception of law"; "perhaps the most elaborate legal theory ever developed from the angle of the practical lawyer"; "great lucidity and practical touch . . . showed that at every stage of the legal process there is and must be creative activity"; "most subsequent philosophical discussions of the juridical process are an elaboration or resumption of Gény's pioneer work."

Gaudemet (149)*II* 6: Gény resolved the traditional antinomy between "stable legal order and everchanging life of society" and demonstrated that legal rules must be "simple summaries of sociological observation without losing their formal normative character." Germann (161)20,143: "harbinger of a new antipositivism"; critic of "the conceptual acrobats"; one of the "prophets of our revolutionary times."

Hernandez-Gil (199)206,209: Gény "is for French and world jurisprudence what Savigny and Jhering have been for German jurisprudence." He links Gény also with the "death blow" to the old school. Today's perspective on practice and even some comparative doctrine—*cf*. Dabin's compliment quoted in the text and his exegetic reasoning a few pages later in the 1962 lecture (92)23–24—make such appraisals look somewhat premature and overoptimistic.

Husson (214)32: "coherent but flexible synthesis" with a "penetrating force . . . lifted the discussion [of legal method] on the level of legal philosophy." Lambert (241)117: "penetrating, suggestive, full of new and fertile ideas." Legaz y Lacambra (250)118: Gény broke the "fetishism of the statute." Llewellyn (268)189,260,422n46: "magnificent *Méthode*"; "simple and glorious formula"; "sweet craftsmanship." Von Mehren (294)825: "a powerful and extremely influential statement of a non-mechanical conception of the judicial process." Olgiatti (313)339: "marvelous realistic spirit [against] the abstract formalism of the traditional method." O'Toole (315) 456n5: "Gény "incisively analyzed the folly of the traditional mode . . . stretching enacted rules by dry logic." Pound (334)293; (332)466: "book of first importance"; compared with Duguit, Gény "may in the end be rated the highest in respect to the permanent contribution to the science of law." Ripert (353)381: "justly praised"; "has renewed the study of jurisprudence." Roubier (358)75: "celebrated work, magisterially conceived." Stone (385)151: "the earnest Gény." Wortley (424)139, 149: "most complete and luminous account of the bases of modern French private law"; "of more than accidental interest to" English legal practice. See also Castán (66)132f, David and de Vries (98)94, di Carlo (63)*I* 234, Jones (225)69, Recaséns-Siches (346)553, Terré (393), and Tuor (400)28.

I now turn to the various "school" labels listed in the text. "Pragmatic" is Duguit's common label for Saleilles and Gény—cited by Bonnecasse (35)*40* —and he defines pragmatism as "the idea that legal reality is purely conceptual and that the truth of legal concepts is measured by their effectiveness." Bonnecasse (35)*42* does not think of Gény as a pragmatist in these terms. For "idealist," see Cardozo (62)27, Allen (cited at the beginning of this note), and Friedman (142)209.

The label "scientific rationalist" comes from Bonnecasse (35)*241*, and is related to the label "neoclassicist." The evaluation by Bonnecasse refers to both of Gény's major works. He called the *Méthode*, with reference to the tone of Saleilles' preface, "the manifesto that was to become the charter of the scientific school" (35)*155*. Elsewhere, he classified Gény with the private-law branch of the "scientific school," dated approximately 1880–1914 and represented also by Thaller, Saleilles, Planiol, and Charmont, all of whom "completely distinguish themselves from the great [nineteenth-century] commentators by their common scientific conception of law, that is, the distinction of science from technique, together with which one also has to mention methodology" (35)*204, 173*. By neoclassicism Bonnecasse means the revival of the traditional school in a refined form in which the "experimental" (empirical) and the "rational" (intellectual-normative) elements were distinguished. This is "scientific rationalism." All these labels have indeed the same denominator: the reference to empirically processed social reality as the objective source of law-making, which is the unbroken thread of Gény's work.

For "legal sociologists," see Esser (127)14. Friedman (cited above) speaks of Gény as a "sociological idealist." For "realist" in the American sense, see Frank (134)6,279; in the European sense, see Bonnecasse (35) *59–60*.

The term "neo-Scholastic" is rather critical as it is used by the legal sociologist Pound (332)451 and the empirical positivist Holmes (203). But, in a hairsplitting feat, an undisputed neo-Scholastic, Dabin, criticizes Gény's natural-law conception, insists that law is completely man-made (*construit*), and at the same time considers Gény too practical and not sociological (*donné*?) enough (93)98f. Dabin's judgment improved as it mellowed (92)27f.

Dabin also described Gény's *donnée rationelle* as "metaphysical realism." The label "metaphysic" appears also in Cossio (80) 114f. Here it is an accusation by a dogmatic neo-Kantian reflecting the school's monopoly claim on "scientific theory" of law. A more moderate member of the Vienna-Brno branch of the school (and my teacher), Sedláček (371)*I* 277, seeks points of contact—though not very persuasively.

Cossio, writing from the standpoint of legal monism, also tacks on Gény the label "eclectic." Compare this with Battaglia (19)409, who says it less aggressively from the standpoint of philosophical monism; Cohen (74)300; Terré (393) 135, somewhat ambivalently, not to say more; and Villey (406) 54 and (407) 102n6.

It is interesting to note that apparently nobody tacked on Gény the label "progressive," at least as fitting as many of the preceding adjectives. Morrow's (306)373n53 term "liberal" comes close, but the context is off.

Into this specific list one must incorporate by reference the various obligatory but not less sincere eulogies in two memorial volumes for Gény: the three-tome *Recueil* (347), edited by Lambert on the occasion of Gény's retirement; and the posthumous *Le centenaire* (308), by the Faculty of Law at Nancy. The bibliography collected in the latter book tends to belie the conclusion by Cossio—already quoted above and one of the few writers who dismiss Gény out of hand—that there is a disproportion between the eulogies and the actual discussion of Gény's doctrine in the literature. See, as a most recent instance, the 1967 Toulouse colloquium on the philosophy of comparative law, with numerous references to Gény, including the epithet "monumental" by chairman Marty (239)7. A genuine projection and elaboration of Gény's doctrine is another matter.

XI

Gény's position on natural law was ambivalent and even went through a circular metamorphosis. The fact that it is discussed in a note only—although other concepts, which have been subject to a comparable intellectual fate, are discussed in the text—indicates a judgment on the relative value of natural law in Gény's doctrine.

I believe it is not difficult to justify this judgment. Starting with the controlling concept of *donné*, all Gény's data are, from the standpoint of positive law, a priori. But their common source is empirical, summarily denominated the nature of things. It could be, of course, argued in a philosophical discourse (which this is not) that the nature of things is not the same as the nature of life or of nature, that it is here a legal concept contingent on perception, and that, consequently, the empirical content of this source is relative and may be fictitious.

Be that as it may, Gény's definition of *donné* as "a datum derived from the nature of things and, hence, susceptible of being understood through cognition or sensed through conscience," adds to Gény's concept of science a dimension without which it cannot be understood. It also distinguishes this complex of data, including the traditionally natural-law item of justice, from natural law in the common philosophical sense.

It is unfortunate that Gény (as well as his critics, friendly and unfriendly, trapped in the traditional dichotomy of positive/natural) insisted on labeling this dimension "natural law." If Gény's data are natural law, then this natural law is something qualitatively so different that it should be distinguished also in name, as I did in the text. (If my term "empirical natural law" appears contradictory, compare it with such an accepted term as Dewey's "experimental logic.") Gény's complex affair with natural law can be highlighted by the following references. In the *Méthode* (1899) he modifies the "outmoded" traditional natural law by stating that "absolute justice . . . can indicate only a direction . . . no more than the legislator does the judge directly apply the just in itself." Even the sharpest critics of natural law (158)*160*n268f.) recognize "effectively the *objectively just*, no matter how reduced in scope" (157)161. "The concept of the just, arrived at through our rational and moral faculties, is . . . susceptible of an infinite number of degrees," and "in its final application to the facts of life it . . . is overcast [literally, flooded] by subjective cognition" (referring to Beudant and Saleilles [158]*161*n291).

In the subtitle as well as the text of Volume II of *Science et technique* (1915), he links *science* with "irreducible natural law" (*l'irreductible "droit naturel"*—in quotation marks as if trying to distinguish it). The concept, shared also by Dabin, originated probably with Cathrein's doctrine of minimum natural law with a variable specific content (67)—*cf.* Lehmann (251) 371—which probably also inspired the terminology of Saleilles (361)109 and is related to Stammler's (381).

The relativity of Gény's "minimum natural law" at this stage of his work and his confusing terminology show in these statements: "Law, as doctrine and belief [value system] can derive it, is essentially a rational construct. . . . In the strictest sense, natural law is the total of rules of law [Gény must mean standards of conduct; *cf.* his distinction between socially enforceable rules of law and 'morals proper' in *Science I 16*, repeated in *II 158*] that reason derives from the nature of things." He continues: "But these objective data, although they condition the very existence of law . . . offer only empty framework. They must be completed . . . by practical action, which involves more decisively human will . . . the technique of law [as distinguished from science], superimposed on doctrine and belief, sometime even in conflict with them" (159)*176–77*. It is perhaps significant that at this stage Gény also softened his attitude regarding *applied* natural-law principles. Compare his strict attitude against divorce legislation in *Méthode* (158)357n215 with the relative statement in *Science* (159) *II* 386: "The principle of . . . basic indissolubility of matrimony . . . as much as [it is] not based on an absolute rational requirement, appear[s] to respond to moral or social aspirations and can be valid only on that basis."

In later years, Gény tended to broaden and thus to distort his rational original conception. So, Volume IV of *Science* (1924) is subtitled in terms of the old conventional dichotomy, "the conflict between natural law and positive legislation," without any adjective that would reduce the natural law here to manageable technical proportion. Contrast his own summary of the thesis of *Science* (*II*, at viii): "Only natural law [system of values], reduced to the essential minimum, more modest and malleable but that much more assured in principle, furnishes the indispensable base for a truly scientific doctrinal [empirically systematic] elaboration of positive law."

Yet, Gény still meant empirically based justice, both as the ideal and the concrete standard of law. *Cf.* (159)*IV*,xii,xv. The summary statement in the same volume, *302*,v—"The 'donné' corresponds about to the basic concept of natural law [consisting of] a stock of moral and economic truths"—vitiates his original insight. One must point out, however, that though Gény seems to have later corrected this deviation in judgment, we are still two generations later witnessing the use of a comparably indiscriminate macro-concept of "natural law," *e.g.*, (372) and (289)s.IX. Gény's article, "The concept of law in France" (1931), criticized by Roubier (358)41, might have been also Gény's reaction to the misunderstanding, past-oriented criticism. But Ripert (352), the French twentieth-century Austinian, probably overstated (for his own purpose) Gény's vacillation between the minimum-empirical natural law and the higher-law concept. There is in fact no incompatibility between Gény's recognition of natural law as an "imperfect idea" (153)255 and his insistence that natural law must not cease to be considered (152)3. However, the first of these references does imply a melancholy longing for metaempirical absolutes, which negates the best in Gény's pragmatic doctrine.

In his *Ultima verba* (1951), published in the year when he reached the age of ninety, Gény's statement that "positive law is the only true law" seems to synthesize his early (*Méthode*) as well as late ("Justice") insights. He is back on the straight conceptual path from which he had deviated in *Science*, perhaps under the personal trauma of the First World War—the loss of a promising son and the shock the warfare gave to Gény's system of civilized values. (*Cf.* the reference to "war, moral crisis, the need to defend the very concept of justice" in the introductory note to *Science II*, written probably while the German penetration into France forced him to leave Nancy temporarily and return to Dijon.

Dabin's intervening correct distinction may have also helped. This leading philosophical neo-Thomist clearly dissociated all of Gény's *données* from natural law proper. Dabin's position was that "au binôme droit naturel-droit positif il faut substituer celui de morale-droit" (for the distinction natural law—positive law we should substitute the group morals-law [93]*216*). In this frame of reference, law is completely man-made (*construit*); the moral conscience alone is a *donnée*, higher, metaphysical. But historical experience shows that, far from being an a priori binding datum, the moral element ("natural law," "justice") can be totally or partially accepted or rejected. This choice is in itself part of the creative lawmaking act (93)133. Consequently, Dabin would reclassify Gény's *données* and put them all as "preliminaries" into the category "law." Most significantly this includes also Gény's moral element—(93)157–58—for his justice is an abstraction from the historical positive law, and his incidental reference to religion still leaves intact Dabin's factor of choice. But Dabin's alternative trichotomy, morals–social norm–law (he quotes with approval Duguit on the distinction between the latter two—*ibid.*, n1), has in comparison with Gény a too crudely formulated central link and is therefore inferior.

Some American reactions and comments on them are of interest. *Cf.* Cardozo's "The same expression [natural law] ought to mean today that law springs from the relations of fact which exist between things" (61)122 and the correct evaluation of this "new school" in Dickinson (107)*II* 522. *Cf.* also Lambert (347)*I* 139–140, contrasting "our timid and impotent natural law" with the "valid American natural law . . . super-positive law [the product of judicial review], imposing itself on legislation as well as on judges." (ref. to Haines (181) and Cohen (75).

XII

Ripert and Boulanger argued that "most often law does not take a crude fact and attach to it legal consequences. . . . The necessary influence of the legal rule on the [selection of the facts] makes the distinction between *le donné* and *le construit illusory*" (355)*I*, *331*, 148n1. But *cf. Gény* (159)*I*, 35, 102–103.

Ripert's and Cohen's dismissal of the science-technique distinction tends to stumble also over the apparent organic nature of some such classification. It pops up in quite varied context. See, for example, the contemporary phenomenological positivism, with its dualism of object and norm, in Amselek (9), who considers Gény's distinction of science and technique to be inadequate, but does not seem to offer perceptible amendments; for succinct criticism, see Friedman (142)206–207. Troller uses (1965) the key terms "Das Vorgegebene" [*donné*] and "Rechtstechnik" and even the formulation "Die gute Formgebung [construit] erfolgt nach dem Willen des Gesetzgebers [*objet de volonté*] (397)59,99,100, apparently without any knowledge of the added bracketed terms Gény wrote in the 1910s.

Among those who appreciated the science-technique classification are sociologist Gurvitch ("the capital distinction" [179]4)—neo-Scholastics Olgiatti (313) and Dabin ("a handsome-looking two-level edifice" [92]34; eclectic Hernández-Gil compared the system of *données* to the stairs-and-steps scheme of Merkel and Kelsen (199)209,224; so does Friedmann—"sociological counterpart of *Stufentheorie*" (142)331. Pound considered science and technique "two of the three elements of which law is made up . . . and which our analytical jurisprudence has ignored" (332)466. Note the vertical hierarchical metaphor in Dabin, Hernández, and Friedmann, as contrasted with the present-day image of linear operational sequence with feedback loops. Gény's model, though hierarchically organized, has more elements of the operational flow (as tentatively articulated as they may be) than his reviewers' own dogmatic background allowed them to perceive. The most complete bibliography of early comments on and reactions to Gény's model is in *Archives de philosophie de droit* I (1925).

Most of the critique comes from the rather conceptualistic Italian jurisprudence. Maggiore (276) considers Gény's distinction "exaggerated" (the original reads *esasperata*, instead of *esagerata*, but that is no doubt a typographical error). Instead he suggests a distinction between "abstract and concrete logic." Even if we overlook the quaint use of the word *logic* and read Maggiore as intending to distinguish between abstract rules and their application to concrete problems, it leaves out one-half of Gény's scheme—the source of the abstract rules. Battaglia's critique (19)209 is equally unpersuasive and his alternative is inferior. He reasons that either technique is merely the elaboration of the substance and therefore nothing else than science itself or it is separate and then one runs the danger of falling back on the old "abstractions." The goal must be to explain the law in its unity. That is impossible to do with Gény's categories; it requires the unifying concept of "spirit, creativity." The formulation indicates that Battaglia mistook technique for method. For if method, in his definition, consists of "the directives mind must follow when it wants to penetrate any object of knowledge," then Gény's "technique" is obviously something more: the process of normative formulation of this knowledge derived from the ultimate environmental, psychological, and ethical data. Bobbio, in a very early work (31) 38, questions Gény's definition of technique, which he understands as essentially a product of volition, science being a product of intellect. Bobbio argues that "technique is also an intellectual product." This critique is primarily formal and semantic, an impression Bobbio's subsequent reference to the concept science tends to support. Most likely it is based on Gény's capsule definitions at the end of the second edition of the *Méthode* (157)*224*. But the word *intelligence* there is counterposed to *volonté* and means clearly knowledge as distinguished from discretion (volition). Both of these are intellectual processes.

Gény indeed tends to confuse the context by designating the process toward the *construit* as "artificial." Note Gény's refinement from "oeuvre de volonté artificielle, sinon arbitraire" (159)*33*(1913) to "procédés artificiels, objet de volonté plutôt que d'intelligence" (157)*224*(1919). This language makes sense in the original only in the absence of better terms. I should have translated it (1961) as "discretionary, object of volition [decision] rather than of knowledge [data base]," not as literally as I did (158)569. Compare also Gény's language added in 1919: "This discretionary power . . . must not become arbitrariness" (158)428. It is interesting to note that on checking the French original against Bobbio's interpretation, when I prepared the translator's introduction (1962), I was apparently so sure about having made a correct conceptual rather than literal translation—*cf.* (283) n110 in fine—that I did not check my carbon copy of the translation for possible improvement in the proofs, the correction of which was happily not my responsibility.

Holmes's judgment on Gény is contained in a short comment entitled "Natural law" (203), which is a charming gem of Holmesian linguistics covered by his own dictum that "one phrase adds no more than the others to what we know without it." Another American, Patterson, an influential teacher of jurisprudence in his time at Columbia, also failed to grasp the full dimension of Gény. His lack of interest and understanding is so complete that it cannot be redeemed even by the nature of the text and the prefatory salvaging clause about "oversimplification or even distortion" (322)viii,343. The ground common to both Holmes and Patterson is that they reacted not against Gény's methodology (Patterson does not even list the *Méthode* in his bibliography) but against his natural law, misunderstood indeed. This is also suggested by Llewellyn (268)422n46, who suspects that neither of the two took pains to penetrate to Gény's technical-legal core. But Patterson's verdict on Gény, which Llewellyn reports—"after all, a second-rate natural law writer"—is more acute than intended if Patterson meant, as he probably did, not writer but philosopher. Llewellyn himself has no difficulty in identifying the "technique and attitude" element in Gény's "natural law," independent of any particular philosophical orientation. *Cf.* also the balanced judgments of Dickinson (107)522 and Rogers (357)573.

Villey, cited in the text, has a unique viewpoint: he feels that Gény's natural law went awry because he read the wrong literature—the second-hand ("mediocre-caricature") deformations (Windscheid, Boistel, Cathrein) instead of the originators, from Aristotle on (406)48f.,54.

It is notable how few writers understood and accepted Gény on his own terms. The realists—conspicuous among them Cardozo, Frank, and Llewellyn—and contemporary writers of balanced outlook (Stone and Esser) start with admiration for the *Méthode* and look to *Science* for continuation and development.

Cohen is one of the few who have concluded that *Science* has not appreciably added to *Méthode*: "Many valuable observations in the book . . . were substantially embodied in [Gény's] earlier work" (74)300. The initial and still-prevailing evaluations—Dabin (92)27, Kayser (230)2, Wu (427) 40, and Terré (393)135, at least by implication, all writing in the early 1960s—consider *Science* clearly more important and superior, though in varying degrees. This was no doubt Gény's initial intent and conclusion. As this essay develops, it may become clearer why one must disagree with the majority opinion. Yung apparently takes this position in by far the brightest contribution to the centenary memorial volume (432), as he makes no reference to *Science* in his thirteen-page comparative contribution. There is a melancholy indication in the last paragraph of the second edition of the *Méthode*, written when two volumes of *Science* were already published and the manuscript of the third volume was substantially finished, that Gény's own feeling about the relative value of his two principal works may have become ambivalent.

XIII

On the conservative side, perhaps more telling than an outright attack, is the subtle dissociation from Gény by Saleilles in his generally commending preface to the *Méthode*: "I do not have to align myself with . . . I do not discuss, nor analyze. . . . Even I might have difficulty in disengaging myself from the [traditional] school, in whose spirit I was formed" (158)lxxxv.

Saleilles was then a figure of national and international prestige, which Gény never became during his active professional life; and Gény dedicated to his memory the four volumes of *Science et technique*.

Some of the glibness at the other end of the spectrum can be illustrated by Boulanger's reported slight—Gény is merely "Portalis one hundred years later." The reference is to the chief architect of the Napoleonic Code and advocate of the concept of insufficiency of written law ("National codes make themselves as time goes on; properly speaking one does not make them"), whom Gény repeatedly and copiously quotes (157)*47,57*. But why only Portalis? Why not "Aristotle 2200-odd years later?" Gény quotes (157)*56*n Aristotle's famous passage from the *Nichomachean Ethics*: "Statute includes only the most common cases and does not attempt to hide its own gaps" (V.10.xiv.4). In Section 5 one finds even an early statement of the free-search method: "When the statute contains a general provision and the individual case is exceptional, it is proper [for the judge] to speak in [the legislator's] place as he would have done if he had known the particular case at issue." And Gény duly quotes it in this context (157)*156*.

So it would be historically more correct to say that Portalis restated—without reference to Aristotle and contrary to Justinian's insistence on the final authority of the legislator to make and interpretate law (see Imp. Justinianus Augustus Demostheni, C.1.14.32 [529 A.D.])—the real limitations of legislation and the necessity to supplement it by decisional law. Gény systematically and critically developed the argument *and the method*. He states his case in the *Méthode,3*. *Cf.* Villey, who points out with admiration still sixty years later how Gény would "straightforwardly [*en règle*]" identify the methodological need and would devote to it "two thick volumes and I do not know how many years" (406)44. Boulanger's reported remark also markedly differs from what he wrote about Gény, and from the admiration he expressed privately to me in 1965. Consequently it must be filed away as a piece of lecture-hall oratory rather than a pondered judgment. Gény reacted to the various "critiques" and "attacks" in a note put at the head of the second edition of the *Méthode* (157)xi.

XIV

Article 5 of the French Civil Code (1804) reads, "Il est défendu aux juges de prononcer par voie de disposition générale et réglementaire sur les causes qui leur sont soumises [Judges are prohibited from deciding cases submitted to them in the form of generally binding rules]." Article 5 is the French legislator's explicit reaction to the so-called *arrêts de réglement* of the prerevolutionary parlements. These were decisions in specific controversies that the Parlement as a court of law utilized to proclaim general rules for the future. See, however, Article 12 of the Austrian Civil Code (1811), drafted and promulgated without any such historical background: "The dispositions in individual cases and the judgments rendered by courts of law in particular controversies have never the force of a statute. They cannot be extended to other cases and other persons."

Article 4, French Civil Code, reads, "Le juge qui refusera de juger, sous prétexte du silence, de l'obscurité ou de l'insuffisance de la loi, pourra être poursuivi comme coupable de déni de justice [The judge who refuses to proceed with a case on the grounds that the statute is silent, obscure, or incomplete, can be held liable for denial of justice]."

XV

These representative quotations illustrate Gény's ambivalent thesis on decisional law, including that resulting from free search. They are listed in the numerical order of pages in the translation of the *Méthode.*

"No matter how broad a power of personal judgment we would give our judges, its exercise still does not constitute an interference with the legislative sphere as long as the judicial decision remains limited to the particular case" (158) 144. He refers to Article 5 of the French Civil Code.

"I do not quite see how the judge could be reproached for finding in his own conscience the decision he is not allowed to refuse to the litigants (Art. 4, Fr.Civ.C.), where the statute does not give him any guidance" (158) 145.

"It could be said that the statute is only a simple beginning toward the actual and definite decision" (158) 146, citing Hugo, 1813, and Bülow, 1885. With Hugo's "initiative toward the actual holding," compare Duguit more than a century later: "The statute is nothing more than . . . a simple base [*document*] for the finding of the legal norm" (110) *1*91.

"It is exact to say . . . that decisional law represents the true positive law" (158) 146n17, with reference to Planiol (added to the 1919 edition).

Gény cites without any objection Betrand (judge, Court of Cassation, 1888): "In reality, the judge participates in [the making of] civil law." But he asks in the next sentence, "Does all this not lead us into the abyss of individual arbitrariness . . . sacrifice [of] the primordial . . . need for certainty in law?" (158) 148.

"Yet it is not necessary to sacrifice to the chimera of abstract stability . . . the whole idea of individual adaptation through judicial discretion" (158) 149.

"Hence I think it temerarious to introduce [in France] ideas current in England and in the majority of the United States. . . . separation of legislative and judicial power in England is less complete . . . than our revolutionary legislation wanted to establish" (158) 328.

"Decisional law studied in its evolution is nothing else than a contemporary history of our positive law" (158) 334.

"If the objective is to erect decisional law into a formal positive source, we must not forget that it is subject to variations and contradictions, and that its structure does not offer the guarantees essential to all lawmaking . . . I do not [share] the most optimistic assumption that the preceding decisions contain a germ of future development and that by strictly following the precedents the judge will manage to satisfy new needs" (158) 335.

"Basically, the whole difference between Lambert and myself is that in his eyes [the status of decisional law] is only a question of fact . . . while

I see here a true question of law. When Lambert objects that courts cannot be forced to return infinitely to the same question, I answer that I request only the *faculty* for each court, *if it considers it proper*, to reopen a question, even if already decided by others, and examine it without being absolutely bound by prior decisions" *Id.*n98.

"I shall therefore continue to refuse to see in our court decisions a formal source of positive private law that could function as an independent creative force next to statute and custom" (158)335.

"In the presence of a rule supported by a firm line of prior decisions, the interpreter [judge] can abstain from a new inquiry on grounds of his faith in the alleged precedents. He has a basis for solving his personal doubts in the sense indicated by the authority, which he should not lay aside except for decisive reasons. . . . This certainly does not represent legislative force . . . such as we attach to written law or custom" (158)336.

"Court decisions are in our modern system the only really fruitful and, at any rate, the most frequent occasion to form a legal custom . . . these decisions [examples] have originated usages . . . based on the conviction of the parties that the rules introduced by the courts were obligatory. . . . we have here assembled all the elements of true customary law of which the precedent is the point of departure and the essential determinant. . . . But it is important to note that decisional law does not constitute here an independent source of law, or even a custom *sui generis*. It functions only as a propeller of the custom . . . a propeller that is so indispensable and the effects of which are so inevitable in our social and political conditions that a simple mental transposition or even simplification of the formula suffices to ascribe to it all the merit of the normative creation of which it is in effect [only] the capital instrumentality" (158)337.

"Thus decisional law, as much as it initiates custom, can be considered in my opinion still today a truly productive force in law. But . . . as we cannot admit that custom is effective if contrary to written law, so we cannot attribute an obligatory force to a usage based on decisions that . . . radically contradict the legal text" (158)337–38.

In 1919, Gény summarized the relevant thirty-eight sections of the original *Méthode* (1899) in two paragraphs that contain these key words: "unless they are formed as custom[ary law], judicial decisions, even the most solid and consistently followed, have value in the sphere of lawmaking only by virtue of their reason (*rationis imperio*), not because of their formal authority (*ratione imperii*)." The result of "free objective search for a rule" when legislated or customary law is not available, "although a pure legal norm, is limited to the *res judicata* and cannot serve as a general rule binding in the future" (158)223,VII,VIII.

A little later, in *Science* (159) *III*, *199*, *200* (1921), he said:

> By putting formal sources, especially written law, in the first place among the technical processes toward judicial decisions, I am afraid I will scandalize many lawyers. Is the statute not the essence, practically the whole of positive law? . . . Statute is [not] the expression of some absolute sovereignty. . . . Statute is only the result of an opinion. . . . The only value

> it merits responds to a technical necessity. . . . a purely historical critique [of Gény's strict] Romano-canonic conception of customary law pretends to find in all the legal past [a basis to] propose that we simply fuse modern customary law with decisional law [reference to Lambert], without apparently noting the insurmountable difficulties that the erecting of judicial decisions as such to a formal source of positive law would create . . . under our constitutional principles.

"When I attempted to define the role and the limits of 'free objective search' in the complete framework of interpretation of private positive law . . . still under the influence of traditional ideas, I considered the independent search for a rule as subordinated or at least subsidiary to the straight application of written law. . . . My present position is somewhat changed: the jurist [*jurisconsulte*] is in my opinion in principle free to search for the positive rule amidst the elements of the *donné*; the written law is merely a technical means . . . simply one factor working in tandem" (159)*278*.

"The principal effort of the lawyer [*juriste*] centers on technique [of which] decisional law is . . . the most instructive model" (159)*303*.

Concerning Gény's position on decisional law, Boulanger comments, "Theoretically the judge can sweep the slate clean with regard to what others have decided or even what he had decided. From this theoretical freedom . . . it has been concluded that decisions are not a source of law. We are not very sure that, with regard to decisional law, the question of sources of law has been examined with a sufficient concern about reality" (37)22. Ripert, speaking of Planiol's treatise published in 1899, comments, "It required courage then to attribute to cases authority equal to the written law" (354)17.

XVI

In France, Labbé had turned particular attention to judicial decisions since the early 1880s, when he had become the first major professor turned *arrêtiste*—writer of critical notes under the decisions of the courts of appeal and of cassation. Shortly after Beudant, Bufnoir, and others began to illustrate the meaning of the code articles to their students and readers by citing leading cases.

This was a very belated recognition of *le Palais* (the seat of the courts) by *l'École* (the law professors), considering facts such as these:

1. Since the passage of the law of April 1, 1837, the decisions of the Court of Cassation, when revising the second appellate decision in a case, have become final and binding in law. The so-called *double pourvoi* is a peculiarly French practice. The first *pourvoi* (petition for cassation on a limited number of grounds of violation of law) results in a *renvoi* (remand with an essentially advisory opinion) to a court of appeals different from the one which made the decision, object of the first *pourvoi*. This second appellate court is, however, free to side with the first appellate court, rather than to follow the, by definition, contrary opinion of the Court of

Cassation. If the second court of appeals confirms the first appellate decision, rather than following the opinion of the cassation panel, and the losing party petitions for a second review (*deuxième pourvoi*), the Court of Cassation sits in a plenum (*chambres réunies*), originally with thirty-six judges, since 1965 reduced to fifteen. If the "full" court upholds the opinion of its chamber, which was seized of the first review, it will have quashed two identical holdings of different appellate courts in the same case. The resulting second *renvoi* is not only an obligatory instruction to a still different court of appeals (the third in the same case) to issue the final order in the case; it is also decisional law (the principal source of *jurisprudence constante*), susceptible of change only by legislation or by the Court of Cassation itself—in spite of Boulanger's dogmatic argument (39)440 (See Note XVII *in fine*).

2. The oldest French case reporter, the *Journal de palais* (1791–), began to be published again in 1837, after an interruption of thirty-six years, and has appeared regularly since. *Sirey*, the second oldest reporter, reappeared in 1840 after an interruption of thirty-five years and was also published regularly until its merger with *Dalloz* in the 1960s.

Although late in coming, the *arrêtistes* started an important trend toward overcoming the "theology" that doctrine had imposed on practical needs throughout most of the nineteenth century. (*Cf.* the famous mid-century dictum by Bugnet of the Paris law faculty: "I do not know civil law. I only teach the Code Napoleón." If Bugnet worshipped on the altar of the code, is Langdell's common law theology some twenty years later—"Law is a science . . . all the materials [principles and doctrines] of [which] are contained . . . in cases" (243) Preface—substantially different?

Bartin returned, still rather timidly, to Portalis in 1892 (18) when he wrote that "the judge . . . really participates in the making of the civil law . . . decisional law [has] a possible historical role." Lambert wrote in 1893 (240) about judicial decisions as a sufficient organ of contemporary customary law—a phrase that Gény notes "made it" and reappeared within a few years as (*a*) "new customary law that borrows from the civil code merely a general direction sufficient to assure its unity"; and as (*b*) "court decisions, the changes in and variations on which represent the law," in a prospectus for the doctoral program at the Faculty of Law in Lyons, Lambert's home institution. (All the quotations in this paragraph are from the *Méthode, 147*.)

Planiol wrote in the preface of his *Traité élémentaire*, published in the same year as Gény's *Méthode*, "Let us take decisional law for what it is, a customary law of recent origin" (330). Capitant, in the second edition of his *Introduction* (1903; 1st ed., 1897), stressed his effort to "give judicial decisions all the importance that they deserve" and concluded, partly against Gény, that (*a*) "rules [abstract precepts] that emerge from clusters of judicial decisions . . . make law"; (*b*) judicial decisions therefore have higher authority than the doctrine of writers; and (*c*) "the judges participate in the creation of law without stepping outside their competence and without any violation of the principles of our public law [separation of powers]." Capitant (56)vii,30,32n cites then the concurring opinions of Tissier, Percerou, and Meynial (all in reviews of *Méthode*) and of Esmein, Langlois (*Essai sur le pouvoir prétorien de la jurisprudence*, Caen thesis, 1897), and Thaller.

A better expression of Esmein's ideas than that cited by Capitant is found in the leading article of the first issue of the *Revue trimestrielle de droit civil* (1902), entitled "La jurisprudence et la doctrine," in which Esmein declared "decisional law . . . the true expression of civil law . . . the real and positive law until the code is changed" (123)12. Esmein's contemporary Lambert went as far as to, in Gény's words (159)*12*, "envisage the subjection of all positive law to a progressive decisional law informed [*éclairé*] by contemporary social development" (242)216–43, (241)809–24, 875–927—a position Gény considered one of "extreme daring."

The depth and, as I will show later, the futility of this debate can be gleaned from the fact that Esmein's son Paul, the editor until his death in the 1960s of the classical treatise of Aubry and Rau, was still compelled to write in 1952 about "the discussion never closed in France about whether decisions are a source of law." Esmein concluded, as his father and other writers cited above did, that "to refuse to see in them a source of law is to misjudge reality" too much (124)19–20.

On the other hand, Carbonnier, who is to me—and by wide consent of his French colleagues—one of the most sophisticated contemporaries, has refined his 1935 formulation ("Decisional law is a superimposition of individual judgments. . . . But by the simple fact of accumulation, *res judicata* cannot acquire an authority that it did not have as a single instance" [58] 482–83), but not beyond saying that "decisional law is not a genuine source of civil law, comparable to statute or even to custom . . . but merely . . . has a considerable authority" (57)*I* 115. This conclusion is based on the same stereotyped historical interpretation of Article 5 of the French Civil Code as Gény's and is contrary to Capitant's correct insight half a century earlier that the "new force acquired by a consolidated rule of decisional law owes its authority only to the mass of [individual] decisions through which it was formulated" (56)30,32.

In Germany, the doctrine of which was Gény's constant critical reference, Bülow, Kohler, Gierke, and others had voiced, since the mid-1880s, similar ideas in favor of decisional *law*, all duly noted in *Méthode* and *Science*.

XVII

As the preceding note indicates, nobody in France has explicitly proposed that decisional law be recognized as a separate formal source, at the time Gény wrote or since then. *Cf.* Dawson's list of recent writers (102)417n3. Capitant came very close to suggesting it when he asserted in response to Gény—and no doubt also under the influence of Planiol—that "we must recognize the separate and independent character" of decisional law, which "it is impossible to relate to the will of the legislator." But this promising lead is soon lost and we are back on the customary law track (56)30,32. More recently, Maury insisted that Article 4 of the French Civil Code represents a formal legislative delegation to the judge of the right to create "rules of law through *jurisprudence constante*." But he puts the result in Hauriou's category "*institution-chose*" (194)44 (institutional fact), rather than classifying it as a separate source (278)37,50.

The second proposition in the text, about the pretorian power, is the heart of Gény's free-search method. There was no difference in principle between him and his critics. Gény met them more than halfway when he attributed to "a firm line of prior decisions . . . the force of the written reason [which] an interpreter [judge] should not lay aside except for decisive reasons" (158)336.

As to the "real dispute," even that begins to look a little silly when it is reduced to the analytical bare bones. It is true that the traditional distinction in France between *droit écrit* and *droit coutumier*, which was even a geographical fact before the consolidation of the northern and the southern law in the Napoleonic codification, should not have prevented Gény from seeing that judicial decisions have always been the transmission belt between social usage and customary law. A social fact, including the *opinio necesitatis*, becomes a legal norm only after it has been confirmed by an authoritative decision in a concrete conflict situation. For judicially upheld usage (customary law) to become "written," is then more a question of technology (recording, printing, dissemination, and eventual compilation and codification) than of analysis. The timing hardly affects the de facto or de jure authority or the degree of creative responsiveness of the judicial system to changing needs or normative gaps.

But when Gény's thesis is carefully synthesized, he turns out to be less dogmatic than his critics or followers. Gény would not have said, as Boulanger did fifty years later, that, once a decisional doctrine has been established (that is, the line of judicial solutions "has been transformed into custom"), "the creative power of decisional law has lost its reason to be" (39)440—a formula akin to the English doctrine of the eternal force of precedents, which the House of Lords overruled only in 1966.

The key to Gény's position is not to be found in these doctrinal disputations, which most of his critics did not seem to discover or appreciate. The key is rather the methodological focus of Gény's interest, even reflected in the subordination of source to method in the title of his first principal work and in his strategy in favor of free search.

XVIII

Planiol's comment deserves an extensive quotation: "Those who are unwilling to recognize that the courts are the organ that gives authority to customary law are very much embarrassed as to how to explain the matter. . . . Gény is led to put the decisions of the courts on the same footing as the teaching of writers. He sees nothing in judgments but the isolated opinions of . . . individuals of greater or lesser significance. That is true of the opinions of treatise writers. Their authority is . . . without any sanction. . . . But it is a grave error to apply the same conception to the judgments of the courts. . . . they make decisions that are executed" (330)*14*.B.n.

On Gény's assimilation of the authority of decisional law to that of the writers, see also Lambert (241)17–18, who suggests that the continuation of the nineteenth-century ideology might produce a split into *la doctrine*, "having merely conventional and fictitious reality," and *la jurisprudence*, "the only really applied legal system." This split would be analogous to that between the Roman civil and pretorian law and between the English common law and equity. Oddly enough, Gény cites this observation with approval (158)38n18. See also (158)*147*n90, where Gény indirectly criticizes an opinion, identified only by the year of publication (1897), saying that it is "docile" for the doctrine to follow court decisions rather than to deal with (that is, manipulate) principles and texts in the traditional manner.

In the broader context, it is a matter for conjecture how much Gény was unable to overcome the traditional compartmentalization between the three governmental branches and to what extent he was not interested in pressing the point. At any rate, Gény reads the crucial Articles 4 and 5, French Civil Code, as literally as possible. Compare the blind alley to which it leads him still in a 1919 addition to the *Méthode* (158)*176* at n576: although the clear meaning of Article 4 is to order the judge to decide and denies him the opportunity to excuse himself because of silence, obscurity, or insufficiency of the code, Gény uses the word *prétexte* in this article to construct a hairsplitting distinction between judicial lawmaking under Article 4 and "free search." *Prétexte* means in French both pretext and pretense. Yet, according to Gény, in Article 4 it cannot mean anything else than "the judge's *claim* [pretense] that the code is silent." The only possible explanation for this acrobatic "nuance which [Gény dares] to formulate only with hesitation" can be the desire to maintain the semblance of a strict division of powers. How else can one draw a line between a judicial decision, where the code is unclear, insufficient, or silent, and the also judicial "free search for a rule," which simply does not exist in the code. Note that the introductory articles of the civil code are considered in France to have a quasi-constitutional authority, which means governing the whole legal system, not only private law. This doctrine was fully established in Gény's time.

XIX

Ehrlich (118)312,342 and Kantorowicz (171)21 related the technique of arriving at a solution and *then* finding the supporting authority—in Justinian's Corpus Juris Civilis—to Bartolus (1314–1357), the most famous of the glossators. But the situation must be distinguished. The Corpus Juris was not an obligatory source of reference; the glossators and their successors were eager but not bound to find their concrete solutions supported by the rules and principles of Roman law.

The modern roots of the hunch thesis go at least as far back as the German judge Bülow in the 1880s (50), whom Gény repeatedly cites. In France, Niboyet cited Bartin as stating (probably in the 1890s) that "the judge makes a decision and then gives it the [legal] frame" (14)*VI* 74. The idea was, thus, sufficiently in the doctrinal environment by the time the

Méthode was first published. Shortly after, Saleilles would write (360)45: "One decides the result at the outset; one finds the principle afterwards. This is the source and scheme of all legal thought." Considering Saleilles' overcautious stance in his preface to the *Méthode*, written two to three years earlier (esp. [157]xxiv, [158]lxxxv), the cited "hunch" statement presents a swing in dogmatism from right to left without much apparent analytical progress.

Gény cites the Austrians and Germans Unger, Fuchs, Bahr via Vierhaus, and Rumpf (158)548n538–41, all of whom were reacting to the "free-law" movement, which got its full shape in Gnaeus Flavius' manifesto in 1906 (171). Kohler, professor of law at the University of Berlin and an early follower of Jhering, but by then a crown counselor (*Geheimrat*) and certainly no radical, could write in 1911 (commenting on an article by J. S. Sheppard on "the decadence of the system of precedent," Harv. L. Rev. 24(1911)1298: "The [American] judge allegedly asks today first 'what is the correct result?' Only then does he reach for the available positive law . . . which he tries to shape as much as possible so as to lead to the desired result. *All just like in our practice*" (235)919 (emphasis added). Note that this was written only a decade after the new German Civil Code entered into force! Note also the affinity with the apocryphal but probable anecdote about Chief Justice Marshall, some eighty years earlier: "Judgment for the petitioner. Mr. Justice Story will find the authorities."

In face of this and more, Gény could still write in 1919: "Unger [then president of the Supreme Court in Vienna] makes interesting revelations about his judicial manner. . . . This manner is not unrelated to the fashion of consulting which 'Gnaeus Flavius' [(171)21] ascribes to Bartolus, according to the legend [Gény did not know about the John Marshall legend], and *which I consider* quite widespread, basing myself on the confidential statements of some French judges [presumably in response to the *Méthode*]. It could be summarized by saying that the judge decides on basis of his conscience and his intimate feelings; *then* he finds the legal grounds. One must agree that *if it were really so*, there would be no better justification for the claims of the partisans of 'free law' " (158)216n538 (first and third emphases added).

An omission that is perhaps symptomatic of the amount of analytic thought Gény gave the hunch thesis is the lack of any implication that the judicial hunch is educated, *i.e.*, that the judicial conscience does not operate in isolation but rather in the framework of the judge's technical-legal training and experience. In other words, Gény makes no connection between the hunch judgment and the positive nature of things, which is the keystone of his free-search concept (and which he discusses, with reference to the same Unger, twenty pages earlier).

The ambivalence and lack of enough distinctions regarding intuitive judgment have continued in France long after. See Maury (278)31, citing with approval Kocourek: "One cannot always rely on the explanations of the reasoning which judges offer after the event" (234)489.

The notion that the hunch is inevitably and subconsciously educated is missing also in this quotation of a "wise [French] judge," apparently sometime early in this century: "The judge looks only for the formula of his decision in the law books. . . . The sources of law [are] much more the means of controlling his personal sentiments than the initial inspiration of his judgment" (Perreau [328]*I* 4, as cited by Maury [278]31n5). Cardozo (61)170 perhaps had these built-in limits in mind when he criticized Saleille's formula above: "So sweeping a statement exaggerates the element of free volition."

Roubier is more sophisticated (358)74–75, via Hutcheson (347), cited below. A well-known case of a judge correcting his hunch after study of the law is that of Judge Ulman in the *Baltimore Tramways* case (402).

For other European post-Gény writers on judicial hunch, see Dualde (109)207, 215f.; Germann (161)10, with an interesting amplification in the 1946 edition of his original 1921 position (161)22; Isay (216), compared with Castán (66)129,163f.; and Liver (265)1,40, who also lists various other Swiss writers. But Liver's reference to only contemporary non-Swiss authors (Boulanger, Esser, Coing) is misleading and fails to give the credit due to Gény's contemporaries two generations earlier–Capitant and Lambert.

In America, the hunch thesis is usually linked with Judge Hutcheson's formulation of "the triumphant precursor of the just judgment" (215)274, contributed also to the *Recueil* (347)*II* 531–73. See also the practically contemporaneous discussion by Radin (342)864 of the "inverted fashion" in judicial process. This term describes the same sequence of decision and justification as the hunch thesis. Radin's terminology raises–but does not lead to the analysis of–questions about what is "normal" in what categories of decisions–routine, difficult appellate, prima facie cases?

XX

Gény expresses the subjective nature of legislated law in two wordy formulae: (*a*) "The characteristic of written law is that it represents with respect to the rule of law it enacts the authority of a specific social organ cast in a verbal form which sets its contours and defines its content binding for all" (158)92 at n96; and (*b*) "statute is valid as an expression of the will of certain persons, formulated in writing and binding on everybody because of the power the authors have" (158)93 at n110. Compare the statement of this idea by Stone: "acts of social authority duly constituted and competent to announce obligatory general rules" (386)153, (384)216, which might be perhaps further trimmed down to acts of (competent) authority promulgating general rules.

The objective doctrine was as such a progress in comparison with the rigidity of the exegetic method. The *ex nunc* interpretation was postulated articulately by commentators as different as Bülow (50), writing in 1885 ("The statute is only a preparation, an attempt to realize legal order. The statute only indicates how the legal order should be fashioned"), and Ballot-Beaupré (16)27, president of the French Court of Cassation, speaking in 1904 ("The judge should not obstinately insist on finding out what was . . . the thought of the authors of the code when they drafted this or that article; he must ask himself what they would have thought if they drafted the same article today"). Gény cites nine additional German commentators in favor of the position that, as he puts it, we ought to "separate the statute from the legislative process and consider it an independent unit which evolves together with the social environment and ought to be interpreted according to its transformations" (158)*104* at n261.

With Lambert's formula of the objective conception of legislated law, compare (*a*) the more conservative formula of Saleilles in the preface to the *Méthode* ("the laws of adaptation of the reality to the [legal] texts, as well as the adaptation of the texts to the development of social life and environment"), which Saleilles ascribes to his teacher Bufnoir and refuses to abandon in favor of Gény's formula (157)xxiv; and (*b*) a more "progressive" hybrid standard proposed by Julliot de la Morandière (77)*I*,406), to interpret the old statutory text with the interpolation of the *volonté* (policy) of the present legislator as derived from contemporary legislation.

As much as Gény's subjective conception implies that legislated law is *primus inter pares*, he merely uses a generally valid classification. But he adds—as Lambert also notes (241)31–32n2—important mitigations, including the admission that the authority of a statute "naturally decreases and may completely disappear . . . under the influence of changing environment." This admission is contradictory, as Lambert suggests, only in dogmatic terms. In reality, and in the mode of presentation, it is still another example of Gény's ambivalence.

Lambert, in turn, makes important concessions in favor of continuous use of the traditional system of interpretation, *e.g.*: "The use of the traditional apparatus of interpretation seems to me indispensable to give our decisional law the firm lines and contours compatible with the natural laws of evolution, to allow positive law to enrich itself constantly by new decisions without breaking too abruptly the old framework. . . . It suffices to compare French law [with] English decisional law, which developed too fragmentarily, without sufficient directives [flowing from the codes], to appreciate the advantages of our own traditional method of interpretation" (241)41.

As implied in the essay text, the simple terminology of subjective-objective is not without ambiguity due to promiscuous usage and the resulting relative and shifting meaning. For example, Hernández-Gil (199)225 defines Gény's position in favor of the subjective conception of legislated law as a stand "against subjectivism," meaning the projection of the individual intent of the interpreter into the legislative text that he interprets. On the other hand, compare the use of subjective-objective in contemporary American usage in reference to judicial attitudes in applying law (72). Still a different type of subjective-objective is inherent in the dual aspect of the French word *volonté* (of the legislator). It expresses both the intellectual willing (intent) and the power to impose its normative result. The corresponding

American distinction is between the subjective intention of the legislator and its objective verbal expression, which may be distinguished by the word *purpose*. (*Cf.* Holmes, as cited by Frankfurter [136]: "When counsel talked of the intention of the legislature, I was indiscreet enough to say I don't care what their intention was. I only want to know what the words mean.") See also Gény's elegant fusion of the intent and the expression quoted in the text following this note. What about the archaic global term "spirit" of the law? If it is understood to mean the intention of the legislator as it comes through his words—as Gény interprets it (157)*100*, with reference to Laurent!—it would be, in spite of itself, more on the "objective" side of purpose. In its modern form, the objective conception originated with the German historical school, which assigned to the formal legislator a back seat compared with the superior authority of the continuously legislating society.

Coordinating the preceding terms with Gény's terminology (the word *scientifique* in his free-search formula means *objective*), one would say that Gény (*a*) advocated the *subjective* conception of legislated law; (*b*) urged an *objective* standard both for interpretation (by insisting on the subjective, *ex tunc* mode, he limits the expressed purpose strictly to its historical context) and for filling gaps in the statutes; but (*c*) did not ignore the fact that the judge will project into the process his *subjective* personality in the form of discretion (as distinguished from arbitrariness).

Gény's insistence on the *ex tunc* interpretation would seem to have required an advocacy of maximum reference to the legislative record, in order to penetrate the original purpose and so to be able to restrict the scope of the statute accordingly. Gény is much less committed than that (157)*104*. He is, at least explicitly, concerned about the "frequent abuse . . . of inductions drawn from these legislative materials" and the "incoherent empiricism" that it represents. More important, he skirts the logical consistency of his position in favor of narrowing the potential applicability of legislated law and thereby increasing the application of the free-search method—a strategy to which I will return.

In line with this position, Gény also insisted that *ordre public* (general, public policy) clauses in the legislation must, on the contrary, be always interpreted *ex nunc*. This further increases the latitude of the judge's discretion to reach the most adequate contemporary decision.

It is also a further corollary of Gény's doctrine, with respect to the wrong classification of analogy as interpretation, that when a judge decides by analogy, he crosses the limits of interpretation proper and enters the sphere of judicial lawmaking.

For accord with Gény's position on general clauses, on both sides of the Atlantic, see Capitant (56)77n and Bruncken (47)138.

XXI

The legitimacy of interpolating modern meanings into Gény's language—in other words, translating Gény for today—imposes itself often not only on the basis of the intrinsic or obviously intended meaning of words in their intellectual context, but also because of better terminology, which Gény cites with approval (or at least without any apparent disapproval) yet does not incorporate into his vocabulary. One of the better examples is Kohler's distinction between philosophy of law and policy (*Rechtspolitik*). The latter has, in Gény's summary, "more directly and essentially practical aims." Gény quotes Kohler early in *Science* (159)*II* 120, but his mind is too much fixed on his conceptual quatuor "science," "technique," "*donné*," and the philosophy of "irreducible natural law." So, though he correctly paraphrases Kohler's definition of the objectives of philosophy as a medium for "adaptation of law to the cultural development," the close connection between his own *donné* and legal policy research and policy making escapes him.

Llewellyn's misreading or overreading of Gény occurs when, looking toward improved handling of legislated text in the hands of American case-method-trained judges, he praises *Méthode* as a demonstration of the "uses [of] an ancient text to handle the most modern cases" (268)422n46. Commons actually suspects himself ("I may not interpret Gény as he intends") and, indeed, is right (78)141. Another example of one who overreads or reads for his own purpose is legal sociologist Gurvitch (179)227, who makes Gény say, in a paraphrase, that "statute is only an opinion," when Gény is in fact saying much more carefully that it is "merely a result of an opinion; even if it is supported by a majority, it cannot pretend to be absolute" (159)*III* 85.

A case in which it is difficult to determine whether the subsequent writer misunderstands or overreads is Allen (3)484, who cites the *Méthode,107* (on analogy) against British mechanical jurisprudence (concretely, Lord Simonds in *Magor* [1952] A.C. 189,191), but talks about statutory law as merely a *donnée* ("part of social and legal material"), a conception Gény developed only later in *Science*.

XXII

Ehrlich suggested the idea of the gap in an "immature and uncertain form" in an obscure "work of my youth" published in Vienna in 1888 (121), that is, eleven years before the *Méthode*. (Gény was then in Algiers.) He summarized it in an equally obscure book, published in 1893 in Berlin (120). From there it finally emerged into wider international circulation in the form of a quotation at the beginning of his famous lecture on "free law" in 1903, in which he discussed the affinities between Gény and himself and stated, "I have no doubt that Gény did not read my work, which has remained quite unknown also in Germany, and that he was in no way stimulated by it." He praised in turn Gény's "unusually rich material on French legal history and decisional law, the great majority of which was new to me" (117)iii–v.

Ehrlich drew on Bülow (50) and, perhaps, on Kohler (236,237). All this literature, including Ehrlich's summary of his "gap" article of 1888 fifteen years later, became known to Gény only when the floodgates of German free-law literature opened sometime during the first decade of this century.

Gény's comments on it appear only in the fourth chapter of the epilog to the *Méthode* (157)205f., published in the 1919 edition.

Another instance when Gény learned about Ehrlich's work with delay—this one caused by World War I—was *Die juristische Logik* (119), which Gény saw apparently more than four years after its publication. Volume III of *Science* was already set, and Gény could add only a note to the preface. There he refers to the parts of Ehrlich's summary and critique on which he would have apparently drawn in his own work. Ehrlich in fact receded in this last major work from the earlier more extreme free-law conception and adopted a position on the role of the judge rather close to Gény's *Méthode* of sixteen years earlier. This convergence is correctly noted by Cardozo (61)121: "Ehrlich has the same thought [as Gény]." Esser (127) repeatedly implies, also with regard to other writers such as his mentor Heck, that Gény was the originator; Stone (385)149f.,158, on the contrary, talks about Ehrlich and Gény in the same breath and suggests the priority of the former.

The reconstruction of the sequences and relations, as much as it is possible, suggests that Gény, if not always first in strict chronological terms, arrived at his ideas independently and formulated them so well that they eventually represented the best synthesis. The danger of concluding more on the available evidence is illustrated by Cohen's opinion (74)378n52 that Kohler's idea of "free creative or sociological interpretation [1886, 1887] received little attention until the adoption of the German and Swiss civil codes [1896, 1900] and Gény's *Method.*" Gény apparently did not have available either of the two prestigious journals (identified after their founders as *Grünhut* and *Jhering*) in which Kohler published, although he repeatedly cites in the chapter on free search Jhering's article in Volume I of the *Jahrbuch* in question. But that might have been an indirect citation through Jhering's later works! At any rate, Gény's "free search" was not "free creative interpretation." As to Ehrlich, there is not enough evidence to conclude one way or the other. Nor did Huber, the author of the Swiss Civil Code, seem to draw on Kohler when he arrived at a formula practically identical with Gény's. (This fascinating example of contemporaneous generation of seminal thought I will recount in the second essay.)

The breadth of Gény's inspiration and his ambitions can be also gleaned from the mottoes of his two principal works. *Méthode* is prefaced by Shakespeare's "There are more things in heaven and earth . . . Than are dreamt of in your philosophy" from *Hamlet*; *Science*, by Goethe's "All theory is gray, dear friend. But green is the golden tree of life" from *Faust*. Both are cited in the original language. See also a submotto of Part 1 of Science (7): "Man cannot more than he knows; true experimental science gives him power only by showing him what he does not know" (Claude Bernard, *Introduction à l'étude de la médecine expérimentale*, 1868).

The "Brandeis brief" is related initially to *Miller* v. *Oregon*, 208 U.S. 412 (1908).

There are interesting instances of interaction between Gény and other legal cultures, in some cases delayed by geographical or language factors.

Among them are, I believe, such items in American literature as Llewellyn's "situation sense" (268), as compared with Gény's "trend at a given time and place" (159)*I* 132f., 183f., *II* 386f., approvingly cited by Cardozo (60)91; or Llewellyn's "equity of the situation" (referring to Cardozo's judging) and Gény's "intuitive equity" (157)*163*; or Fuller's use of "irreducible minimum natural law" (subtitle of Gény's *Science*, II) as a jurisprudential household word that requires no reference (147)388; see also Friedman (141)827, who relates the very distinction between reason and fiat (the operative words in Fuller's article) to Gény.

Among other writers from the Anglo-American orbit who relate Gény's ideas directly to their own positive systems are especially Jones, Wortley (not very fortunately in [425]II 16), Stone, Friedmann and some of the American contributors to the *Recueil.* Wu (427)42,46 is able to relate Gény's *données* to Sir Matthew Hale's conception of the growth of the common law from the seventeenth century, as well as to Walter Lippmann's *Public philosophy* (1955).

Two comparable European examples are Puig-Brutau (339), especially the introduction, and Spiro (379), although the avowed direct reference of both is not Gény but American realists. See also the pervasive underlying reflection of Gény's idea in the Chilean Alvarez (5).

XXIII

Villey and Julliot de la Morandière evoked the climate during Gény's centenary symposium (308)42–44,69–70 with these vignettes, most of them taken from the *Méthode* 1–19: "The philosophy underlying the exegetic method . . . the philosophy that triumphed in the French revolution and came from Rousseau, Locke, and above all Hobbes . . . practically conquered public opinion at the end of the nineteenth century. The ideas that reigned were those of Laurent, Aubry and Rau, Baudry-Lacantinerie . . . Demolombe ('My adage, my article of faith is: Above all *les textes*'), Bugnet ('I do not know civil law; I teach only the Code Napoleón')." Against the explicit provision of Article 4 of the French Civil Code, Blondeau stated in 1841 "without any dissent" that since "the sole source of any decision is the statute . . . the judge must reject the complaint if the legislative texts are silent." (About fifty years later a "learned judge," Crépon, still wrote in the *Répertoire* of Fuzier-Herman, under the heading "Cassation": "One of the basic principles of our society is that nothing must be left to the discretion of the judge; he can never decide except on the basis of an express provision of the statute.") Liard, the rector of the University of Paris, said in 1894, five years before the *Méthode* was published: "Law is legislation. Consequently the task of the law faculties is to teach how to interpret statutes. The resulting method is deductive. The articles of the code are so many theorems, the relations between, and the consequences of, which must be demonstrated. A lawyer is a geometrician." Gény (157)*26* cites Liard (260)397f., but prefers to overlook the parallel with geometry in favor of siding with Liard's plea for introducing "social sciences" into the law curriculum (260)*1*. See also his rather incidental and gentle denunciation of "jurisprudence as a kind of social geometry" at the end of the first edition of the *Méthode, 186* in fine.

No wonder Villey (406) speaks repeatedly of Gény's "courage" in taking on this multiheaded doctrinal dragon systematically and, despite all the possible critique of ambivalence, uncompromisingly. For instance, Gény's devotion to Saleilles does not prevent him from criticizing his mentor's position on interpretation *ex nunc* (157)*95*.

In the matter of the conservative-progressive mixture, there is an interesting parallel between Gény and Cardozo. In his classic *The nature of judicial process*, written one generation after Holmes's "not logic, [but] experience," Cardozo started his analysis of the judicial process with the method of logic rather than other methods or sources more relevant to his central thesis; he continued with this formal hierarchy even after all possible reasons, logical and chronological, which may have shaped the initial outline, had disappeared. While arguing in the opposite direction, he felt it necessary to describe Chief Justice Marshall's opportunistic dictum on the sole task of the judges being to give effect to the will of the legislature as "lofty . . . well and finely said" (61)31f.,112,169.

XXIV

With reference to Gény's "belonging," his close associate at Nancy, Voirin, may be right when he states in a necrology that Gény, "resisting the attraction of the capital, pursued untiringly in the calm and silence of his study, first at Dijon, then in Nancy, the work . . . that was to give him worldwide fame" (408). But it is also a fact that in a country where academic roads still lead to Paris, despite the recent policy of *aménagement du territoire* (decentralized regional development), Gény's highest recognition within the system was a one-year chairmanship of the *concours d'agrégation*, the competition for assistant professorships in French law faculties, in 1929. By this time, sixty-eight years old, he had already collected the first four of his nine honorary doctorates from widely spread European universities. See also the somewhat ambivalent statement by Julliot de la Morandière: Gény, "who was a correspondent [of the Institut de France, the assembly of the five official academies], would certainly have become one of the [forty] titular members, had he lived in Paris" (304)67. But Gény did not have to live in Boston for the American Academy of Arts and Sciences to make him an honorary member!

Gény's tendency to be overly modest and self-deprecating may have worked against him in the academe. Note his claim of writing the *Méthode* originally only for himself (157)*5* and calling it merely an "essay," though "critique"; or the list of his biases ("preconceived ideas, prejudice of origin, education, environment and interests") and bona fide intention to reduce their impact on his work—while, correctly, denouncing valueless science ("a kind of scientific snobism, giving up considered opinions"), both in the introduction to *Science* (159)*I* 19.

Regarding Gény's "good manners" in equaling decisional law with doctrinal writing, one may wonder how much Gény could have been also semantically trapped by the then current global term *interprète*, which included both judges and law professors. (This conception of the equality of both "subsidiary" sources was written into Article 38, Statute of the International Court of Justice, in 1919 and has remained unchanged in the present 1945 version!)

XXV

My point is that Gény's doctrine was evaluated by many participants in this symposium in terms that I have defined elsewhere (279) as "noncritical . . . antiquated concepts, or concepts not sufficiently distinguished or refined, through comparative method where indicated"—in sum, on a level inferior to Gény's and incapable of carrying on his doctrine. Dabin spoke of "silent statute" (308)20, without the slightest hint that silence is not only absence of words, that a statute can speak and yet be silent regarding the normative values that determine the justice of the particular decision—the "teleological gap" widely publicized in connection with Swiss decisional law some thirty years earlier. He claims (at 24) that decisional law "is not binding" in certain national systems, without any recognition of the purely formalistic nature of this proposition. Villey (at 45) claims that "in pure logic [relevance?] there are no gaps in the positive legal order," without any indication that this proposition requires a redefinition of "positive legal order" to include both its verbal form and the changing value content of the rules. (This statement, made on an occasion commemorating Gény, comes two generations after Heck, *following up on Gény*, revised in his jurisprudence of interests the nineteenth-century concept of the completeness of the legal system.) Julliot de la Morandière counterposes so rigidly "decision" and "legal norm" (at 74) and the legislative and judicial functions (at 82) that it is impossible for him to recognize the obvious *and* necessary continuity between the particular rule in a litigation and the generalized rule of a decisional doctrine (*jurisprudence constante*)—in practical, operational terms the equivalent of legislated law, in any country—and to view the two branches, legislative and judicial, for what they are (or should be) in reality: partners in the continuous labor to keep the legal and social system synchronized. See also his crude conception of free search (at 81); or his proposition to evaluate Gény in terms of the number of decisions of the Court of Cassation that he directly influenced; or the faith in the myth of the "certainty of the statute" as contrasted with the "uncertainty and variability" of decisional law (at 82), an unproductive, analytical position and difficult to believe sixty years after the *Méthode* and thirty years after the writings of Jerome Frank and others.

The preceding sample includes only some of the more extreme remnants of the nonempirical approach to law and jurisprudence, revealed in tribute to one of the founders of the modern empirical doctrine. Other examples, many of them much more technical and subtle, are discussed in the second essay.

Notes

XXVI

The various combination of all the factors noted in the text might account for the scarcity of reference to Gény in the older German literature, in perfectly apposite contexts. Gény himself hints at the "customary exclusivity" of the German doctrine. Nevertheless, the *Méthode* was reviewed immediately, though not in any detail, by the prestigious Oertmann (311).

Of a different kind—caused by lack of comparative awareness, though the linguistic limitation is often a contributing factor—is the absence of reference, which I shall illustrate by two recent American publications. One is technical; the other, jurisprudential: (*a*) "A symposium on statutory construction" (389), where several authors managed to discuss fundamental issues raised by Gény without once mentioning him or his ideas; and (*b*) Davitt's general text (101), with no specific reference to Gény on such topics as interpretation, judicial function and method, not man-made law versus man-made law, etc., formulated generally in terms inferior to Gény's.

The phenomenon of "intellectual immunity" to Gény has merely continued a state of affairs that existed at the time Gény wrote his *Méthode* and on which he repeatedly commented. The writers in question have spent themselves on giving stale answers to conventionally framed questions, occasionally disguised by new vocabulary; or they fall within Ascarelli's too kind dictum that "one notices a certain contrast between the language of the doctrine and the practical reality" (13)203, originally addressed to Latin Americans from Ascarelli's Brazilian exile, but alas universally valid (and Ascarelli himself was no more than conservatively modern); or, at best, they frustrate their potential insights because they are unable to discard completely useless traditional concepts or because their method is not comparative.

I will illustrate the last point by a concrete example of this wasteful conceptual provincialism so frequent in the researched literature on both sides of the Atlantic. A judge of an important appellate court, despite plentiful American references (David and de Vries, Mehren, Loussouarn, just to mention the most immediately preceding publications), merely *hypothesizes* that *stare decisis* cannot be wholly escaped even in "civil-law" countries (409)204, instead of pushing from this axiom onward.

Even authors who deal with the same problems as Gény and quote him, the "first group" listed in the following text, illustrate how difficult it is for some to shed completely the old conceptualism, apparently because of substantially the same environmental influence that produced Gény's overcautious formulae. Germann (161)140–42 was more rooted in the past than he would admit. Ascarelli's confessions and terminology, *e.g.*, (12)iii–iv, show the same. Castán (65)144, although deliberately critical along Gény's lines, still says in 1953 that "we must abandon the thesis that the statute is the sole and exclusive source of law . . . the coexistence of legislated law and decisional law has caused prestigious commentators to admit a pluralistic conception of the legal system, which perhaps does not satisfy formal logic but which alone expresses exactly the reality." Even Esser, one of the most sophisticated writers, occasionally administers a formalistic shock—*e.g.*,

(127)311f.—when he seems trapped by the traditional concept of the *Juristenrecht.*

The present state of English jurisprudential thought at large can be reconstructed on the conceptual framework in Evershed (128), essentially unchanged fifteen years later (Dennis Lloyd 1974, 1976), despite *implied* critique and insights.

A very special case is Holmes, to whom I have made previous references. The case is one of allergy rather than of immunity. I speak in the text of *apparent* ideological difference between Holmes and Gény, because Holmes could no doubt be criticized for not using his brilliance to understand the modest, restricted, and pragmatic meaning of Gény's neonaturalism and instead reacting in the stereotyped fashion. Had he confronted Gény profoundly on the germane technical level, rather than superficially on the secondary and misinterpreted philosophical basis, the potential cross-fertilization may have brought measurable advancement in jurisprudential thought. The only instance I have found in the literature where Gény and Holmes are related is in Kocourek (234)466.

XXVII

Note this small sample of reactions to the continuing formalistic conceptualism: Ascarelli (12)xi, criticizing the notion that the alternative to logic is arbitrariness, and (13)xxix n21, extensive comparison of mathematical and legal reasoning (*cf.* Ehrlich's critique of the "mathematical-game method of decision" [119]295); Germann (161), continued conceptual "in-the-past-rootedness"; Dualde (109)178,186, critique of the assumptions underlying the preferential status of legislated law; Djuvara (108)*I* 220,271, critique of the notion that legislated law exists authoritatively without contact with social realities; Esser (127)177,181,222, "text absolutism," "closed system," implying that the genealogy of Heck's concept goes back to Gény, 290 ff.

One example of the osmosis mentioned in the text is the collection of articles by a Spanish writer, Jerónimo González (173), written mostly in the second quarter of this century under apparent influence of Gény but without specific acknowledgment. I was led to this source through an exchange with the Catalan Puig-Brutau, who, together with the Swiss Spiro, represents the better example of another mode of propagation of Gény's ideas—the circuitous route. In Puig and Spiro's cases it was via the American realists, as already noted.

XXVIII

The term "projection" of legislation is Wurzel's. For him it stands "in the middle between subsumption and analogy . . . employed by legal reasoning in bringing together a fact and a legal concept . . . without changing the nature of the concept. (*Cf.* Levi's [254] legal concepts with shifting meaning, "a moving classification system," and Dualde's critique (109)180 of "projection" as a "gratuitous application of a precept to something that is not envisaged by it.") "Analogy is different from projection only in degree, not in kind" (428)345,357. Gény draws the line between interpretation and analogy, the latter belonging to free search. For Wurzel, the rule used as a base for analogy gets an extended application "by substituting another of the images forming the concept for the until then representative central image" (428)349. For Gény the rule/model has merely a statistical value in the process of avowed judicial rule making. Gény's correct classification is hidden in Wurzel's convoluted language.

It would be incorrect to connect the doctrine of the "logical completeness," sometimes also styled "hermeneutic completeness," exclusively with the code system. The best-known advocate of it in England, independent of any continental influence, was Blackstone. See his notion of the common law as a complete and perfect system in which the judge simply finds the norm of decision, dubbed by Frank (132)189 the "Columbus theory." This doctrine differs from Heck's "closed system" (197), in that Heck has in mind axiological, not normative, completeness—at least in Esser's reading (127)222n372, to which I submit.

XXIX

The term "to make law" is really too amorphous and colloquial to be useful without further study. It is not clarified by saying that "the legislator makes laws, but not law." I discuss in the third essay the necessary distinctions as well as operational synthesis of the various forms and phases of law-making. This note is an opportunity to pull together various comments about Gény's insistence on strict statutory interpretation (*ex tunc*) and the misunderstanding by many of the strategy, if not subterfuge, in favor of more latitude for free search.

Here are some samples of the misunderstanding of Gény's motivation. Degni (103)*90*, as quoted in Castán (66)136, completely misses the element of subterfuge. Clearly misunderstanding Gény's thrust is Jones (224) 376,384. The corollary of Gény's position is the conclusion that analogy can be considered interpretation only on the basis of a fictitious legislative intent; in reality it is already judicial rule making that uses the existing positive law as persuasive datum. Friedmann (142)212 (1944 ed.) may be overreading Gény or missing the *au délà*; he does not mention the double element of the superiority of legislated law and its limitation to the original intent/purpose, not fictitiously extended. Loussouarn (271)243 gives a completely opposite impression (that Gény favored reinterpretation of statutes without respect to the original legislative intent) in a manner that would have to be considered a typographical error were it not expressed in a whole paragraph. See also the striking misunderstanding by Becker (21)70,91. An example of criticism based on confusion about the crucial executive aspect of Gény's postulate is in Gómez (172)22. Ripert's summary comment (353)12 seems deformed by a crude preconceived conceptual framework rather than by missing Gény's point. This impression is reinforced by Ripert's rhetoric (at 384–85), where he suggests that the limitations on the interpreter, rather than those built into the very constitutional framework as Gény assumes, are an afterthought, the result of a concern over interference with the legislative prohibition of lawmaking by others.

Gény's thrust was not overlooked by the "traditionalist" critics, who considered Gény's tack much more "destructive" (which means effectively innovating) than the open approach of a Duguit. See, for example, Bonnecasse (35)41. Lambert correctly distinguished Gény from the exegetes—Gény "restricts statute to its narrowest limits and thus believes to leave a sufficient place for spontaneous [nonlegislative] development of law" (241) 32—and certainly did not miss Gény's point. But he was too constrained by his own argument and tactics to bring out Gény's underlying strategy and the brilliant shift it achieved. In fact, Lambert may even have engaged in the same kind of scholarly twisting, of which he suspects Gény, with regard to some German authors (241)152n1.

Contrast an obscure Romanian contributor to the *Recueil*, Vasilesco (403), who grasps and expresses the conception that social environment, from being merely a standard for an interpretation *ex nunc*, often fictitiously tied to the legislative intent, becomes a source for avowed contemporary judicial rule making. This indeed distinguishes Gény's conception from Lambert's "extremely daring position, which envisages all positive law being subjected to progressive decisional law enlightened by contemporary social trends" (159)*I* 40. (Vasilesco's comment is paraphrased in this essay.)

Among the later writers, Esser stands out by fully understanding the subtlety of Gény's "Socratic intention to force on the judge the creative act of free search by forbidding him systematic statutory construction" (127) 175, meaning the construction of legislative purpose in a new fact situation that the legislator never had in mind.

XXX

That Gény influenced Kantorowicz (Gnaeus Flavius), the spark plug of the free-law movement, cannot be doubted. The comments in literature on the material relation between the two doctrines—free search and free law—are confused, ranging from an identification to sharp distinction: *e.g.*, Dualde (109)178; Hernández-Gil (199)255; and Roubier (358)78–79. Radbruch (340)162f. names as the main sources of the free-law movement Gény (1899), Ehrlich (1903), and Kantorowicz (1906) and considers Fuchs's 1929 synthesis ("Was will die Freirechtschule?") "the ripest fruit of the movement . . . which was the strongest sign of life of the German jurisprudence since Jhering." Cardozo takes, by implication, Gény's side in his warning against *Gefühlsjurisprudenz*, emotional decision making when feasible objective standards are abandoned (61)106.

As for the not very significant development of Gény's free-search conception in the literature, see Betti (25)379, who apart from a valuable distinction among Gény, the free-law movement, and Heck merely says the obvious; see also (26). Thus he adds to the evidence of how much the problem is still with us—and not only in the doctrine. Ripert's insistence on the extreme fiction-propped objective conception—if daring interpretation of an unclear text is required, "the principle of the legislative authority is respected by the fiction that the statute is applied in the sense desired by the legislator" (353)348—might be considered old-age stubbornness. But compare the probably realistic appraisal by Loussouarn that the "current French interpretative doctrine is a mixture of the exegetical [method] and that of [free search]" (271)243; and Tunc: "Civil law is conceptualistic" and therefore can be taught and understood with limited historical background (398). For comparison, see Gilmore (169)1045—a creditable popular summary entitling the author to the benefit of doubt with regard to the somewhat loose language in the last part of the quotation—speaks of the development from the nineteenth-century principle of narrow construction to the "principle of statutory radiation." Judges "apply the legislative mandate even beyond the area to which the statute, according to its own terms is limited . . . the courts have been learning to treat statutes as if they were codes."

The difficulty of improving on Gény's formula rather than only using different words is also illustrated by one of the better Swiss writers, Germann. His (161)9–10 is pure Gény. Germann's formula of the statute as "a limit and guidepost" seems even closer to the actual practice, which requires systematic interpretation of legislated law before reaching for other sources and methods of decision. But, on the whole, Germann's formula is inferior to Gény's. Occasional semantic messiness ("some" directive and "clear" directive are used interchangeably as standard in the same context) and degeneration of reasoning into hairsplitting (*e.g.*, 117) imply insecurity about the inner structure of the formula. It is true, indeed, that Germann is unable to rest his theorizing on unequivocal Swiss practice.

Closely related to Germann's thought are Ascarelli's insistence that there is a creative element in the process of interpretation and his warning against *equitatismo*—a premature refuge in equity, before the legitimate content of the legislated law has been fully drawn out (12)64,71f., and vii–ix. This problem is in fact perennial. See two examples taken from spatially, materially, and doctrinally widely separated areas: (*a*) analysis of the Korean prisoner-of-war repatriation problem (285)437; and (*b*) the dissent by Chief Justice Negrón in *Rosado* v. *Rivera* (81 P.R.R. 15 [1959]).

Another tack is Heck's distinction between "adjustment" (of norms to new circumstances) and "transposition" ("crude method of adjustment," interpretation out of the historical context, under the objective conception of legislated law), tied with his formula of the "thinking obedience" (*denkendes Gehorsam*) of judges (197)107,108. When one cuts through Heck's semantics and ornamentation, his emphasis is on the judicial projection of interests and values into the legislative norm instead of its syllogistic application. Gény, in turn, encourages the finding of gaps so that these interests and values can serve as direct sources for decision. This is a more straightforward approach and therefore doctrinally superior. However, the line between the legitimate limits of legislated law and the free decision is indeed fluid with Gény as well as with the other authors. Stone's criticism of a fictional element in Gény's assumption, that "the transformation of the content of provisions" originally put in by the legislator "could be entirely avoided," is relevant here (385)743n196.

Djuvara (108)253 ff., 272 and Ascarelli (12)iii–iv and (13)202–203, both very much influenced by Gény, point out by implication the weakness in the master's thesis: his concentration on legislated law, instead of considering also the analogous characteristics and limitations of decisional law in relation to the supplementary free search. Here Gény was indeed trapped by his own formalism—the classification of decisional law outside the basic formal sources. But the sound of the critical trumpets is too uncertain to deserve more than a listing.

In sum, Gény's comparative judgment about his formula stands: "None of these efforts [specifically, the free-law movement] have resulted in a synthesis that would equal the so simple and yet so complete formula of Article 1, Swiss Civil Code" (157)*222*, which he identified with his own free-search concept.

But there is a legitimate question, already generally suggested in the text, to what extent Gény went *au délà* of himself in his original free-search thesis. In an early comment, Sugiyama (388)455 stated that free search required further "scientific" (theoretical) development not quite achieved in *Science*. Perhaps a more comprehensive and fair judgment would be that Gény had the great merit of being one of the first to recover from the onslaught of the positivistic primitivism and to begin to put together the lawmakers, the method, and the sources in a meaningful manner. If *Science* nevertheless represents only formal, analytical progress compared with the elementary statement of these ideas in the *Méthode*, it is not only Gény's fault. He stated correctly in the *Méthode* that the social sciences were not in his time—and are only beginning to be now, two generations later—mature enough to provide the free-law maker (and any lawmaker) with the empirical data necessary to fill the doctrinal outlines and put them to work.

XXXI

With regard to the expression "existing normative apparatus" in the text: by his insistence on customary law as part of this apparatus, subordinated to legislated law only in case of conflict, Gény merely corrected an excess of the prior doctrine, which was not universal anyway (*i.e.*, it was never seriously advocated in Germany or Switzerland). Hence this point did not invite any reaction or development. As much as Gény cultivated customary law to prepare the ground for the classification of decisional law (*cf.* the German doctrine of decisional law as judicially made custom, *Gerichtsgebrauch*), the subsequent comments have been largely critical—one would say deservedly, if this whole question were not cast in analytically wrong terms.

It is perhaps significant that a most interesting and thorough recent effort at a theory of justice by Boehmer (34) proceeded on a lower level of abstraction: an analysis of the living *jus aequum* in German decisional law.

Alongside Stone's dictum and to set it in the fuller historical context, it must be pointed out that Gény's doctrine of *donné* was not principally a theory of justice, but belongs in the family of those schools of thought that began to turn jurisprudence away from metaphysics (inclusive of the positivist variety) toward a more complete and therefore potentially scientific analysis: the sociological and interest schools (Ehrlich, Pound, Rümelin, Heck); the teleologists, drawing on and refining Jhering's conception of social purpose; and the various value-jurisprudence writers (Ascarelli, Dualde, Boehmer, Germann, Esser).

XXXII

Another formulation by Gény is found at the beginning of *Science* (159) *IV* 36–37, where Gény in fact makes a connection with his free-speech doctrine and appears to correct himself:

> Then [in 1899], still under the influence of traditional ideas, I considered free search as subordinated or, at least, subsidiary to the application of written law. I asked myself only in what sense written law impeded absolutely free search in the sense that it alone could govern certain relations, the nature of which took them out of the realm of free value judgment [*appréciation*]. This was the result of the very ground plan that I followed in the *Méthode*. At the present, my position is somewhat changed. Since I believe that the jurist is, in principle, fully free to investigate or explore positive law in the environment of the *données*, the role of written law has been reduced to an element of technique. The question is under what circumstances would this element, instead of being merely an adjunct, show itself so indispensable that its absence would make impossible any legal regulation of the matter under consideration.

The preceding statement raises a number of comparative concepts—absolute gap, justiciability, retroactive force of judicial decision—which Gény never pursued further and which this is not the place to pursue. More important in our context, it confirms the judgments of those who recognized all along Gény's effort at a balanced synthesis, contrasted with the more extreme reactions of an early Ehrlich or Kantorowicz. For a much later (1945) English version of such extremism, see Glanville Williams' "Law consists of emotive [value] judgments" (420).

Speaking of confusing semantics, see these formulations, both written around 1961. (*a*) Dabin (92)36–37n88 defines policy (*politique juridique*) fairly closely to the mark as "judicious choice of the best norm, taking into account the goals of law and the capabilities of realizing them." But then he adds, "Hence there is a technique [*sic*] (or rather art, a wisdom) that envisages the base of the rules, and a technique that deals with their formulation [*mise en forme*]. Rules that prescribe the form depend of course on the base of law and, consequently, on policy." (*b*) Terré (393)137n8 makes the strangely insecure statement that "the concept of the 'objectively just' [referring to Gény's *Science II* 393n172] is not without relation to [the contemporary] 'theory of values.'" In fact, it is *the* central concept of legal axiology, the theory of values in law!

More relevant critical perspective on Gény's scheme would be likely to show that, since it is focused foremost on the problem of the sources and ingredients of a specific rule (or on the legal system as a complex of these rules), it does not capture the dynamics of the living legal order: the continuous progress from (1) the conflict of interests toward (2) the essentially political, explicit or tacit agreement on an orderly solution, (3) expressed in a formal legal norm, which will be molded or discarded as (4) new types of conflict or a new content of the order ("living law") require (5) new solutions (law). The concept of conflict in this terminology is a functional aspect of Gény's basic data (*données réeles*); *order* is the function of values (the other *données*), but overlaps into Gény's technique in that it includes a material formulation of the norm; the legal solution (legislative, judicial, or administrative norm) is of course completely technical in Gény's sense, but with a double function: to protect the established order and to provide the basis, framework, and mechanism for the orderly solution of new conflicts. Thus positive law (the set of norms) is both the final product and a point of departure—a procedural framework toward new norms that will express different future values and needs.

This analysis, as well as much of the terminology in my interpretation of Gény in this context, has been taken from an outline I developed in the early stages of my teaching of international law (*ca.* 1950), without any reference to Gény, and has been progressively refined over the years. I may be allowed to set it down for comparison:

I. Elements of conflict (environmental-resources, social-historical, psychological-ideological)
II. Choice between solutions by
  A. Force
  B. Other means
    1. Mutually convenient usage
    2. Negotiation (agreement, settlement, political process)
    3. Arbitration-adjudication
IV. Resulting order
  A. Tacit
  B. General or specific political (diplomatic)
  C. Specific decisional (with possible general repercussions)
V. Resulting forms of law
  A. Custom
  B. Treaties (constitutional and ordinary legislation)
  C. Decisional law

This outline inevitably shows what its original focus was (*i.e.*, the precedence of negotiation or diplomacy over adjudication, typical in international law), but seems to need only some terminological touch-up to apply to law in general.

XXXIII

When one reads the two most outstanding conventional European writers—Ascarelli (12)vii ff., 195, (13)xxi, and Germann (161)116–117—one longs for the relative simplicity of Gény. These works no doubt represent substantial contributions to local jurisprudence. But their relative standing on the scale of jurisprudential progress is perhaps not too unfairly represented by Ascarelli's arguments in favor of "sociological and broadly statistical study of legal institutions" (12)viii. This is Holmes seventy years after!

Dualde's thesis is that "to interpret . . . a statute . . . requires that we investigate the causal series within which the statute is situated." The aim is to apply to law the method of interpreting natural ("scientific") phenomena in their full cause-effect relationship (*e.g.*, meteorological phenomena: rain-wind-evaporation of water–low pressure area, etc.) Compare Heck's formula (197)107: "The judge is to take into account all norms and values, not only those pleaded by the parties. He is deciding an individual case but with reference to the whole legal system." The idea was developed also by Müller-Erzbach (307)14–15, going beyond Heck essentially in Gény's direction, but listing Gény only in the general bibliography.

The state of legal axiology can be gleaned from the fact that in an even-handed survey by Hartmann (193), a philosopher interested in law and citing all the outstanding writers, legal axiology earns eleven lines in a thirty-one-page essay (compared with twenty-five for values in political theory).

Philosophical inquiry into values (*e.g.*, justice) is a source of working hypotheses and therefore is a needed and legitimate element in any theoretical endeavor in law. Things have gone wrong in two directions. (*a*) Traditional philosophers dealing with law have revealed that they are as burdened with outdated concepts and method as the most conventional legal writers. Two recent symposia, one European (239), one American (207), contain substantial evidence. (*b*) Efforts to construct new analytical bases, such as those by the New Haven School, *e.g.*, (246,247,292), have not gotten beyond taxonomy. It is, indeed, difficult to see any real jurisprudential progress from Hohfeld (200) to Lasswell and McDougal as far as theory goes.

The main thrust toward systematic social science, providing lawmaking data as postulated by Gény, has been American. At first, in the 1920s, it followed the fiction that the way to science in law is to gather ever more data. But such studies as Moore's on parking regulation in New Haven (303), Beutel's on bad checks (27,28), and especially the Chicago jury project (227), have been path-blazing in assembling and conceptualizing the raw substratum of law in operation as a basis for lawmaking.

This endeavor must not be confused with efforts to develop adequate methods of handling legal data with the help of mathematical and cybernetic methods, inclusive for the purpose of predictive retrieval. This research operates on a much higher level of formal legal material rather than of the data in Gény's sense.

XXXIV

The full text of the three mentioned articles of the Swiss Civil Code (ZGB) is:

> *Art. 1.* Application of the law.—The statute determines all legal issues covered by its text or interpretation.
>
> If no rule can be drawn from the statute, the judge shall decide according to customary law and, when even that is not available, according to the rule he would make as legislator.
>
> In this he shall follow established doctrine and decisional law.
>
> *Art. 2.* Content of legal relations.—Everyone must exercise his rights and fulfill his obligations acting in good faith.
>
> Obvious abuse of a right shall not be protected by law. . . .
>
> *Art. 4.* Judicial discretion.—Where the statute refers the judge to his discretion, or to evaluation of circumstances, or to important [just] grounds, he shall decide according to law and equity.

Article 3 contains the Swiss version of the clean-hands doctrine of English equity.

In the preceding translation I follow as closely as possible the German text because this was the language in which Huber thought out and originally drafted these articles. Compare Liver (266)N.61–62. Differences between the German and the French and Italian official versions are obvious at first sight. The present translation I believe to be more faithful to the text seen within the legal-cultural system than my 1961 translation (158) xliii n156, 509 at n305, which was done in the context of Gény's comments based on the French text and before I had available the Swiss bibliography on which the present analysis is based.

Among the translations into English of Article 1, the one prepared by Schick (366) in 1915 for the Comparative Law Bureau of the American Bar Association was allegedly "corrected" by Huber. (According to the foreword, Huber suggested that the German version was the most satisfactory basis for the translation, not however for the reason I state above, but rather because there were already in existence the translation of the German Civil Code (Wang) and a commentary on it (Schuster) and because it was in the interest of developing uniform terminology in English!

Schick's translation of Article 1 is the most accurate, but some linguistic critique is relevant. (*a*) Schick uses ten words more than necessary (partly because instead of "covered by" in the first paragraph he uses the word-for-word translation "for which it [the statute] contains a provision according to its terms or its exposition"). (*b*) Although this extended version stresses a textual dimension that may have influenced the application of Article 1(2) by the Swiss federal court (Bundesgericht), the legal meaning of *Wortlaut* is (statutory) text, not terms (which has different specific meanings in the legal English, such as technical expressions, conditions, periods of time, etc.), and *Auslegung* in law means interpretation, not exposition. Hence it should read literally: "contains a provision according to its text or interpretation." (*c*) Schick translated *Gesetz* as code instead of statute (code is *Gesetzbuch*). (*d*) In paragraph 2, I translate *Vorschrift* as rule. A more literal but still idiomatic rendition would be prescription in the basic sense of "written or explicit direction or injunction" (316)1299. Schick's "command" comes from the then current terminology of Austin, the German equivalent of which is *Befehl*, not *Vorschrift*. (*e*) Schick translated *entscheiden* (which completely corresponds to the word *decide*) as pronounce, which is a Gallicism (the French version of Article 1(2) says *prononce*). (*f*) His translation, "customary law, and failing it," is not precise according to the German text (as per my translation) or to the other two texts, which use the phrase "and in default of it." (*g*) Although the Italian text uses the word *adottare* ("*che egli adotterebe come legislatore*"), the simplest and most precise common meaning (in French, it is *établir* [establish]) is not "to adopt" as Schick translates (the general dictionary meaning of *adopt* supposes something preexisting) but to set (*aufstellen*) or, more idiomatically, to make. Legislators do not adopt rules; they make and enact them. Between these two *practical* synonyms, the Swiss judge was obviously not given the power to enact legislative rules (the German expressions for this are *veordnen, erlassen*) but to make or confect the missing rule, acting *qua* legislator. (*h*) In Article 1(3) *Ueberlieferung* is not "tradition" as Schick translates it, except in a figurative, cultural sense (*cf.* du Pasquier [320]29–30); legally it is what is handed down or transferred to followers, *i.e.*, decisions as examples or precedents. The qualifying adjective *bewährte* in German, as well as the French and Italian versions (*jurisprudence* and, more exactly, *giurisprudenza piu autorevole*) confirm the meaning of "decisional law." So does early Swiss doctrine. Gmür (170)Art. 1,N.33, interpreted the term *bewährte Ueberlieferung* in 1908 as "the consistent practice of our highest courts." Compare Meier-Hayoz (295)N.466–67, Esser (126)169, (127)269. Contrast Reichel (349)346 and du Pasquier (320)30. The latter defines the preferred word *tradition*—without any basis in the text or its history and without reference to Gény—virtually in terms of *donnée idéale*. But the argument in favor of "tradition" as the meaning of *Ueberlieferung* would fall even if the purely linguistic lead were not as persuasive as I explain above. On logical grounds, since customary law and doctrine, the two major means of tradition of the axiological-normative apparatus, are listed separately, the term *Ueberlieferung* must refer to the remaining mode, the judicial decisions and the doctrine and custom built upon them. This conclusion is not contradicted by Meier-Hayoz' suggested rewording of Article 1 (296)275, if the individual decisions (*Präjudizien* [precedents]) are distinguished from the decisional doctrine and custom (*Ueberlieferung*). Compare the German conception of the judicial custom as law (*Gerichtsgebrauch*), the French *jurisprudence constante*, and the Spanish *doctrina legal*, all resulting from more than one prior decision. Finally, the grammatical form of Article 1(3) is declaratory with a clear implication of a mandate. Literally it would be in English "he follows." I translate it "he shall follow," thus stressing the implicit order. Schick's conditional "should follow" has no basis in any of the three texts; nor is it the usual grammatical form of statutory language.

Another early translation, widely known because cited by Cardozo (61) 140–41, is by Perick (327)238, sec. 5. It follows the French rather than the German original and is wordy (seventy-nine words instead of the fifty-six above), quite contrary to the leanness and directness of the original. Huber was among many other things also a journalist, briefly even the editor-in-chief of the *Neue Zürcher Zeitung*. For biographical data see Yung (431)206–207.

On the differences between the three official versions of the ZGB, see generally Meier-Hayoz (295)n106f. The Italian version is not less official, because it was prepared only after the German and French texts were formally and legislatively approved. Some additional comments are of interest.

Concerning paragraph 1, the "text or interpretation" is in French "letter or spirit," in Italian "letter or meaning [*senso*]." Reichel points out that the disjunctive form is incorrect, for text *and* interpretation are indivisible (349) 295. In this sense, *Auslegung*-interpretation would be understood correctly with an emphasis on the goal rather than on procedure, *i.e.*, as "spirit" or meaning. Huber's use of the term "interpretation" could be explained by his probable reluctance to use the German *Geist* (spirit), which has a different principal connotation, though *Sinn* (meaning) would not be equally objectionable.

In paragraph 3 there is a striking difference between the German and Italian texts on the one hand and the French text on the other. (The generally closer similarity between the Italian and German texts indicates that the later Italian translation was made from the German original.) Where the German and Italian texts say the judge "follows" (*folgt, si attiene*), the French text says "*s'inspire*," literally "he takes his cue from" established doctrine and decisional law. There is a much more subtle phrasing, more obviously so with respect to writers as source, but also with respect to decisional law, even if it is *jurisprudence constante*. If judges always had to *follow* prior decisions without any alternative, there could be no changes in decisional law—a fact belied by Swiss practice, as well as in various degrees by all others. The German and French texts of the last preliminary draft were closer to each other, and more realistic, speaking of counseling (*beraten*) and guidance (*le guident*). See Meier-Hayoz (295)N.44. But there is no basis to conclude that the finally adopted French term was meant to express a deliberate sophistication pointing the way to the modern theory of precedent as I will discuss it in the last essay. See also Carbonnier (57)121.

In Article 4, the terms used are in German judgment (*Ermessen*), in French evaluation (*appréciation*), and in Italian prudent criterion (*prudente criterio*). They are the equivalents of English discretion in connection with the injunction to use "law" (the power . . . to decide, within the limits allowed by . . . law" [316]*III* 435). But they also represent a special concept, since the additional reference to equity in Article 4 broadens as well as restrains the judge's discretion in the common sense of the word. So the translation of these terms as "discretion" must be read in the full context.

In the French text there is a curious and probably not critical enough reference to "rules of law and equity." Although Meier-Hayoz' comment (295)N.98, may apply to other parts of the ZGB, Article 1 and the ancillary Articles 2 and 4 do not bear out the conclusion that the terminological differences are "shadings of meaning tied with the peculiarity of the specific language that cannot be rendered in another language."

The official presumption is that all the three texts represent an "adequate expression of the legislative will. . . . The aim of judicial practice can be only to find the true meaning of the statute, even where the texts differ and a norm possibly restrictive of civil rights [*Eingriffsnorme*] is involved" Meier-Hayoz (295)N.99,113.

An interesting comparative generalization between Article 1 and Article 2 is in Yung (431)203: "Where Article 1 abolishes the absolute rule of written law, Article 2 condemns the absolutism of private rights." Generally on Article 4, see Meier-Hayoz (295)421–22.

The Swiss doctrine makes a dogmatic difference between a decision under Article 1(2), which imposes a "legislative method," and under Article 4, which aims at "casuistic . . . solution best fitted to the special circumstances" (295)N.16–18. But in the newer doctrine, as well as in the court practice, "there is a tendency toward generalization in decisions under Article 4 [since] a decision under Article 4 must be objectively grounded. . . . The difference between these two methods of filling gaps is extensively wiped out in practice and remains rather only 'a difference in the point of departure and the gravity center' " (295)19,21, (168)186. A more sensitive comment was made by a discussant of Boulanger's report on judicial interpretation in 1949 (42): "Art. 1,2, is useful in the sense that it attracts the attention of the judge to the need to decide in *law*, not in *equity*, as he would be perhaps inclined to do" (300). This distinction must be of course read on the level of the rule-making process. *Policy* still appears to be the best rallying concept. *Equity*/justice is then one particular input in the broad quasi-legislative consideration (lawmaking for the particular case) that Article 1 mandates.

XXXV

Some additional details and marginalia are due.

The kernel of the opinion of Meier-Hayoz is that "the origins of the final text of [Article 1] (2) . . . cannot be stated with certainty."

> A direct influence of the formula of Aristotle in the *Nichomachean Ethics* (V. xiv) cannot be proven. . . . The phrasing found in the explanations of the draft (*Erläuterungen*, 38: "The judge should decide in such cases as the competent legislator would have done had he though of them") indicates an influence of Vangerow (*Lehrbuch der Pandekten* 1, 55 [1863]), who in turn does not seem to have been influenced by Aristotle but arrived at his formula in connection with the analysis of analogy on the basis of Roman texts: "Gaps are most easily filled through the prescription that the judge should decide unprovided cases as the competent legislator would have done had he thought of them." The question whether Gény's *Méthode* and his reference to Aristotle influenced the drafting of Article 1, ZGB, remains obscure. It is a fact that Huber knew the work of Gény and appreciated it [Fritzche (143)207]. But the question whether Huber knew it before the editorial deadline remains open. . . . Also the influence of neo-Kantian thought and of the jurisprudence of interests on the origins of Article 1 should not be underestimated [referring to Huber's friendship with Rudolf Stammler and Max Rümelin].

Notes

The passage from Aristotle's *Nichomachean Ethics* (V.[xiv]. 5) reads: "When the statutes contain a general provision and the individual cases are exceptional, it is proper, where the legislator failed to rule or erred by speaking in absolute, to correct him or to supplement his silence, and to rule in his place as he would have ruled if he had known the particular case at issue." Merlin's statement (*Répertoire*, 1827) bears the imprint of Portalis and is concerned with judicial filling of gaps through equity derived from the spirit of the legal system. The formulae immediately precede in Gény's book the definition and coining of *libre recherche scientifique* (158)354 n203.

Some older Swiss commentators (1912–1915) suggested also the Aristotelian source of Huber's formula for Article 1(2). See Tuor (400)36 and Egger (114), as cited by Williams (421)73. Reichel (349) finds the genealogy of the Swiss formula in the Roman *ex aequo et bono* as a source of filling statutory gaps ("Si quid in lege praetermissum fuerit, id ex aequo et bono debet praestari"), but considers the modern formula a "vast improvement."

Germann (166)397n10 and Yung (432)97 refer to the Kantian influence, apparently first spelled out by du Pasquier (318)*216*. The reference is to Kant's injunction in *Metaphysik der Sitten* (1797): "Act so that the maxim of your will [the particular decision] could always become also the principle of universal law [general rule of law]."

Yung (433)329, offers this interesting comparison between Portalis' *Discours préliminaire* and the beginning of Huber's *Exposition of motives*. Portalis: "It is the task of practice to fill successively the gaps we leave. The national codes make themselves as time goes on; properly speaking, one does not make them." Huber, a hundred years later: "If one compares the manifestation of legal practice in the sphere of civil law with the creative activity of the legislator, one is soon convinced that the results of the latter are relatively modest."

Perhaps the most important single piece of evidence is a copy of Huber's draft of the ZGB (1900) discovered sometime between 1962 and 1973 by Oscar Gauye, the director of the Swiss Federal Archives. This particular copy carries Huber's handwritten legend "citations from previous drafts." In the margin of Article 1(3)—later to become paragraph 2—Huber annotated the key words from Vangerow, as quoted above. Gauye also documents a possible lapse in Gény's memory—developed into a thesis by Capitant (309)34—about his and Saleilles' visit to Huber in Bern "in 1896 or 1897." In fact, their first meeting seems to have taken place in mid-1900, on the occasion of the International Congress of Comparative Law in Paris (150)274. However, Gauye's arguments may be somewhat less than complete (the evidence of the 1900 meeting for being the first one is circumstantial at best) and perhaps constrained by an interest in proving Huber's independent originality.

Rather than to try to prove either/or hypotheses, for which there is not enough data anyway, it is preferable to look at such events as comparable responses to comparable stimuli and as a result of the imponderable ever-present element of intellectual osmosis. As to the longer-time frame, note the hundred-year span between Portalis and Huber and the thread running from the *Interessenjurisprudenz* of Huber's close friends back to Jhering ("right is legally protected interest"), back to Article 4 of the French Civil Code, the deepest meaning of which is identical with the Swiss Article 1: it is an order to the judge to give remedy for the protection of a recognized interest even if there is no specific statute to protect it.

XXXVI

The original draft of Article 1 (1900) reads: "The civil code governs all matters covered by its letter or interpretation.—In the absence of any statutory provision, the judge shall decide according to customary law and, in its absence, *according to established doctrine and decisional law.—If he cannot draw the rule of law from any of these sources, he is to decide* according to the rule he would make as legislator" (translated from the German original: *Schweizerisches Zivilgesetzbuch: Vorentwurf*; the difference between the draft and the final versions is italicized).

With small verbal changes and simplifications, this was the 1904 version. But published correspondence between Huber and the president of the drafting committee (151)116–18 illustrates an intervening drama involving more than semantics. As already noted, Huber introduced his exposition of motives with the thought that the locomotive of progress in law was not legislature but practice, principally adjudication. The 1900 draft of Article 1(3) also contained a stronger "creative" language. What I translated above as "draw" is in the German original *schöpfen* (to create).

It seems not farfetched to surmise that Huber's motives and language were the reasons—the point is not discussed in any documentation available to me—why the drafting committee inserted in January, 1904, the word *verständiger* before the word legislator: the judge must act as an "intelligent," "judicious" legislator. Huber protested in so many diplomatic words (in May, 1904) that he did not share the fear about "the arbitrary and not diligent enough judge" and that the proposed formulation was open to all kinds of ridicule. He suggested first the wording "the judge will decide in conformity with the general principles and purposes of the legal order." Two weeks later, he proposed a change in the last sentence of the word *würde* (would) to *müsste* (should, would have to [make as legislator]).

It is, of course, also possible that the drafting commission had in the back of its collective mind simply the image of a "reasonable man" (with pedigree going back to the Roman *diligens paterfamilias*) raised to the judicial power. Huber's arguments in the second letter suggest, on the other hand, an exaggerated idealism about the intellectual content of legislative lawmaking. See also (431)192,197–206.

At any rate, Huber prevailed. During the subsequent debates, both the left and the right made unsuccessful moves. The left wanted a radically shortened Article 1, in which paragraphs 2 and 3 would have been substituted by this formula: "When the statute contains no provision, the judge decides according to his best knowledge and conscience" or, as an alternative, "in the spirit of the law [legal system]" (295)N.8–9. The right wanted the whole Article 1 scratched, as had happened *mutatis mutandis* a century earlier with the French Civil Code.

In the final draft (September, 1907), Article 1 emerged in its present form, which preserves the creativity in the French version (*s'inspire*), but uses the more imperative term in the German version, with the Italian translation somewhere in between. There is a choice.

The Swiss formula is clearly superior to similar provisions in other codes. Compare: (*a*) Article 7(2) Austrian Civil Code (1811): "If the legal controversy remains in doubt [after the standard interpretation and use of analogy], it must be decided with regard to carefully collected and considered circumstances following the principles of natural law." The original reads "*natürlichen Rechtsgrundsätzen*"; a permissible translation would be "organic [natural] principles of law." Article 21, Louisiana Civil Code: "In all civil matters where there is no express law, the judge is bound to proceed and decide according to equity. To decide equitably, an appeal is to be made to natural law and reason or received usages, where positive law is silent." This article reproduces the original formula of Portalis in *Projet de l'an VIII*, left out from the code as not belonging there. See (56)78n2. (*c*) Article 7, Civil Code of Puerto Rico (1901): "When there is no statute applicable to the case at issue, the court shall decide in accordance with equity, which means that natural justice, as embodied in the general principles of jurisprudence and in accepted and established usages and customs, shall be taken into consideration."

Additional references from other countries and comments are in Meier-Hayoz (295)N.22–30, to which add Article 3 of Japanese law (1875) and Article 6 in Spain. Meier-Hayoz states the superiority of the Swiss formula in the sense that it cannot be criticized as limiting "the claims, also based in natural law, which the jurist can make with regard to the development and completion of his methodology." Aftalión (1)445 is the only author I know of who considers the Swiss formula inferior to the similar provisions in other countries, including his own Argentinian Article 16.

The absence of any reference in Article 1 to equity as a source (it is specifically included in Article 4, ZGB) can be explained by two arguments: first, in Huber's opinion, all law rests in the last analysis on "reasonable legal conscience" (*vernünftiges Rechtsbewusstsein*), which might be translated less literally as "sense of (concrete) justice"; second, established doctrine and decisional law" refers to practical applications of this sense of justice, fostered and systematized by legal writers.

This appears to be a more technical conception of the real meaning of "continental equity." It contrasts with the widespread distinctions from the "Anglo-American equity," which have been made in the past, *e.g.*, (95)415, (38)530. The "controversy" is, I believe, easily solved when equity is translated into operational rather than dogmatic terms: it is the element of justice that operates in concrete cases when there is no law or when the positive law is unjust. That was exactly the function of equity in medieval English law, and that is what Portalis must have had in mind when he designed in his original draft (Article 11) the judge as *ministre d'équité*. In England, equity became Equity—a system of law counterposed to common law—only when the common law courts began to reject new writs intended to correct concrete injustices caused by rigid application of the common law, thus falling prey, for political more than legal reasons, to the tendency expressed in the time-honored Romanist saying *summum jus, summa injuria*. The chancellor as "keeper of the king's conscience" then began to hear such cases in his own court. This decisional law and practice eventually grew into equity as a separate branch of the English legal system.

In this sense all verbal-dogmatic comparisons miss the two main points that all these articles have in common, from the most austere French Article 4 to the most explicit Swiss Article 1: (*a*) they belie the hermeneutic legal theology of the nineteenth century (note that the date of the French code is 1804; that of the Austrian, 1811; that of Louisiana, 1825); and (*b*) they direct the judge to decide controversies justly, even in the absence of positive law.

More specifically with respect to Switzerland, the judge must obviously decide under Article 1, as well as under Article 4, always "according to law and equity." The verbal difference is that in Article 1 he is not specifically told so, whereas under Article 4 he is so told in the just quoted phrase. The practical but not very important difference between the two situations is this: Article 4 presupposes some legislated norm that incorporates by reference the equity element of the judicial-pretorian function and that depends on it, by legislative fiat, for all or a great deal of its material implementation—*i.e.*, the equitable exercise of the judicial discretion. Under Article 1, the explicit pretorian function of the judge not only contains the fundamental equity motive, but the judge also implements it procedurally and substantively by giving a remedy.

Thus, the distinction between the quasi-legislative and the pretorian functions suggested by Boulanger (38)533 and which some might relate to the distinction between Articles 1 and 4 (*cf.* the implication of Liver's conclusion [265]), is barren. See also the argument by Meier-Hayoz (295)N.520, which gives the impression of hairsplitting. No matter how verbalized, the function of the judge when he decides without specific reference to positive law (*i.e.*, *praeter* or *contra legem*) is always pretorian; that is, it recognizes an interest by giving a remedy. This is what Article 1(2 and 3) orders the judge to do: (*a*) to give remedy even in the absence of legislated or customary norm; (*b*) to use a quasi-legislative method; and (*c*) to follow certain sources. In this the Swiss provision is unique.

The classification of sources in the final version of Article 1 was subsequently received in Article 38 of the two statutes of the International Court of Justice (1920, 1946), with a small adjustment: the power to decide *ex aequo et bono* takes the place of Gény's free search and of the formula "judge as legislator" in the ZGB.

Notes

XXXVII

Among the more important Swiss commentators on the origins and meaning of Article 1, Meier-Hayoz stands out in terms of completeness, both in his early work (296) and the full doctrinal development a decade later (295). Du Pasquier's study of Article 1 in function of gap filling (320) is an updated follow-up on his earlier study of judicial modernism and Swiss decisional law (321).

Only the more original additional works are listed. Germann (161,162, 166) touches upon this subject in several chapters, some published originally as articles. Liver (265) discusses it incidentally to his broader main topic. Reichel (350) makes an analysis that is understanding but too conceptualistic and, even in his chosen framework, sometimes remarkably crude. Spiro (379) limits his analysis of decisional law to the general part of obligations, as indicated by the title. But he makes some relevant generalizations, built doctrinally on Cardozo (*The nature of the judicial process*, which was subsequently published in German in 1949 as *Lebendiges Rechts* [the living law], translated by Thiele-Fredersdorf). Tuor (400) deals with the subject in the introductory part of his textbook.

Yung presented a superior paper on Gény and the Swiss Article 1 at Gény's centenary memorial conference in Nancy (432). There he also cites an early appreciation of Gény by the Swiss Picot (329)260–62.

The qualitative poverty of relevant Swiss literature is characterized by Spiro's remark in 1948 (379)xviii, forty years after the ZGB was promulgated, that only Egger (114) and du Pasquier in his earlier work (321) had analyzed this subject with regard to the fact situations (*i.e.*, not dogmatically or conceptually). Meier-Hayoz suggests (296)78 that "the Swiss doctrine . . . often merely reproduces what it has received from the schools of the 'jurisprudence of interests' and 'free search.' "

XXXVIII

BGE stands for *Bundesgerichtsentscheidungen*, decisions of the federal high court.

The reference problem is just one example—France is another, though somewhat more homogeneous and manageable—of national provincialism in our field. The local differences in government structure, positive law, and procedure do not require that the notation systems be incompatible. In fact, some of these systems are defective in the manner of poorly marked city streets or road signs on the assumption that local people know their way around without them.

Theory of law in the sense envisaged here heavily depends on comparative input. This by definition requires that researchers look analytically at legal systems other than their own. Even social scientists (other than the practitioners of empirical jurisprudence) encounter today no difficulties in the study of other countries except those linguistic difficulties not yet spanned by a conceptual lingua franca and by quantification. By contrast, comparative legal research (by which I mean work at the edges of knowledge and synthesis, not descriptive rehash) is an obstacle course combined with detective work that only hardy addicts can carry through, even with the time and wherewithal to spend a year in the given country—a condition not imperative in any other field, though admittedly desirable in subject matters that have such a strong historical-cultural dimension as law does.

In the Swiss situation, it is easy enough to figure out, as soon as one finds at least two case citations that have dates, that the formula is: Date (year) = 1900 + (No. of BGE volume − 26). But not even treatises contain lists of cases cited, although there is a de facto *stare decisis* in Switzerland and the federal court frequently cites prior decisions. Thus to make, for example, a list of leading cases according to the frequency of citation among the writers or to find out their bias in citing or not citing apposite decisions requires the compilation of one's own card file.

The abstract case notation gives the literature a pseudoscientific aura, but on a deeper level it reflects a continued manipulation of abstract concepts in the tradition of the nineteenth-century *Rechtswissenschaft.* A pleasantly surprising critique comes from an old-timer from within the Swiss-German legal establishment. After citing a litany of adjectives designating what Meier-Hayoz calls "genuine gap"—law-systemic, proper, open, external, visible, logical, inherent norm-application [gap], subsumption [gap], true"—Gutzwiller comments that a "number of examples equal to the number of foreign words would have gone farther" (180) 147. To which I should add: the examples should come from properly and correctly identified cases and fact situations.

The Bundesgericht, in contrast to many writers, refers in its own opinions to leading cases by name, to other decisional law by the volume/page reference—for instance, as one of numerous possible examples, the repeated references to the "judgment *Torre*" (BGE 85 II 431 [1959]) in *Turicaphon*, discussed in Note XLIX. See also Appendix D, *Switzerland.*

XXXIX

It is indicative that Meier-Hayoz, whose commentary I quote in the text, can cite the BGE here only in connection with one of four situations that hypothetically permit a deviation: evidence that the legislator made an error. With regard to "deep-going changes in the evaluation of the interests involved," he cites only one law review article (1948). The most important contingency, a "practically unsatisfactory consequence of following the historical meaning," is listed without decisional or doctrinal underpinning. Yet, the last two contingencies seem to be perfectly illustrated by a 1960 case of fraud in a social security insurance situation, which Meier-Hayoz does not list—at least not in the context I cite—although his discussion of interpretation is general, not limited to civil law. The introductory articles of the ZGB have, just as those of the French Civil Code, a quasi-constitutional status reaching beyond civil law to the whole system. Swiss writers discussing interpretation often refer to public, civil, and social as well as penal cases, side by side. See, for example, Germann (163) and du Pasquier (319,320).

The fraud case referred to above is *Kanton Schwyz g. Füssler*, BGE 86 IV 92 (1960). The issue was whether an employer who falsified documentation in violation of Article 66 of the KUVG (health and welfare insurance statute) is also subject to sanctions for fraud and forgery under the penal code. After stating that the court "decided the question affirmatively in *Trayvand* (BGE 82 IV 138). This decision is to be followed," the court turns to the lower decision: "The cantonal court considers as determinative the will of the historical legislator who clearly aimed at the exclusion of general penal law. This is not to be agreed with." A summary follows of the legislative history, including compromises in the conference between the national and the cantonal chambers, political considerations in view of the popular referendum ("to phrase the penal provisions mildly"), which "leave it open to doubt whether the intention was to govern the sanctions exclusively through the KUVG."

The federal court continues:

> When the will of the historical legislator cannot be derived with unequivocal clarity from the legislative record, the statutory text is not an obstacle to an interpretation that takes into account the general development of law and contemporary circumstances. [Referring to *Pantet*, 83 IV 121 (1957), a penal case discussed later in the text, but also to two public law cases (1955,1956), the first of which Meier-Hayoz cites (N.164) as an example of the "objective-contemporary" mode. The formula of the court is identical with the formula of Meier-Hayoz above in the text. The lack of any reference in either direction—decisional law or commentators—indicates that the formula is part of the Swiss legal environment.] In this perspective it must be taken into account that social views have changed in the fifty years since the KUVG was deliberated upon. . . . According to contemporary perceptions of justice it would be inconceivable to have to convict of fraud under Article 148 of the penal code an employee who had fraudulently drawn benefits from the "Suva" [social security insurance; this was *Trayvand*] while the employer who is in arrears on premium payment through fraudulent machinations would get away with an administrative fine under Article 66, KUVG. The reasonable meaning of the statute can be only that both the employer and the employee are subject to the same penal sanction. [Analogy is drawn with more recent social legislation, *e.g.*, unemployment insurance, where penal sanctions were decreed without any distinction between the employers and the insured.]"

The decisions of the Swiss Bundesgericht are published in the official reports in German, French, or Italian, depending on what language the opinion was originally drafted in. The principal headings in the older official reports are in German. The syllabi of the decisions are "increasingly" (as of 1960) being published in the three principal languages (295)N.480, with the language of the original opinion at the head. There are two private unilingual case reporters, *Praxis des Bundesgerichts* (Basel) and *Journal des tribunaux* (Lausanne).

The language differences are occasionally the cause of friction. A reported incident (305)47n106 tends to confirm a certain minority complex of the French-speaking judges (no comparable reference is made to the still smaller Italian-speaking minority). On the other hand, legal writers from the French-speaking cantons feel superior over some palpable differences in legal-cultural orientation between them and the German-speaking majority.

XL

The adjectives upholding the objective method are "critical," "juridical" (lawyer-like), "autonomous," "normative," "rational," "teleological," "sociological," meaning "mostly the contemporary mode of the objective method." Reference is also made to "the body of intelligent/competent readers" (the same quality of *verständiger* that Huber fought off in connection with Article 1) or to "reasonably interpreting popular intelligence" (which may really mean *Volksgeist*).

The objective method is said to "reject . . . any reference to a subjective sense, whether it is the will of the historical legislator or an interpretation informed by the will of the now deciding judge." The Bundesgericht said in an earlier opinion in a civil case (which culminated in the 1955 public law case cited in the text) that "it is not decisive what the legislator willed when he enacted a provision but what is to be derived from the statute in the light of the general principles of law" (BGE 63 II 155–156[1937]). The citations are from (295)N.149,222; (320)13.

"The aim of interpretation is to ascertain the *objective* meaning [*Sinn*] of the legal norm" (295)N.140. *Sinn* is the conceptual antonym of *Wille*. The distinction seems to be identical with the one drawn between the purpose of the law expressed in the text and the intent of the legislator—Gény speaks of expressed intent (157)98, in fine; so did Justice Holmes, independently—both of them reducible to the common denominator of the policy of the law. In these terms, the difference would be between the expressed policy (made concrete, if necessary, with the help of legislative record) and policy that can be read into the statutory text. But the Swiss doctrine does not seem to venture into the policy alley, except for an occasional reference, *e.g.*, to *ratio legis* (295)N.134, or is even against this organic conception (Gmür and others).

Looking at Article 1 in this light, the Italian formula *lettera od il senso* is closest to the text-and-policy formula. Since the Italian version was translated from the German, Huber's original *Auslegung*, which I translate as interpretation, would appear to mean what it should: search for the policy of the statute to ascertain the intended or applicable meaning of the words in a marginal situation. To use the expression spirit, as the French version does, appears too broad, "less precise" (295)N.134, and even conceptually musty.

The lack of discriminating terminology, which points to insufficient analysis on the level of the organic-theoretical deep structure of the process, is further compounded when, for example, Meier-Hayoz entitles one of the sections "A *single* legal thought despite the noncorrespondence of the content of the three texts," using the term legal thought to mean policy (295) N.106, although elsewhere he speaks of the "legislative-political [in the sense of policy, not politics] basis of the norm" (295)N.134. Gutzwiller points out in a review of Meier-Hayoz (180)146 that in practice the judge will have to select that linguistic version (in an example he gives it is the Italian) that best corresponds to the legislative policy, concretely the protection of the public in corporation law; but Gutzwiller speaks here of *Wille*, not of *Sinn*.

Everybody can have his pick among these terminologies and methodologies, taking his cue, according to his preference as to the medium, from (*a*) an actor: "Language is not so important as long as the intention is clear" (Menasha Skulnik, referring to the counterpoint between Zulu, Yiddish, and English [New York *Times*, 14 June 1970]; (*b*) a poet of the "flower child" generation, who entitled her article about Harvard "Reality is more often what we think we say than what we say we think" (*New York Times Magazine*, 7 June 1970, p. 70); (*c*) a music critic: "Music is constantly being made new; the notated score is only a guide" (Peter Yates, *Twentieth-century music*, 1967); (*d*) a theologian: "Catholics have learned to put brackets around the elements of the system that do not seem in harmony with the gospel as they now understand it" (Gregory Baum, University of Toronto [New York *Times*, September 15, 1970]).

XLI

Radbruch (340)163 compared the more extreme form of the objective mode with the art of the prestidigitator who "surprisingly pulls out of the statute a ruling that he first magically implanted in it." But he agreed with the function of interpretation as the "thinking through of what the legislator thought"—"*Zuendedenken eines Gedachten*" (341)211.

Carbonnier introduced in his leading contemporary textbook on French civil law (57)129–30 additional confusing terminological wrinkles: (*a*) "method of social purpose [teleological interpretation] which is more objective than the intent of the legislator." Does he mean to distinguish psychological intent and stated purpose? Probably not, because it reads later, "The same purpose can be realized through different means that the legislator could not imagine. (*b*) historical (evolutive) method: this seems identical with Julliot de la Morandière's thought about, in Carbonnier's words, "what would be the thought of the historical legislator if he had to legislate today [with the possibility of arriving at] even a meaning contrary to the literal formula." (*c*) free search; this is Gény's conception.

On this side of the Atlantic, the notion of the judge acting in the guise of interpretation as he thinks the legislator would act in the face of the present situation seems to be reflected in such recent ideas as that of Charles Reich (Yale) as summarized in a newspaper column on Justice Hugo Black: "Central governments have acquired power beyond the imagination of those who framed the [U.S.] Constitution. Thus judges, to preserve the relative weight of the protective clauses of the Constitution, must read them generously." Justice Black, the editorialist adds, would never agree, but surely he had tried to carry out the Bill of Rights not so much in its original words as in its original significance (as construed by the judge from his contemporary vantage point?) See A. Lewis, "The authentic voice," New York *Times*, 5 October 1970.

XLII

Huber recognized in principle gaps in law "when the statute contains no norm that might be applied in the given case directly or by analogy" (209) 354—written twenty years after the drafting of Article 1; *cf.* (166)174. This is the "genuine" gap (*echte Lücke*), according to Zittelman's terminology taken over in the Swiss doctrine from Gmür, Egger, and Burckhardt through du Pasquier (320)19–20 to Meier-Hayoz (295)N.271f. Gény devoted to Zittleman a whole section in the second edition of the *Méthode* (157)*212*.

The rediscovery of gaps around the turn of the century was a reaction to the hermeneutic doctrine of the nineteenth century, a conception of the codes as closed units in which exegetic interpretation could find all the needed answers. Gény quoted with satisfaction in the first edition Menger's reference (1890) to "the absurd fiction that the civil law has no gaps and that law and life cover each other completely" (157)*166*. Article 4, French Civil Code, was a similar reaction against the revolutionary concept of "*référé législatif*" (42)62, which would have limited judges to a *mechanical* matching of the statutory words with the facts in controversy, ordering them to refer any case not clearly decided by this "slot machine" method back to the legislature. The pendulum then swung to the other side and the *Projet* of the Year VIII stipulated that "in the absence of a precise text, the judge is a minister of equity. Equity is a return to natural law or to customs integrated into the positive law." Portalis perhaps somewhat weakened the formula by stating that "the judge is the minister of the law when it has spoken; he is the arbitrator of controversies when the law is silent" (42)63. Carbonnier would supplement the present Article 4, French Civil Code, with a reference to equity (thus making of it a combination of Article 7, Austrian Civil Code (1811), and Article 1, Swiss Civil Code, on the ground that "the preliminary book of the *Projet* was shortened for technical reasons, not for reasons of principle." Instead, the exegetics of the nineteenth century endeavored to "shift Article 4 into the sphere of law [instead of equity]" on the basis of the alleged hermeneutic nature of the code (57)23.

The *Suffragettes* case (*Quinche c. Vaud*) raised the issue of justiciability —essentially an absolute gap that cannot be filled even by the teleological method because it is, by definition, outside judicial power. Gény recognized the possibility of an absolute gap in a typically scholastic manner:

> It remains to be considered whether written law is not sometimes such an integral and necessary part of this technical elaboration [in the *science-technique* context] that the jurist should in certain legal matters decline to

> decide in any manner in the absence of a state or regulation. . . . I lightly touched upon this problem when I attempted to define the role and the limits of 'free objective search' in the complete framework of interpretation of private positive law [*Méthode, 169*]. At that time still under the influence of traditional ideas, I considered independent search for a rule subordinated, or at least subsidiary to the straight application of written law. I asked myself only to what an extent written law could absolutely set free search aside in the sense of being exclusively competent to regulate certain matters, the nature of which made them escape from the reach of free search. My present position [*ca.* 1924] is somewhat changed: the jurist is in my opinion in principle completely free to find positive law amidst the elements of the *donné*. Hence, written law is merely a technical means. The question is in what cases this technical element, instead of being simply one of the factors working in tandem, would reveal itself so indispensable that its absence would set aside any possibility to solve the issue judicially [(159)*IV,278*,36–37]

Although Gény formally thinks only within private (civil) law, the Swiss, German, and of course French experience is evidence of the indivisibility of the doctrine of interpretation. See the extension by the German federal court of weapons law to an attack by hydrochloric acid, despite the formal proscription of analogy in the interpretation of criminal law; see also (166) 98–100n88; (163)216n33,232n92; (161)119–23.

XLIII

What I call "semantic" gap, on grounds explained in the text, the Swiss doctrine refers to as "logic" (Burckhardt, cited by Meier-Hayoz), "systemic" (*rechtssystematisch*, though this term should properly cover, and perhaps does, both the gap in words and in their meaning), and perhaps also "cognitive" gap (*Erkentnisslücke*). This last classification is complicated by a distinction of gaps *intra legem* and *praeter legem*, within and without the statute (295)N.268,274,278 and is considered to be the principal type of gap to be filled under Article 4, Swiss Civil Code (295)N.313. Commenting on this and further vocabulary, which is irrelevant here, Gutzwiller sighs: "We have become more 'refined'; have we also become proportionately more just?" (180)145.

The Bundesgericht is being cited (by 1965) only as having declared in 1954 that, in case of doubt, "the text of the statute is not an exclusive determinant of the interpretation" (BGE 80 II 316). In BGE 87 I 16 (1961) and BGE 88 I 112 (1962), the court deviated from a verbally clear text to adhere explicitly to the logically true sense. Germann speaks in this context about the "*possible* meaning of the words" (166)60 (emphasis added).

XLIV

The "teleological" gap is "not genuine" (*unechte*), is "ethical" as opposed to "logical," and is "related to the policy of the legal system" (*rechtspolitisch*), as distinguished from "the policy of the statute (*legislativpolitisch*)

—all summarized in (295)N.274f. Previously, Meier-Hayoz suggests a simplification—"statutory" versus "law-[as-a-system]" gaps (*Gesetzlücken, Rechts-lücken*)—but does not conspicuously apply it (296)253. The reference to purpose and/or policy, both of them having value content that changes while words remain fixed, still appears the simplest and clearest terminology.

The purpose/policy of a statute can be based on inadequate knowledge and thus balancing of values/interests. So, after the court concluded that, had the legislator possessed full knowledge about the vast aquifers and the present technology of their exploitation, he would certainly not have assigned them to private ownership, it held that Article 704, Section 3, ZGB, was "inadequate and due to erroneous views of the legislator on the nature of subterranean water resources. It should be eliminated when the civil code is revised. Meanwhile the cantons should remedy it by transferring important water resources [according to the standards set by the Canton of Zurich, at issue in this case, it would be resources that yield three hundred liters per minute or more] into the public domain" (BGE 65 II 149 [1939], cited in [320]16). This is an example of the "famous formula" that du Pasquier cites in the neighboring context—"to step out of legality in order to return to law"—and that he regrets the Bundesgericht has not consistently followed.

The definition of teleological gap by the court and the subsequent practice are discussed later in the text.

In terms of Gény's doctrine, it needs to be kept in mind that, even if the teleological extension substantially refines the concept of the gap, it amounts to a simulated extension of legislated law, instead of recognizing that the relevance of the legislated law has been under these circumstances reduced to a verbal shell into which the judge creatively reads the most important substantive ingredient—a contemporary value content.

XLV

Contrary to the Bundesgericht's two decisions (BGE 74 II 109 [1948] and 76 II 62 [1950]), which are part of the retreat from Article 1(2) as discussed later in the text, the Swiss doctrine, summarized and approved by Meier-Hayoz (295)N.137f,346f, considers analogy not as means of interpretation but of gap filling. The writers, however, do not go all the way with Gény: a gap exists according to Swiss doctrine only when it cannot be filled by analogy! This says nothing about the classification of gap filling by means of analogy; thus it never reaches the crucial insight of Gény that this activity is already judicial free search, which should not be covered by the fiction that it still represents interpretation of the text. Compare Burckhardt (51)280, as cited (166)108n128: "There is no difference between gap filling and interpretation. [Both are] creative activities . . . value judgments . . . supplementing the statute in the sense of the right law." This was written in the 1930s, at the zenith of the practical influence of Article 1(2).

Esser (126)169 points out correctly "the uncontrollable mass of cases of an *interpretatio extensiva*, which is in reality analogy." The keys to analogy are, of course, common principles that become increasingly general as the judge moves farther from the statutory context in which he should have been able to find the decisional norm. The most general of these principles is the "[law and] equity" formula of Article 4, ZGB. Boulanger (41) suggests this classification adopted by du Pasquier (320): (*a*) rational principles, including the Roman—or better, Latin—litany of interpretation canons; (*b*) principles induced from a text; (*c*) structural/systemic principles; and (*d*) policy (*ordre public*) principles. More important seems Boulanger's related comment that Gény's "free search . . . consists, to a large extent, of search for [general] principles" (41)65.

Another dimension of this doctrinal edifice, which badly lacks some unifying theoretical framework (so also Esser, *ibid.*) is the already mentioned problem of *equitatismo*, which means turning to the most general principle (equity) before the content of existing legislated law has been drawn out through legitimate methods of verbal, logical, and policy (teleological) interpretation. Related are the widely criticized German "jurisprudence of sentiment" (*Gefühljurisprudenz*) of the early twentieth century and the Swedish practice of ad hoc decisions based on the justice of the case (166) 216n206, citing F. Schmidt, *Scandinavian studies* (1957), 163.

XLVI

1. As was the case with Mendeleev's periodic table of elements, a hidden symmetry was revealed in the process of constructing the table of the elements of judicial search for a rule reproduced below. "Empty spots" appeared and were filled in from the literature or in the form of working hypotheses.

For instance, Stone's critique of a fictional element in Gény's assumption that "the transformation" by the interpreter "of the content of the provisions" originally put in by the legislator "could be entirely avoided" (385) 743n196 required that the pure *ex tunc* interpretation be followed on the scale by a mode that is still *ex tunc*, but is not purely objective since it makes a realistic allowance for the different frame of reference of the present interpreter (item B, 2). This is no doubt the real situation, not Gény's puristic assumption that is probably psychologically impossible. The question to what extent this different frame of reference must remain unconscious has not been explored. An interesting but fiction-oriented alternative suggestion by Julliot de la Morandière, in the sense that the present interpreter might substitute the ascertainable policy of the present legislator for the historical policy, is interpolated as item C, 6.

2. The scale of the various modes ranging from interpretation *ex tunc* to judicial quasi-legislation looks as follows:

I. Interpretation

A. Subjective

1. *ex tunc*, with reference to the original (historical) legislator only

B. Mixed

2. *ex tunc*, with an allowance for the different frame of reference of the present interpreter
3. *ex nunc*, by delegation from the original legislator (discretional [general] clauses)
4. *ex nunc*, with material reference to the original legislator
   (a) positive reference (analogy) for the purpose of
      (i) interpretation (selection between contrasting legislative norms
      (ii) decision (extension of a positive norm to cover the present case; *analogia legis*)
   (b) negative reference (*argumentum e contrario*)
      (i) interpretative: as 4, (a)(i)
      (ii) decisional: formulation of a new rule inconsistent with the one that suggests itself by way of analogy

C. Objective

5. *ex nunc*, with a purely formal (constructive, feigned) reference to the original legislator
6. *ex nunc*, substituting openly the constructive policy of the present legislator for the expressed or assumed policy of the original legislator
7. *ex nunc*, with reference to general (constitutional, equitable) principles (*analogia juris*).

II. Rule making

8. Explicit order by legislator to judge to give remedy or to decide even where the legislator is silent, accompanied by an explicit order to have recourse to "natural law (or justice)," "equity," "general principles," etc., or tacitly presuming reference to these equity sources
9. (a) Quasi legislation (Article 1(2) Swiss Civil Code)
   (b) Free search (Gény)
10. German "free-law" conception: substitution of the judge's ruling for a positive legislative rule that is considered unjust or otherwise unacceptable.

3. The scale makes it obvious how crude for analytic classification purposes is the simple subjective-objective distinction. Meier-Hayoz in fact mentions the possibility (citing Burckhardt, 1925) of "conceiving the difference between interpretation and gap filling not in terms of [opposite] principles, but of degree [and] thus putting emphasis more on what they have in common" (295)n139. But he leaves the matter there.

The really important operational considerations are the following. (*a*) Can a gap be filled by reference to legislative rule without the use of unnecessary fictions; if not, is it or is it not proper to admit judicial gap filling by free search? (*b*) It should be recognized that the line between interpretation by analogy and judicial rule making is drawn essentially on the verbal surface. This still leaves in the hands of the judge the most important preliminary: the classification of the facts and the values involved for the purpose of determining whether or not to "interpret" by analogy—that is whether to make use of a specific rule that the legislator did not enact for that particular purpose. Thus, rather than to put analogy clearly on one side or the other, it may be more correct to say that the line of division tends to cut through the middle of the technique of analogy—interpretative analogy (positive and negative) being on the side of interpretation, decisional analogy (especially the rejection of an apparently analogous rule through *argumentum e contrario*) being on the side of rule making.

Certainly to try to draw the line between modes C, 5–7, and II, 8–9, and to call modes 5–7 interpretation on the ground that there are some substantive legislated words to start with, whereas in cases 8 and 9 there is only the legislated order to proceed to adjudication, would be an unworthy example of exegetic dogmatism.

To use a different current term, it seems almost artificial to draw a sharp (or any) line between "discretion" proper (under Article 4, Swiss Civil Code, or under the so-called general clauses, mode B, 2) and quasi legislation (Article 1(2). In both cases the judge has decisional independence from a *specific* legislated rule.

XLVII

Note the different thrust of the amendment of Article 1, proposed by Meier-Hayoz in 1952 (296)275–76, so as to make it "more precise and complete" though "the proposed supplements are already partly realized in contemporary judicial practice": (*a*) paragraph 1 remains the same; (*b*) paragraph 2 remains the same; (*c*) paragraph 3: when filling gaps, the judge shall appropriately apply statutory provisions governing similar situations (*Verhältnisse*) and shall be governed by principles inherent in the spirit of the legal order; (*d*) paragraph 4: only for exceptional (*besondere*) reasons shall he deviate from the prior decisions of the federal jurisdiction; and (*e*) paragraph 5: he shall be advised by established doctrine and decisional law (*Ueberlieferung*); he shall be inspired by comparison with foreign law.

The changes are less striking than it might seem. The use of analogy is axiomatic. The question is rather how it is classified, as interpretation (requiring the fictitious reference to the legislative intent) or, frankly, as free search. In his later work (295)N.137–39,251–53,346,349, Meier-Hayoz classifies analogy as "gap filling." The reference to general ("inherent") principles (*analogia juris*) is again axiomatic. All law or decision making is subject to this outer social-axiological frame of reference. Rather it is important to realize that the concrete formulation of the ultimate general principle of justice (as well as any other general principle) for the purpose of decision is a function of the judge's value judgment. With respect to *Ueberlieferung* (see Note XXXIV): (*a*) *quaere* whether the intended difference is between individual "precedents" (paragraph 4) and decisional doctrine (paragraph 5); (*b*) in either case, however, the strict standard for deviation is less important than the fact that it is again the specific court that determines whether the reasons are exceptional enough and, if they deviate from prior decisions, whether they can be considered established decisional *doctrine* or are merely individual prior decision(s). Thus we face a basic analytical limitation even in such a good work: whether *Präjudiz* or *Ueberlieferung*, it is merely a prior decision (or sequence of decisions), not an absolutely binding precedent until the specific judge has determined that he will in fact use it as a rule.

XLVIII

The Swiss *Bundesgericht* is small compared with, *e.g.*, the French Court of Cassation (some seventy magistrates), but considerably larger than the U.S. Supreme Court. It has twenty-six judges. The tendency toward "shadings," which inevitably arise in a corps of even this size, is increased by the regular rotation of the presidents, who themselves are directly members of only one of the several divisions. These are: public law and administrative; civil I and II (each with six judges); judgment execution; the criminal law group (public prosecution, criminal chamber, federal criminal court, and cassation court). See (305)17–22.

Germann (163)226n70 illustrates the point. With regard to the crucial criterion of interpretation (referring to legislative record), the civil law chamber I gave an opinion substantially different from that handed down by the civil law chamber II only several weeks before, without even citing the prior case, not to speak of arguing the point away (BGE 68 II 106, 111 [1942]; BGE 68 II 124 [1942]). When the *Quinche* (*Suffragettes*) case came fifteen years later, the court had a convenient choice available—and chose the dictum of the civil law chamber II, without reference to the other decision.

Since 1943 (Article 16, law on the organization of the federal judiciary), a chamber of the court can overrule decisional law followed by another chamber or established by several chambers sitting en banc only with the approval of the other chamber or by a decision of the united chambers.

XLIX

The political nature of the decision in *Quinche* is supported also by circumstantial evidence. The case originated and was decided in a period of considerable agitation about women's voting. The eventual popular referendum in 1959 rejected it by more than a two-thirds majority. Only three French-speaking cantons, among them Mme Quinche's home, Vaud, approved it (305)187.

The same *Bundesgericht*—but possibly a different court—had no difficulty in admitting Mlle Dr. Roeder to the bar in 1923 (BGE 49 I 14), overruling an 1887 decision on the ground of "changed economic and social conditions" (166)256.

The two different 1942 civil decisions mentioned in the text in connection with Germann's criticism are those cited in Note XLVIII.

The six restatements of the objective doctrine between 1942 and 1957, three by each civil chamber, are listed in (163)227n71,72. The dates indicate in fact that the civil chamber II, on whose 1942 dicta the Bundesgericht relied in *Quinche*, reversed itself in 1953 and twice affirmed thereafter (1954, 1956). That makes the reliance in 1957 on the 1942 dicta a shaky doctrinal foundation indeed.

The *Quinche* case is extensively commented from a comparative political science viewpoint by Morrison (305), who also appends a full translation at 290–302. The excerpts above in the text have been translated directly from the original French text of the decision.

L

The statement about the unchallenged position of the objective doctrine since *Suisa* deserves some elaboration.

The subjective-historical method of *Quinche* was applied, with verbatim quotations and direct reference, in *Pantet* (already cited in the text). Here there was no political motive for the court's conservatism. Rather the collective logic went apparently awry. The subjective interpretation was built on a statute not in force at the time of Pantet's violation—a 1932 cereals control law, replaced by World War II economic protection regulations, was applied to black market sales of flour and related merchandise that occurred in 1948–1949—and it was used to the exclusion of general penal law, which came into force after 1932 but before Pantet's misdeeds. As a result, violations of this particular type were put in a favored position compared with similar fraudulent acts under the penal code. This the court disposed of by casually noting that the "result in the present case is not completely satisfactory"—as distinguished from the "absolutely inacceptable in practice" formula in *Quinche*, cited two pages earlier—though the result clearly violates the principle of equality under law.

Pantet was inevitably reversed at the nearest opportunity in *Füssler* (BGE 86 IV 92 [1960]). But the language of the court could be "at most [described as] an effort to prevent a direct contradiction" with the subjective-historical doctrine (163)225,228–29. Only a year later (BGE 87 II 118 [1961]) the criminal cassation court of the Bundesgericht set the historical method completely aside and went back to "any interpretation that corresponds to the true meaning of the law as it can be logically derived from the implicit value content and intended purpose of the statute."

In civil law, chamber I, which had never abandoned the objective interpretation, confirmed in *Turicaphon* (BGE 87 II 320, 331 [1961]: royalty rights of eight plaintiff phonograph record makers against owners-lessors of automatic record-playing pay machines) that "above all, the so-called historical method has no decisive weight in statutory interpretation." Even the more conservative chamber II gave almost simultaneously (BGE 86 III 146, 153–55 [1960]: certain rights in bankruptcy proceedings) the legislator the following choice: "Should the preceding interpretation [broad, contrary to the legislative record] not correspond to the intentions of the legislator . . . he would have the right to expressly bring about the limitation in the scope of the statute" (163)230.

The reference to legislative record, which is the principal tool of the historical method, is infrequent and/or spurious. According to Germann's statistics, in the fifty-seven decisions between 1958 and 1961 in which the court expressly referred to the *ratio legis* (meaning, purpose), only in eleven was there any reference to the legislative record (163)243n117,124. That means that in the other decisions the *ratio* was constructed *ex nunc*, whether true or not to the historical legislator. In the first seven years after the promulgation of a new penal code (1935), less than one-third of the published decisions made reference to the legislative record and most of them were simple dicta: they confirmed what could be derived from the text itself without further reference.

LI

With reference to analogy and to "concrete justice," see Germann (166)397:

> Where other codes (the Austrian, the Italian) filled gaps either by reference to legal norm provided for analogous cases, or to "general principle," or even to what is called "natural law," and thus required that the judges regularly base their decisions on preexisting rules or principles, the Swiss Civil Code relies in the case of gaps in positive law *on the judgment of the judges themselves*. Thus it gives them more independence and more responsibility. . . . The code advises the judge to "follow established doctrine and decisional law" (if there is some), but leaves him entirely free in this respect so as to permit him to reach at every stage of the case an equitable decision.

On the last point Germann refers to Egger (113)63, published in 1928.

More on concrete justice from du Pasquier (320)13–14: "When the text causes any doubt, the court . . . presumes that it is to serve justice and social utility. It freely discusses moral or practical arguments in support of various interpretations in search of a useful and just decision, without reference to the intent of the legislator, or attributing to him the intent that conforms with the decision reached."

On the tendency to use analogy, du Pasquier comments (at 26): "The court has a tendency to search for the *ratio legis* on which to base its decision at the very core of the legal system; hence its frequent recourse to analogy." Properly this would refer only to *analogia juris*, since the "core" comprises general principles, not specific provisions transferable by *analogia legis*.

LII

Liver, who became in the 1950s the spokesman for judicial restraint (265), with possible influence on the court's attitude toward gaps (432)95, insists that Swiss judges act like other judges, relying on their equity powers under Article 4 and on general principles of law. Germann (166)405–406 says really the same, though he emphasizes the advantageous position of Swiss judges under Article 1(2), contrasts it with that of French judges restricted by Article 5, French Civil Code—prohibition to decide in form of general rules; see Note XIV—and considers the methodology of the Bundesgericht "largely exemplary" (166)8. On the other hand—and incongruously, if Article 1(2) is considered the pivot—he approves of the "heuristic" value of the legislative record "when the statute is obscure, so as to find any possible meaning at all (BGE 56 II 74 [1930])" (163)242n122.

See also René David (97)96: "Article 1, ZGB . . . has not remained a dead letter, nor has it caused any revolution." Boulanger (38)341 concluded that at least "with regard to the procedure the judge is to follow, the direct effect of the text [Article 1(2)] is doubtful."

The most authoritative summary is by Meier-Hayoz (296)203: "As to the great judicial freedom that Article 1, ZGB, sanctions in the opinion of the doctrine, one can feel some of it in the decisions, but not exceedingly much." Du Pasquier (320)28 summed up the record as "getting by with . . . interpretation whenever possible instead of sounding the rather solemn trumpet of Art. 1,2."

A complementary evaluation of the Bundesgericht in the public-constitutional sphere is in Morrison (305), with a suggestion (at 238) that the ease of constitutional amendment made it unnecessary to develop interpretation techniques different (*i.e.*, more "creative") from ordinary legislation; the judges have sought "to avoid, as far as possible, acts of judicial legislation."

LIII

The question must be projected from the Swiss sample to a broader and more general phenomenon: the various historical periods of exaggerated dominance of positive law always were accompanied (preceded) by a corresponding weakening of jurisprudential doctrine. The last of these periods, the nineteenth-century positivism based on the fiction of the closed (hermeneutic) nature of the codes, was the cause of precisely such reactions as Gény's or Huber's.

Terré (393)128 suggests with regard to anti-Gény trends in France that "it is proper to look for the reason not in the fact that petitions for cassation must invoke a legal text—a requirement that is easily satisfied—but in some kind of prudence that is intrinsic to lawyers. . . . Just as the legislator who, putting on his best appearance, disguises retroactive statute in an interpretative form and makes legal constraint penetrate the contractual mold, the statutory interpreter insists on specific text but does not pretend to himself that the new meanings are not as artificial as any stipulation subsequently read into a contract."

Radbruch (340)163 pointed out that the Swiss Article 1 could serve as "credo" to the German free-law movement and added this apposite point:

> Though [they] believe to state what actually exists in practice, they nevertheless assign highly important consequences to the transfer of what has been done unconsciously into the consciousness of the judge. As long as the

> judge believes that he must apply law where, in reality, he has the duty to create law, he will, instead of following in good conscience the loud voice of the spirit of the law [*Rechtsgefühl*], easily press out of the silent statute a decision that is contrary to this spirit. And even when he follows the voice of justice, he will not justify his decision with the enlightening arguments based on justice, but with artificial, shadow arguments, irrelevant expressions in the statute with which the legislator probably did not mean to say anything, even less to provide a rule for the present case. We frequently find in the justification of decisions not so much the wisdom of the judge but the skill of a prestidigitator, who surprisingly extracts from the statute a decision that he before inserted into it. This fact may have a great deal to do with the estrangement between the law and the people.

Morrison makes his observation cited in the text with direct reference to *Quinche*, but without much sophistication.

LIV

The judges of the Bundesgericht are elected for six years by the Federal Assembly meeting in joint session. Although "any Swiss citizen who is eligible for the National Council" may be elected to the court, in fact only lawyers are elected, many of them academics who are typically also practicing attorneys or former law secretaries of the court itself. Since 1970—the *Quinche* syndrome legislatively healed and the change sanctioned by a referendum—women are also eligible.

Federal judges are the highest paid public officials in Switzerland except for the members of the Federal Council.

Morrison (305)99,104 points also to age and prior experience as factors that might influence the judge's psychology and attitude. Paradoxically, youth and judicial "activism" are not necessarily correlated. But Morrison cannot make a more definite judgment than to say that "a man who served nearly all his life within a judicial system dominated by positivist legal principles might have a different view of law than an individual who only began to judge cases after years in another occupation." In 1965, according to Morrison's statistics, fifteen of the judges then serving entered the court before the age of forty-three (six of them before the age of thirty), and eleven entered between the ages of forty-three and sixty-two.

LV

Unless carefully analyzed, Article 1(2) gives the impression that the judge is to legislate. I myself, when I first translated Article 1, was victimized by a lack of subtlety. I expressed the *aufstellen* of the German original, which is *établir* in the French version, as *enact*, the whole sentence reading "the rule he would enact as legislator."

But Article 1(2) does not tell the judge that he *is* a legislator. It only tells him that under defined circumstances he is supposed to act as legislator, which means make or confect a rule using the same sources, data, intellectual processes as the legislator does when he formulates his problem, policy, and legal solution. To call it enact, with the connotation of formal promulgation, is too much.

LVI

As to the conceptual framework, see Germann's list of the remnants of "the spirit of positivism not yet overcome in the Swiss practice . . . although both practice and scholars stood firmer on the ground" then in Germany and France (161) 109–11. If the "spirit of positivism" includes also the continued use of outworn concepts and their uncritical manipulation, then Germann's evaluation, though probably correct, is only relative. Compare, for example, the following:

1. The use of the concepts "policy" and "general principles" for the purpose of distinguishing the positions of the legislator and the judge, indistinguishable in the given context (265) 40.

2. The hairsplitting distinctions among analogy, interpretation, and gap (320) 32, when the analytical scheme is really simple and straightforward: any reference to another rule or principle, applicable on the basis of factual (inclusive axiological, value-oriented) similarity or relation, represents the use of analogy. It makes no difference whether this is done for the purpose of interpretation of another norm or of rule making to fill a gap. Compare in general the macroscopic analysis of the concept of gap by du Pasquier, but this is shared by the doctrine and the courts alike. Contrast the outline and comments in Note XLVI.

3. The inability to make the not so subtle distinction—*e.g.*, (320) 22–23, though the awareness of at least one element is present, *cf.* 69—between (*a*) judicial lawmaking through the continued material validity (*i.e.*, repeated and consistent application) of the principle of a specific decision, because its normative quality continues to be recognized by subsequent judges; and (*b*) legislative lawmaking, which is formally valid whether applied or not, though its material effect depends on judicial recognition of normative value for the purpose of doing justice, just as it does in the case of decisional law (more on this in the third essay).

4. The inclination toward the formal rather than the real/operational, even when the analysis or critique moves in the right direction. See, for example, Germann (167) 133, where a potential promising argument (I might be overreading it) in favor of incorporating values among the facts that determine the applicability of a positive norm is stillborn, because the value concept is tied to the normative form rather than to the factual foundation (the *donné*) and because of the insistence on categorization and verbalization in the established framework instead of developing an adequate fresh setting. A quite different illustration of the same criticism is Reichel (350), who spends his insight on terminological exegesis instead of substantive analysis.

5. The inability of boldly breaking out of the established conceptualization, suggested above, is perhaps best generally illustrated again by Germann himself—one of the more sophisticated Swiss writers, possibly

handicapped by his intensive interest in criminal law and doctrine. Germann repeatedly ends up with the correct insight after he has almost paralyzed his argument by all kinds of conceptual *ifs* and *buts*. *E.g.*, after the complicated argument criticized above, Germann correctly concludes (though still with the use of unnecessarily complicated semantics) that in the last analysis the choice and responsibility are those of the individual judge reaching the individual decision. This thought is contemporaneous and, in its full context, is almost identical with Cardozo's "Judges have . . . the power, though not the right, to ignore the mandate of a statute, and render judgment in despite of it" (61)129. It also recalls the solemn insistence on the irreversible nature of a precedent set by the House of Lords, tempered by the incidental afterthought that "the humblest judicial officer can disregard the most authoritative declaration of the House . . . unless he considers that the precedent cited is 'on all fours'" (3)164 (1927 ed.).

These conclusions, especially on the lack of jurisprudential subtlety and the prevailing traditional climate of thought and approach, are supported even by two very advanced works of younger authors. Spiro (379) does not get jurisprudentially farther than to adopt the rudiments of American realism, including the emphasis on facts (but see the conventional treatment of such fact-related concepts as *Sachverhalt* and *Tatbestand* or of *ratio decidendi* on the very first page. Meier-Hayoz' work (296) was a *Habilitationschrift*—a thesis presented and defended to qualify for a university lectureship—which excuses the various stereotypes (*e.g.*, the syllogistic scheme of judicial decision on the first page). A more serious concession to the Establishment is the emphasis on legal certainty (p. 274), belied by his general approval of Article 1(2), ZGB.

The best example of lack of follow-through from insights to conclusions is perforce again Germann, the leading and most comparative Swiss writer on methodology. Just to give one outstanding example, compare (166)213–24, where he builds his thesis up to the correct organic decision theory—starting with relevant facts and aiming at the (just) decision of the concrete case (though with some debatable dicta on differences between "casuistic" and "rule-making" methods)—with the following chapter (229,239,249) where he makes conventional and in operational terms demonstrably incorrect distinctions between the single decision and the general rule of which it can be the starting point. The explanation of these discrepancies cannot be found in chronology. There are only three years between the various chapters, the first written in 1963, the second in 1959–1960—almost twenty years after Germann wrote his first major work (161).

The concern about judicial abuse is the underlying tone of all the major commentaries, though at least in one (296) it gives the impression of lip service. Liver, in a most recent contribution (265)45, goes much farther than anybody else in emphasizing that (*a*) the general clauses (which fall properly under Article 4, ZGB) are really more important than Article 1; (*b*) the Swiss judge plays under Article 1 a role "not substantially different from the judge in the neighboring states when he is referred to general clauses" (of course not, but that is a willed, not inherent, result!); and (*c*) the word *Rechtsfindung*, generally used to describe judicial activity, also properly expresses its content—the finding of the law, not its making (*Rechtsetzung*). Except for the last item, which suffers from the inevitable and unenviable comparison with the Blackstonian folklore in English and American law, Liver's conclusions are probably correct on the facts of the Swiss practice. Doctrinally they support the generalization I made in the text above: instead of leading the practice toward a better materialization of the spirit of Article 1, which was at its promulgation ahead of the French and German practice, Liver's descriptive approach and conclusions indicate a satisfaction with the leveling off.

LVII

There is enough in Huber's language to warrant subtler and truer-to-life reading. In the sentence preceding the quotation in the text, Huber makes it clear that he tries to distinguish the judge's action under Article 1(2) from one that would be discretional in the narrow sense. The judge "must not decide arbitrarily, according to momentary circumstantial impression, compassion, indignation, or personal bias." In the sentence that follows the quotation he says, "The judge must decide in the same manner as the competent legislator would have decided had he thought of such a case." The "decide" in the contexts above can be read as a continuum in the rule-making process: the legislator—as much as he envisages a particular situation for the purpose of establishing a general norm—is deciding while making a rule; the judge is making a rule while deciding.

In any case, the actual process is an uninterrupted flowing of one power into another, with the inner divisions or steps moving and blurred. Nevertheless, the Swiss doctrine could not shake off the dogmatic dichotomies. So Tuor (400)5IV: "The judge must decide the case for which there is no rule on the basis of a general norm that he will create through such [*i.e.*, legislatorlike] objective considerations." Egger (113)Art. 1,n36: "The judge proceeds formally like a legislator." Du Pasquier (318)*216*: "The judge . . . must rise above the particular case before him . . . and putting himself in the position of legislator, rule [*statuer*, not *decider*] according to a principle susceptible to be erected in a general rule." Yung (432)98: "Thus the judge must divide himself in two [*dédoubler*]: first he acts as a legislator and sets an abstract rule. He draws on general principles, abstracting from the particular case. Second, he applies the rule he has just enunciated to the case as if it had been promulgated by the legislator."

In subsequent correspondence—after I had expressed incredulity that "anybody" [could] really believe that any decision of the Swiss Bundesgericht since 1912, under Art. 1(2), has been arrived at by following this quasi-syllogistic pattern, no matter in what form the judges may have felt obligated to write up their opinions" (279)715, and subsequently discovered Boulanger's parallel doubt (38)341—Yung suggested in a personal communication (1968) that he "had perhaps emphasized the *dédoublement* too much trying to make his thought a little more striking" for the foreign audience of the original lecture. He then supplied references to other Swiss writers cited above.

Two comments are necessary. First, in their broader context, all the quotations above (except the ones by Egger and by Yung proper) can be also read less dogmatically. Huber emphasizes the decisional process; Tuor in fact talks mainly about the decisional sources; as to the result, he says it must be as good as if the legislative lawmaking process took place; only the term "*general* norm" perhaps reveals the dogmatic basis. Du Pasquier, who is elsewhere much more pragmatic, is possibly victimized by Kant's terminology, which is his paradigm.

Second, Yung's rationale should be commented on. The idea could not have been new for most of his French and international audience. See, for France, Maury (278)29, speaking of the "classical problem"; for the common law world, Wasserstrom (411)138f, whose discussion of the "two-level procedure" Stone (384)286 considers "thoughtful"; for Spanish–Latin American literature, Recaséns-Siches (404)*I* 578: "the Swiss formula could give the wrong impression that the judge creates an applicable norm in the moment when he decides an unforeseen case. In reality, the judge understands that the unformulated norm has already governed [in a general form] before he makes his decision; he simply pronounces and concretely applies it."

Gény strongly implies the same model (which might be more appropriately styled *split*-level) when he says, "Faced first with the task of discovering a general and abstract rule susceptible of being adapted to particular concrete cases." But the context is sociological rather than legal-dogmatic. His references to "notion of normalcy," "probable expectations," need to "envisage the most general fact situation that raises the [concrete] question" are prefaced by exhortation to the judge to "first try to penetrate . . . human and social reality" and observe "society . . . as the indispensable element of legal method" (157)*169*. One is reminded of rather contemporaneous practice–Cardozo's decision in *McPherson* v. *Buick* (1916), a puny fact situation in which Cardozo recognized a harbinger of a vast socio-legal problem to come and that Llewellyn extolled as an example of "situation sense" (268)430f. The similarity of the context and the rhetoric to Gény's is striking.

Yung feels that, beside other arguments (protection against arbitrariness, harmonization of the ad hoc rule with the whole legal system, the capability to invoke the ad hoc decision in the future as an "obligatory" precedent), the "most profound" reason for the two-tier procedure is the "premise that human spirit discovers justice more assuredly when it constructs a general rule, valid for everybody, than when it decides in the single perspective of a particular case" (432)98.

Meier-Hayoz (295)N.520 thinks it "questionable whether it is the judge's task to set up a rule under which the concrete case would be then subsumed or whether he should decide the case directly in equity, without making first a general-abstract norm." But he discusses this in the context of the relative precedential importance of an *equity* ruling (under Article 4 or Article 1) compared with a general *quasi-legislative* ruling (under Article 1[2]), not in terms of the formal versus operational conception of Article 1(2). The precedent theory underlying this argument is, as I shall argue in the last essay, dogmatic, not empirical-pragmatic.

Germann (164)306 and du Pasquier (320)64 present much less dogmatic opinions (Germann's specific context is very empirical-pragmatic). They discuss the problem in terms of the need to decide equally similar future cases (BGE 49 I 300 [1923]); of "class" or, to use a term so debated in the United States in the early 1960s, "neutral" principles; of the dynamics of successive case decisions (versus the dogmatics of the doctrine). But neither draws all the possible implications from these correct insights.

Carry (64)537–38, of the Geneva law faculty, correctly compared the judge's reasoning toward a particular decision with the legislator's selection from various possible rules, as explained in the legislative record. But, again, there is no further projection. Compare Horack's argument in the opposite direction (208)52 that the effectiveness of legislative hearings to get various alternatives considered before the decision on policy and law is made is comparable with trial arguments before a judicial decision.

LVIII

Germann is again more empirical and thus more advanced than the other writers. He introduced even a rudimentary concept of quantification into evaluating the force of past decisional law (165). This is almost contemporaneous with the efforts of American jurimetrists (367), but not further developed, conceptually or mathematically. Even the potential insight is marred by what seems to be an exaggerated straining for certainty. It may be significant that Frank (134)14–23, who debunked the yearning for certainty in law in Freudian terms—one would be on safer ground today to use, for example, modern physics as measure—and linked it to the sources of legal orthodoxy, was judged by Germann (166)274n21 to be an extremist, though in a different *specific* context ("law consists of decisions, not of rules").

The performance of the writers invites a postscript on the relative priority that the *Lehre* was given over the *bewährte Ueberlieferung* in Article 1, ZGB. (*a*) Although the meaning of the latter term is decisional *law/doctrine*, it appears that even a single *arrêt de principe* has carried the day more than once—with acquiescence of the "more equal" doctrine of the commentators (433)333. (*b*) With regard to the whole doctrinal environment in which the fate of Article 1 (2 and 3) was decided, see Ernst Rabel's early critique (1910) of the "conceptual and normative uncertainty" in the procedural aspects of the Swiss Civil Code, in the face of the need for "organic development of new systematic jurisprudence" (266)n157–158.

Notes

LIX

Huber's bankruptcy metaphor comes from an article in *Wirtschaft und Recht* (Economy and law) X(1958)10n5, which I cite via Germann (see the reference in the text). In the same context Huber writes: "The fact that [the Bundesgericht] does not want to exclude any method is in itself an abdication of responsibility in the field of methodology [of interpretation] since the court insists at the same time that cantonal authorities must apply only legitimate (recognized) methods and must reject others as arbitrary." In the law review article cited in the text, Huber considers the attitude of the court to be "formal and positivistic . . . compared with contemporary constitutional doctrine [the reference is particularly to the German constitutional court] and revealing a certain lack of confidence in . . . interpretation. . . . When the court defends itself by stating that any method that seems to reveal best the meaning of the norm in the particular case is acceptable to it, one is almost shocked. The determination of the method of interpretation must, after all, not be left to discretion, but must be something that had been determined . . . as permissible or not permissible. . . . This is not to say that a combined method of interpretation could not be applied under circumstances" (211)466–67. Contrary to Huber, McWhinney concluded on about the same record that the German Verfassungsgericht exercised self-restraint in the American style (293)21n64, cited with approval in (375)238n118.

With reference to the postulate implicit in Huber's critique, it is interesting that the amendment of Article 1 proposed by Meier-Hayoz (Note XLVII) does not include any obligatory or recommended steps or canons of interpretation of existing law, before recourse is had to the quasi-legislative power under paragraph 2. Indeed, Meier-Hayoz' dissertation was written almost ten years earlier, but already in an environment of considerable flux in the court's practice.

Yung's metaphoric evaluation of Swiss practice in 1962, exactly fifty years after Article 1 entered formally into force, was: "The heroic era seems to be over. Prudence has won over boldness" (432)99. Whether the result was "more wise and moderate," as du Pasquier concluded (320)28, seems to be a wide-open question.

LX

It is well established, in the American practice at least, that the choice of facts that form an integral part of the decision (sometimes, such as in *Dobson*, 320 U.S. 489 [1943], they were called "ultimate" or "legal" facts) will be upheld on appeal unless it is arbitrary to the point of abuse. The often considerable difference between the statement of these determinative facts in the majority opinion and in the dissent shows how far the trier of facts can go without abusing his discretion. When the fact discretion is upheld on appeal, this is not done independently of the rest of the case but because the decisional facts were originally so chosen as to fit into the framework of the words and principles of positive law that lead to the result the appellate court considers correct.

LXI

The focus on the judicial function in this essay is, thus, not determined by Gény's frame of reference, but by an intrinsic dimension of any system of justice under law and by the postulate of the rationality of reality—to borrow a term from contemporary structuralism (anthropology, linguistics)—which should perhaps acquire its own meaning in jurisprudence. This realism would have only a limited interface with the so-called American realism. See Hurst's critique (213)366, which I read as stemming from a reaction to the one-sidedness of this realism, not as directed against fresh qualitative inquiry set in the full framework of the legal process.

In sum, the concentration on the position, function, and powers of the judge does not come from any lack of awareness of the total spectrum and of the free play of various agents with whom the judge must participate in a coordinated way in a well-functioning legal system. Many decisions are made and much law is interpreted with practical finality without ever reaching the judicial sphere. These functions of the counselor, the administrator, the legal draftsman deserve to be analyzed and better understood. The theory of political process must be integrated into the comprehensive operational model of jurisprudence. It is not an either/or situation, but one that calls, first, for a revision of the terms of reference using an empirical-scientific method and then the assembly of all the pieces, not only the legal ones in the narrow sense. What I suggest later in this essay is simply a set of critical terms, which I consider a necessary beginning in this process.

I have defined a well-functioning legal order as "a continuous process which at once maintains the established social order and channels new conflicts of interests toward orderly and legal solutions consonant with democratic principles" (287).

LXII

Possible examples from the English and American sphere range widely. See, for example, the following. Lord Evershed, then master of rolls: "Very few, if any of the English judges of today have thought it necessary to ask themselves 'What is the true nature of the judicial function which I am now [in the light of the modern development of English law, especially the proportionate increase of legislated law] called upon to perform?' " (128) 761. W. V. Schaeffer, then chief justice of the Supreme Court of Illinois: "I suspect that what is lacking is not candor but technique and tools . . . sensitive enough to explore the mind of a [judge] and report accurately its conscious and subconscious operations" (364). Professor Auerbach, with reference to "Theory of judicial decision": "How much is [the judge] restricted by the 'taught tradition of the law;' . . . to what extent are policy grounds chosen deliberately by the judge or apprehended intuitively by him?" (15)361. In sum, the "black box" (81)508–509, is still the thing.

LXIII

Despite the correct definition in the text, Pound's achievement has been more encyclopedic than integrative. Holmes, unfortunately, never pulled together his brilliant insights either. Cardozo, the most comparative of American students of Gény, was intuitive and impressionistic rather than rigorously analytic and synthetic. Kantorowicz (228)698n5 summarized well the European state of the art: "Judges and lawyers . . . lack . . . also a rational theory which will integrate [their] research with the concept of law." As the documentation gathered in this study indicates, this is true in the 1970s as it was in the 1920s. See this 1975 example selected to illustrate the wide time-space distribution: "The academicians must develop doctrinal studies which uncover influences, seek internal coherence of the new system, and suggest pitfalls of the law where the coherence is incomplete" (374)1104; see also (148) cited above in the text.

Hurst referred to American jurisprudence when he concluded that "effective [legal research] will require . . . more philosophical investment than went into most legal writing of the last 125 years" (213)367. But when the qualifier "more" is changed to "different, more adequate," it applies to both sides of the Atlantic. Consider, *e.g.*, what a lame philosophical underpinning for a "rational" jurisprudence is the Roman *Lex est aliquod rationis*, dusted off in a major recent comparative treatise (97)361. It is not the reasonableness of a *statute* that is in question, but the full understanding of the operation of *law* and the routine application of this rational model.

LXIV

In an earlier analysis (283)liii–lv, I filled two and a half pages of small footnote print with brief quotations from American and English decisions and literature related to the highlights of Gény's doctrine. The sample was random, with no effort at even a semblance of completeness. Virtually all the quotes originated in the immediately preceding three-year period (1959–1962). The headings speak for themselves: on the effects of a rigid separation doctrine, on the various doctrines of interpretation, on judicial quasi legislation, on judicial psychology and the influences shaping it, blunt or antiquated conceptualizations.

This sample could be expanded many times, to illustrate both the continued existence of several irrational doctrinal attitudes, against which Gény spoke out so clearly, and evidence of the convergence in terms of this essay of the two *grands systèmes* of the Atlantic world. Only some generic sampling can be attempted here:

1. The insistence in America on *ex tunc* interpretation, without the saving grace of Gény's strategy in favor of free search: from Justice Black—*e.g.*, dissenting in *Katz* (30)—through Crosskey (89) to Justice Rehnquist's dic-

tum that the justices' duty is not to enforce their "perception of modern life"—on the equality of sexes, in 1975 (dissenting in *Taylor* [348]542)! There is even a Julliot de la Morandière twist (*cf.* Note XLI) in Justice Harlan's dissent in the *Jones* (*Paddock Woods*) case (1968)—supporting his argument for the dismissal of the case, based on the 1866 Civil Rights Act, by reference to an open-housing law, passed by the Congress in 1968 but not yet in effect at the time of the decision in *Jones*.

2. The loose analysis and rhetoric in the United States in defining judicial activism and the opposite standard of a "strict constructionist" in the selection of candidates for the Supreme Court. Underlying is often a clear misunderstanding of the complementary functions of the legislator (Congress) and the judge (Supreme Court), stated for modern times by Portalis 175 years ago and then again by Gény, and of the consequent difference between "policy making" and "deciding on policy."

3. The frequent failure to distinguish for analytical purposes between the political process and goals and the judicial function and technique of specific gap filling through decision. The doctrinal analysis—*e.g.*, (86)165f—is then almost indistinguishable from popular discourse (175). Although the mixing of politics and law can be rationalized on other grounds, lack of analytical separation, where it proceeds, has been typically related to early stages of disciplinary maturing (*cf.* the gestation of international law within theology before it became a separate discipline).

4. The call for deciding on "neutral principles" (412), which means deciding *deliberately* more than the concrete controversy (as distinguished from assuming that the concrete rule *may* serve as a guideline, judicial or extrajudicial, in other cases where a comparable fact and principle are involved), is akin to the practice of *arrêt de réglement*. See Note XIV.

5. The judicial formulation of the right of privacy, such as in *De Gregory*, is a perfect example of the technique of free search as defined by Gény.

6. The circle appears closed when American commentators warn against the "exaggerated contemporary cult of the legislator" and against assumptions about the self-sufficiency of the statutory system in the United States, citing European nineteenth-century experience under the codes (324)36,46.

LXV

For instance, the failure, from Gény (157)*85* to Carbonnier (57)*I,42–43*, to openly accept *stare decisis* as a fact of life and to systematize it in an orderly doctrine has also deprived French practitioners of efficient instruments for research in decisional law on the order of the American citators. This may be illustrated by a personal experience. In the course of research in the operational concepts in the process of judicial decision in France, I attempted to reconstruct the elements of certain decisional doctrines and to trace their development through the chain of decisions. I did this by working my way backward in time, beginning in each case with the solemn decision of the Court of Cassation (chambres réunies or assemblée plénière), which is binding by law on the lower courts. To do this I had to use the case reports, articles of doctrine dealing with these decisions, commentaries. I logged considerable mileage between the library of the court and the files of its research service, spending long days in the process. With American citators and indices, I would have constructed the desired genealogy in a matter of hours.

The situation in France illustrates also the fact that, when a need exists, practice finds its way no matter what the *École* may insist on pretending. The magistrates of the Court of Cassation have a research service (Service de documentation et d'études), which is a reasonable facsimile of the apparatus of reference openly available to all American lawyers.

The core of the service is the *fichier*, a card catalog of all the decisions of the court back to 1950. By 1975 it contained some 200,000 cards in civil law alone. When a magistrate requests a memorandum on a case (in which he is typically the rapporteur), the service proceeds like a law clerk to an American judge (22). Using an index, the research associate of the service pulls out of the catalog all relevant decisions (if any) and then reduces them to an analytical memorandum. The subsequent proceedings are a trade secret, but not a "black box." A well-founded suspicion is that, if the magistrate likes what he reads in the memorandum, he incorporates the *motives*, the *rationes decidendi*, of the prior cases into the draft opinion he is preparing. If he does not like them or some of them, he has the professional duty to persuade himself and his colleagues in the chamber that the prior decisions of the court do not apply to the case at hand or that the decisional law they represent ought to be changed.

Carbonnier, who is a reluctant witness ("The memory of the court is now on file cards!") states the underlying rule of *stare decisis* as follows: "The Court of Cassation never quashes any lower decision on the ground that it violates its own prior decisional law, always only on the ground that the statute was violated. But the court considers it to be a violation of the law [and as such a ground for cassation] if the statute in question was interpreted differently from the court's prior decisions" (57) *I* 118,120.

For all its value, the service is only a partial substitute. It is available only to the high judges, not to the very powerful intermediate appellate courts. Until 1968, the memoranda on prior decisions were obligatory only in cases dealing with social legislation. They were prepared on express request in a small number of other cases. The service did not encourage increased use because it had available a fraction of its statutory manpower (22). The rest of the judiciary and the advocates have had to make do with the traditional and rather makeshift research tools. Obviously they could not devote to the preparation of their cases the same time a professor on sabbatical leave could devote to comparable research.

LXVI

A few random illustrations of the points of critique in the text:

On the "iron forge" concepts, here is an American example. The chapter "The psychology of judicial decision" in a widely used textbook of jurisprudence is conceived only in terms of the relations between "legal rules" and "mental process" of reaching a decision or rationalizing it. The mental process is here an undifferentiated, global stream-of-conscious notion, which takes no notice of the contemporary development in the related behavioral sciences and has no reference to concepts as tools of thinking, to value judgments or biases, etc. (322)*5.06*. A European example: the continued use of historical macroconcepts, such as "civil law" and "common law"—recently culminated in the conception of *grands systèmes* (97)—which invite simplified disjunctive comparisons instead of a refined analysis that starts with and constantly returns to the empirical *données* postulated by Gény. It is, indeed, true that the construction of the empirical model has not been seriously attempted. The differences between "theory" (presumably empirical) and "empiricism" are discussed in macroconcepts comparable to those above (57)*I*31. On the capacity of empirical conceptualization in America, see Note I.

On confused semantics, one typical example must stand here for the many. Note the apparently unconscious shifting of meaning of the term "law" (*droit*) commented on in the brackets in the following passage on "the relations between decisional law and the statutes": "Cases of first impression . . . are governed by the law, since the statute, an occasional manifestation of the law, is not omnipresent, but the law is immanent. [This makes sense only if law means here the judge's *obligation to settle conflicts* under Article 4, French Civil Code.] Thus the judge will refer directly to law, which he will derive from its living sources [here law means *decisional factors*] a role that momentarily makes him like a legislator . . . to leave the domain of interpretation in the proper sense and to enter the domain of direct creation of law [meaning here a *positive rule* between the parties]" (36)216–17. It is impossible to build rigorous jurisprudential analysis on such semantic quicksand.

On the "geometry" of jurisprudence, see the remarks of André Lichnerowitz, French mathematician and educational planner (shortly before the 1968 student revolt in Paris), that geometry was still being taught in a classical Greek framework and analysis in the spirit of the seventeenth and eighteenth centuries (263). If we substitute legal doctrine and education for geometry and analysis, the comment is not far from the mark.

LXVII

The following sample of dicta from the French literature illustrates both the insights and the conceptual barriers to integration.

Dupeyroux: "Gény commits . . . the error of neglecting the fact that Article 5 now prohibits only *arrêts de réglement*" (111)357n28, "something very different from established decisional law [*jurisprudence acquise*]" (278)30.

Maury: "Separation of powers in France . . . only prohibits the judge from doing the legislator's work, that is, to promulgate a general and permanent rule. . . . No principle of French positive law excludes decisional law from being a formal source of law. . . . Decisional law comprises not rules . . . made in a single judicial decision . . . but general, imperative rules derived from the so-called *jurisprudence constante*. . . . The question [related to Article 4] is whether the judge in deciding an unprovided case establishes a particular rule valid only with regard to the specific case (Article 1351, French Civil Code) or whether, on the contrary, having to determine how he will solve the case, he ends by creating an abstract rule of general scope. Gény sustained the first position" (278)29–31. Article 1351 states that the force of *res judicata* extends only to the matter that was in judgment.

Ripert: "The sovereign was in older times both legislator and judge. Both powers are of the same nature. The judge is the legislator in particular cases. . . . The rule penetrates the legal environment only through judicial power, which has the task to apply it; this power of application consists of making the rule alive and useful" (353)119,393.

Boulanger: "A decision of the court of appeals and, *a fortiori*, of a trial court cannot establish decisional law in the technical sense: it can be only the beginning of a future decisional law . . . a jurisdiction can have the sense of being bound by a precedent only if this emanates from the Court of Cassation" (40)79. "When decisional law is so settled that it has been transformed into custom [referring to Planiol, 1899: decisional law is 'customary law of recent formation'] the creative power of decisional law [*i.e.*, of the Court of Cassation] loses its *raison d'être*" (39)440.

Court of Appeals, Paris, 29 June 1965, JCP II 14,296 (1965): "A court has the power not to follow a dominant decisional law [*jurisprudence constante*] even the best established decisional law . . . is subject to renewal through necessary evolution, especially in an era when even principles [*thèses*] that could have been considered perfectly established are being freely questioned."

Dupeyroux: "Maury does not intend to say that the pluralist perspective [both legislator and judge as lawmakers] is contrary to logic . . . only that it lacks the elegance and thus the logical simplicity that is so seductive to the spirit. . . . But even if it cannot be explained so as to rally all the support . . . the observation [by Maury] imposes itself in the presence of such decisional rules in our law" (111)356.

LXVIII

Byrd's argument and those of similar critics are also conceptually crude. First, they do not distinguish between, on the one hand, cases in which the Supreme Court filled gaps that other branches of the government could and should have filled but did not (the 1954 school desegregation cases came 10 years before the Congress completed the cornerstone of contemporary civil rights legislation); and, on the other hand, cases of judicial review. Second, the scope of usurping legislative power in this second category has been less than ninety instances in about 180 years. The well-known policy of the U.S. Supreme Court is, to paraphrase du Pasquier's comment on the Swiss

Bundesgericht (Note LII) to "get by with deciding on other grounds whenever possible, rather than to sound the rather solemn trumpet of constitutional review." There is, of course, one important difference between the source of the power of these two federal courts. The U.S. Supreme Court can overrule the legislator through a different interpretation of the Constitution and, in turn, be overruled by the legislator through a constitutional amendment. The Court's power is customary in nature. The Swiss court, on the other hand, is invited by an expressed, legislative mandate to substitute itself for the legislator who did not legislate.

Neither the analysis nor wide understanding on the American side is fostered if the problem is discussed in terms such as these: "The criticism . . . that the Court is too political . . . is misguided . . . if it means that the Court should make no decision that can in any sense be deemed political, but should follow some certain body of rules called Constitutional Law. . . . The Law as so conceived is a myth . . . and hence the Court, in order to function at all, must make law rather than simply follow it. Therefore, it must make what are bound to be, in a sense, political decisions" (29). Note the use of "political" rather than "policy-oriented, based on policy considerations," of "make law" rather than "make decisions even if the law has a verbal or teleological gap." A decision "makes law" only between the parties (individual or class), with no assurance at that time that it will become a more general norm, "law" in the sense Bickel used it.

LXIX

The various aspects of competent working jurisprudence in the text can be illustrated by numerous decisions. It does not happen often, however, that they are all present or absent in a single case. Such a one is *Rosado* v. *Rivera*, Supreme Court of Puerto Rico, 81 P.R.R. 157 (1959). It violates every major rule of rational jurisprudence and, in the process, the very purpose of concrete justice. It is a complete anti-Gény. The interest of the case is further heightened by the fact that Puerto Rico is a so-called mixed jurisdiction, the judges and their method being American by training and orientation; the case at issue involves a code of European mold.

The facts and the law in *Rosado* are these. Plaintiff Rosado returns from military service overseas and shortly thereafter marries the defendant. Soon he discovers that she married him dissimulating the fact that she was pregnant by another man. Rosado separates in fact and sues for divorce on the statutory ground of mental cruelty (fraud is not one of the grounds for divorce enumerated in Article 96, Civil Code of Puerto Rico). The divorce is denied, and the ruling is confirmed on appeal to the Supreme Court on the ground that, since the impregnation occurred before the marriage, it could not be causally related to the pleaded ground for divorce, because grounds for divorce must, by definition, originate in the course of the marriage.

A concurring judge agrees with the majority on the sole ground that it is for the legislature to fill the gap in the code, that is, to add fraud to the list of grounds for divorce. The first dissent argues that the gap in this case ought to be filled through equity (Article 7, Civil Code of Puerto Rico, similar to Article 21, Louisiana Civil Code). A second dissent, extensively documented by French decisional law and doctrine, urges the judicial introduction of fraud as a ground for divorce. (The plaintiff argued, and the majority of the court extensively discussed and rejected, the reception of fraud *per analogiam*, with reference to various state jurisdictions in the United States.)

The analytical and policy errors in this case range from the first step in the process toward decision—fact classification for the purpose of interpretation and application of the code—to the ultimate determination of the need for free search and the identification of the source of an ad hoc rule.

First, on the fact classification, it is true that the impregnation of Rivera occurred before the marriage was contracted. But the act of mental cruelty occurred when Rosado learned about the fact. That happened admittedly in the course of the marriage and thus qualified as a ground under the code. Since all but one judge (on whose opinion I shall comment below) accepted another classification of the facts, demonstrably erroneous, they had to conclude that there was no ground for divorce or, in the case of two judges, that there was a gap.

Second, the adopted classification of the facts was in function of a particular conceptualization of the purpose of divorce proceedings: to establish the guilt of one party as the justification for the decree (where the pleaded ground admits the allocation of guilt; thus not in cases of insanity). In this frame of reference, the fact analysis is perforce focused on the party alleged to be guilty. The guilty act of the defendant occurred before she was married. The court considered another aspect of the guilt—concealing the pregnancy from the plaintiff before and at the time of the marriage contract—but found here a gap in the code.

Third, the court did not investigate (and the plaintiff did not urge it to) the underlying premise of guilt in the light of the applicable provisions of the code and of their context. The guilt conception of divorce is, in fact, not the will of the Puerto Rican legislator. It was grafted on the law by one single judge (indeed without a dissent). The first step was a trial court decision early in the century, modeled on the doctrine of the English ecclesiastic courts, and routinely confirmed by the Supreme Court. Then, in 1940, the concept of guilt was enthroned when this same judge was president of the Supreme Court. It is a decisional law *contra legem* or, at best, *praeter legem*. As such it should have been perforce examined in a hard case such as *Rosado*.

Fourth, even after the incorrect fact classification, which created a problem where there was none, the court still had two options: to decide on the basis of a mechanical exegesis or to determine that the concrete justice required the finding and filling of a gap. It opted for the first alternative.

Fifth, this happened in spite of the fact that the finding and filling of a gap in this particular case was not only invited but also facilitated by the expression in the code of a *clear legislative policy*: marriage ought to be terminable on various grounds (ten in all), any of which makes its continuation individually damaging or socially useless. The existence of such a policy meant that, even if a gap was found in Article 96, it was only a *verbal* gap, not a *teleological*. A simple reference to the words *and purpose* of the historical legislator (purpose is the immediate second referent when the words do not solve the case clearly *and justly*) was not only a routine obligation of the judges, but also would have put them on the track of free search.

Sixth, in the typical exegetic fashion, which was Gény's target exactly sixty years before and which Pound called slot-machine jurisprudence a little later (*cf.* also Cardozo's free-search decision based on social policy in *Hynes*, 1921, a case structurally very similar to *Rosado*, though the gap there was in the common law doctrine of trespass), the *Rosado* court decided on a strictly verbal-normative level. Its inability to conceive of the words as expressions of social-legislative purpose and then to act on the apparent gap was a combined result of the common confusion between *deciding on policy* and *making policy* (this is true especially of the concurring judge) and of an erroneous general doctrine of *stare decisis*.

Seventh, by deciding on the analytical and conceptual level criticized in the preceding comments, the court (*a*) did not apply clear legislative policy, (*b*) thereby committed a concrete injustice, and (*c*) in fact not only neglected the existing policy of the code but substituted for it its own policy. As a result, the decision in *Rosado* set the divorce provisions of the Puerto Rican Civil Code in a policy context contrary to the legislative intent. The policy now reads: The integrity of marriage ought to be preserved (1) except in cases of divorce grounds expressed by the legislator in Article 96, (2) even if the facts of the case can be subsumed under one of these grounds but are not, as a result of wrong pleading or because of prior judicial gloss on the legislative intent, (3) even if the facts indicate that the continuation of the marriage is individually damaging or socially useless and thus falls within the scope of explicit legislative policy, and (4) even if the code had not been revised in several decades (more than fifty years preceding *Rosado*; nor has it been revised since, despite the concurring judge's gentle prodding).

In sum, then, the court's applied jurisprudence in *Rosado* is primitive. It proceeds from the model of strict separation of powers. It misunderstands the power and duty of the judiciary to do concrete justice and thus to share responsibility for the continuing adjustment of law to new social needs and values. It misunderstands the scope and impact of a policy decision in an individual case. It does not distinguish between a particular private law case like *Rosado* and a decision on public constitutional law principles.

The court restricts itself to the narrowest possible reading of the text. It makes no effort at extensive interpretation, not to speak of gap finding and free search.

Although pretending to proceed in a constitutionally proper fashion, it not only commits concrete injustice, but in fact greatly exceeds its power, as it substitutes its own policy for the clear policy of the legislator.

Apart from the analytical aspects, the court's attitude was in fact also intellectually dishonest. Although announcing various fiction-studded principles, the majority of the judges was reliably reported as having acted with the knowledge, nowhere implied in the decision, that the plaintiff would shortly have a chance to dissolve the marriage on another ground, that of a three-year separation. This involves, however, another serious value question: the divorce on ground of separation must be mandatorily decreed in favor of the wife. Thus a demonstrably injured party like Rosado finds himself with the additional injustice and burden that the court record shows him to be the guilty party; and, should a question of custody be involved, additional proceedings would be necessary to transfer custody from the "winning" party, the in fact guilty wife.

In view of the facts and law involved, the first dissent is a classical case of "premature refuge to equity," *equitatismo* (12)viii, before the legislated law could be fully drawn out because of a too crude analytical-conceptual equipment. (This is a perennial syndrome. See Note XXX, the United Nation Command's arguments in the Korean POW repatriation crisis).

The second dissent is little more than an informative exercise in comparative law. It makes the error of reaching out to "exotic" sources before "exhausting local remedies," *i.e.*, local law and the most indicated "persuasive authorities." These were, in this case, various United States state laws, since no relevant Spanish commentaries were available (Spain is the immediate model for the code as a whole, but divorce does not exist there) and French sources were generally linguistically not accessible to the court. In principle, the judges ought to be able to verify in the original what a dissenting colleague argues.

In addition, this particular judge identified the alternative fact classification, but did not conceptualize it in the terms suggested above, (that is, with focus on the complaint rather than on the origin of the complaint). Instead he proposed a fiction: that the "guilty" act of the defendant before marriage continued as if repeated until and into the marriage; thus it could cause the actionable ground of mental cruelty. This fiction is similar to an early nineteenth-century case, *Adams* v. *Lindsell*, not expressly acknowledged in the opinion. In *Adams*, the act of mailing acceptance of an offer was fictitiously considered as being repeated until the moment the offeror in fact received the mailed acceptance. This fiction "satisfied" the contemporaneous requirement of a simultaneous "meeting of the minds" and permitted contract formation at a distance. In *Rosado*, however, basic facts of physiology required and permitted that the single act of impregnation be distinguished from the continuing state of pregnancy.

Taking Gény's doctrine and its projections in this essay as a base, the scoreboard in *Rosado* would look something like this (x standing for a point, y standing for a partial, conditional, indirect one-half point):

DECISIONAL MODEL	MAJORITY	CONCURRING	DISSENT I	DISSENT II
Facts: appropriate classification	–	–	–	*y*
Concrete justice: concern and identification	–	*x*	*x*	*x*
Legislated law: comprehensive interpretation (text *and* purpose *and* contemporary social context)	–	–	–	–
Decisional law: comprehensive interpretation in the light of applicable legislated law (as above)	–	–	–	–
Gap identification: verbal	*x*	*x*	*x*	*x*
teleological	–	*y*	*x*	*x*
Free search	–	–	–	*y*
Sources: compatibility	*y*	–	*y*	–
Reasoning: straightforwardness, absence of fictions	–	–	–	–
TOTAL (out of a maximum of 8)	1½	2½	3½	4

In the phase of legitimate interpretation of the legislated law as a norm-purpose (policy) complex, the Puerto Rican court seems to fall squarely within Stone's conclusion reached fifteen years earlier and based on English practice: "The common lawyer, despite the growing importance of legislation, has not acquired the techniques of handling legislative materials in a similarly creative manner to that in which he handles case-law" (387)50. There are additional striking analogies between *Rosado* and cases or doctrine from widely separated jurisdictions. With regard to the expectation that the legislator will take a hint and reform the statute the court felt it had to apply mechanically and unjustly, already Gény spoke of "legislative slumber"(157) *186*. A German treatise, incidentally published in Spanish the same year *Rosado* was decided, criticized this syndrome: "With a stubborn insistence on positivist attitudes [judges] attribute, with occasional gestures of lament, to the legislator the 'guilt' for reaching an unjust decision; they even sometimes impress on him the need to proceed with reform of the legislation" (34)170. What in *Rosado* was a tacit assumption—that the petitioner would have shortly another remedy—was spelled out by Justice Harlan dissenting in *Jones* v. *A.H. Mayer Co.* (1968): "The relief [which Jones seeks] will become available within seven months under a presumptively constitutional Act of Congress." Therefore, Harlan concluded, the Supreme Court should refrain from deciding the case and should "dismiss the certiorari as improvidently granted" (at 476–480).

Rather than being distinguishable on the basis of civil- or common law tradition and method, such cases share positivistic mode and inadequate jurisprudence. See my discussion of a uniform field theory and practice of interpretation, which encompasses and harmonizes the uses of legislated and decisional law (pages 67, 98–100).

LXX

The parallels are striking. In the following excerpt from Ulam (401) only a few words would have to be changed to make it look like a quotation from a book on jurisprudence: "Instead of work on special theorems which now number in the millions, instead of thinking in terms of rules operating with symbols given once and for all, it may be that mathematics will consist more and more of problems, or desiderata, or programs for work of a general nature . . . outlines of larger theories, of vaster enterprises, and the actual working out of proofs of theorems will be left to students or even machines."

In reference to ecology and its social implications and applications, see (282) esp. 66–82; and Mayda, "Ecology of change: Toward planetary eco-management," in *Creating the future: Agendas for tomorrow* (Columbus, Ohio: Batelle Memorial Institute, 1974), 2–8. See this reference also with regard to the concept of technoculture in the subsequent text.

LXXI

Montesquieu's conception in the *Esprit des lois* (1748)—the immediate source of the modern doctrine of separation—was, in fact, inspired by an idealized rather than analyzed notion about the English constitutional system. He was concerned primarily with the relations between the executive and the legislative powers. And he spoke only of a "certain distribution of powers" (288).

The impact of the strict doctrine in Europe was amply demonstrated by the Swiss example in the second essay. See for Italy (32), for Germany (34). Recent and continuing dogmatic current in the United States is reflected, *e.g.*, by (*a*) academic arguments, such as that "legislators are better entrusted with law making than are courts and agencies" (324)40; (*b*) congressional rhetoric: "strict constructionist," "genuine conservative constitutionalist" (Senator Richard B. Russell), "legislation [not lawmaking!] by the Courts" (Senator Edward V. Long); and (*c*) subtle evasions by justices-designate in confirmation hearings, apparently not perceived by their congressional questioners. Senator Ervin: "I'm going to utter a prayer that . . . he'll act as . . . a judge and not a legislator"; Justice-designate Byron R. White: "It's clear that the Constitution vests the power to legislate [not 'to make law'] in Congress, not the Supreme Court" (New York *Times*, 12 April 1962); Senator Eastland: "Are you going to be . . . a 'creative judge' or are you going to follow the law and the precedents?" Justice-designate Potter Stewart: "Certainly, if I can find precedents [not law *and* precedents] that are applicable, I'm happy" (New York *Times*, 10 April 1960).

Several European writers have expressed or implied reservations about the strict separation doctrine. Most prominent among these voices, and one of the first, was Gény's contemporary Capitant (56)32: "The principle of separation of powers prohibits the judge from emitting a rule that has the force of [legislated] law. But . . . this participation in lawmaking is being accomplished without the courts exceeding their prerogatives and without affecting in any way the principles of our constitutional law." See also Boehmer (34) 15; Spiro (379) 345; and Castán (then president of the Supreme Court of Spain): "If the doctrine of separation is not a myth, we must consider it as of little real substance" (65) 5–6. Among recent American writers, Hurst (213) 366 listed the functional study of the separation doctrine as first among three major foci or badly needed legal research. Levi (255) 17 discussed the weakening of the separation doctrine in terms of an "almost disappearance of any doctrine of unlawful delegation." He returned to the subject as attorney general in 1975 in a long lecture (257) in terms of "allocation of power among the branches [with] an understanding that each branch, within its sphere, represents and serves the people's interest." Between the branches of government "the relationship was not to be an adversary one . . . Justice Stone and others have written of the importance of the Court's sense of self-restraint. . . . Institutional self-restraint does not mean . . . a government of hesitancy." He continued, paraphrasing Scott Buchanan, "Separate functions, organizations and powers [within the government] will operate with different modes of reasoning. Each mode is important to the processes of law formation and to the generation of popular consent to the law." Bickel (29), after some semantic stumbling (see Note LXVIII), raises the "recurring institutional problems . . . of *allocation* of competences . . . *division* of powers" (emphasis added).

The functional effectiveness of the various systems is achieved by very different institutional mixes and interfaces. I will mention only two major systems. In the United States, the major components are these: (*a*) judicial power is subject to congressional power of legislative or constitutional amendment; (*b*) both branches exercise their ultimate controls, but are overshadowed in day-by-day decision making by the executive and administrative agencies; and (*c*) the executive exercises considerable control over federal judiciary through the selection of nominees, but this is subject to congressional confirmation and the uncertainty whether the past record of a nominee (especially if he does not have substantial prior judicial record) is a reliable indication of his future performance as a judge, especially on the Supreme Court. In France, apart from (*a*) the conventional relationship between the legislature and the judiciary (*cf.* Capitant's remarks above), which is (*b*) influenced by the bureaucratic (*i.e.*, executive-controlled) nature of the judiciary, there is (*c*) an administrative-judicial hierarchy stronger and more independent than the "fourth" branch in the United States. It operates in complete independence of the judicial "branch," since it has its own highest appellate level, the Conseil d'Etat, which flexibly mixes the functions of administrative adjudication with special assignments on behalf of the executive. It has created its decisional law by an openly practiced and admitted mixture of flexible *stare decisis* and free search. Because of its particular jurisdictional competence, it was this administrative "council of state," not the supreme judicial court (Cour de

Cassation) that has performed the function of protecting individual rights against public power.

The proposition in the text, in the sense that the reinterpretation of the separation doctrine requires a shift from the adversary perception of the political process to the concept of equal-justice-through-law purpose of all the policy-setting components of the government, is based on historical evidence. The strict doctrine (including its judicial consequences) has been a reaction to the abuses of absolutist regimes—the monarchies of previous centuries, the authoritarian regimes of the 1930s and 1940s. The historical pattern, confirmed in its organic nature by modern studies of primitive tribal societies, was different. Historians have concluded that in the Middle Ages the sovereignty of the monarch rested more on judicial that on legislative power (196). In the scholastic disputations about the nature of the ruler, his function as *rex* (adjudicator among conflicting interests) was stressed over the function of *dux* (military-political leader) (326).

Despite the rationalizations of the renewed advocacy of the rigid separation doctrine, the deep psychological reasons may be akin to Frank's thesis (134) of the "quest for certainty" (*i.e.*, security). Seen in this perspective, the authority of the democratic legislatures was simply substituted for that of the autocratic sovereigns, incorporating a distorted conception of the function of *rex*. The sources of this distortion go politically and technically as far back as the pattern underlying Justinian's codification and philosophically more immediately to the eighteenth-century natural law.

The "organic linking of law and justice/social values" postulated in the text is but another facet of the often posited need for "comprehensiveness" (Hall), "synoptic position" (Cairns), the restoring of communication between society, law, and jurisprudence—achieved for their times by the Aristotelians, vulgarized and eventually disrupted by the monists of the natural-law and the positivist-analytical variety. Despite the deceivingly simple (and correct) juxtaposition over the portal of the U.S. Supreme Court—Equal Justice Under Law—the effort at a successful doctrinal integration has failed such an accomplished legal technician *cum* jurisprude as Llewellyn, the very acute philosopher about law Ortega y Gasset (281), and numerous lesser writers between these two professional, philosophical, and cultural poles.

Yet, it does not seem difficult to conceive an organic operational model to substitute for the dichotomous chicken-versus-egg philosophy. It would have to follow approximately this conceptual sequence:

(i) *concrete justice* (individual, social, balanced) is the

(ii) *purpose of positive law* (general-legislative, particular-decisional), if it is informed by a

(iii) *policy-value system*, which operates within a system of institutions and procedures that make possible

(iv) *free formulation of social consensus*, and thus the definition of the

(v) *ideals of justice* at a given time and space, and which provides institutional means and political will for their

(vi) *implementation and enforcement.*

This synopsis expresses above all the fact that the ideals of justice, such as equal protection without discrimination on any ground, equal access to education and resources, basic human rights, etc., are not metaphysical events. Their concrete content changes (note the present social-legal revolution in the United States); their effectiveness depends on the availability of institutions (*e.g.*, access by the disadvantaged to legal aid and the courts, national and international); and they are an inherent moral element of the body politic anywhere unless their free play and metamorphoses are interfered with by power. Also, some "self-evident" slogans tend to lose their meaning in this context, for example the formula "Government of law, not of men."

LXXII

The most famous formula that states the need for this kind of interaction between legislator and judge is by Portalis, the chief draftsman of the Code Napoléon: "Positive law can never replace natural reason in the affairs of life. The needs of society are so varied, social intercourse so active, men's interests so multifarious and their relations so extensive, that the legislator cannot possibly provide for everything." The identification of judiciary with natural reason may not be always justified, but the operational implications of Portalis' conception are unmistakable. Article 4 of the eventual French Civil Code merely ordered the judge to decide (procedural equity) without specifying the obligatory substantive sources (*e.g.*, Portalis' "natural reason"), but other codes, culminating with the Swiss Article 1, completed the formula.

The conception outlined in the text above is echoed by such contemporary commentators as Loussouarn (271)257: "There is neither duality nor competition between legislation and case law"; Breitel (44)21–22; Levi (254)32 and more recently (253)8,11: "There is a doubt about the courts' competence or authority to become problem-solver for society. . . . At the same time, there is great reluctance to deny access to the courts, or to deny protection of rights when . . . other institutions have defaulted. . . . Judges . . . are in a special sense law makers. . . . The courts can be compelled or at least are willing to decide complex issues as a matter of law or right, in circumstances in which the legislature or executive has avoided or deferred decision."

The fourth paragraph in the text not only supports the thesis of the functional equality of the legislator and the judge, but suggests practical superiority of the judicial capacity of concrete gap filling. It deserves an elaboration.

In principle, there can be no judicial decision, exercise of discretion, or gap filling unless there is a case. The plaintiff must start with establishing a cause of action. The existence of a cause of action means that the existing law contains a policy in the sense that a defined interest in conflict should be protected if the alleged facts are proved. Even in a routine case, the determination whether the claimed interest is covered by the policy of the law brings into the play exercise of judicial discretion in the selection of the decisional facts and their matching with the apparent policy (*cf.* the *Rosado* example in Note LXIX). *A fortiori*, this happens when the cause of action is urged against positive law as allegedly inapplicable (teleological gap) or without any reference to genuinely applicable positive law (full gap). These were the instances that put in motion the pretorian *formula in factum concepta* or, in England, a new writ or equity injunction.

To prevent the situation in which occasional judicial quasi legislation turns into massive ad hoc lawmaking, Justice Tate (Supreme Court of Louisiana) suggested, with specific reference to water and mineral law in Louisiana, the institution of a *référé*, a regular report by the courts to the legislature, drawing attention to the need for comprehensive gap filling through legislation (seminar, "Interpretation of authoritative legal texts in civil law and mixed jurisdictions," Baton Rouge, 1973). This *référé* differs from the classical variety (*e.g.*, the first draft of the French Civil Code), which stood in lieu of judicial gap filling; it attempts to institutionalize the present ad hoc mechanism of indirect—and not effective overall—stimulus of the legislature through decisions only.

See also the sharp insight into the incremental "rejuvenation of law [through decisions] without the often awkward intervention of legislator" (40)86, arrived at despite Boulanger's wandering around in the preceding context.

LXXIII

Levi (256)405 seems to be saying this, in a roundabout language ("*Brown* . . . should have been decided with the same result but with less of an immediate jump and on the partial basis of an old and accepted theory"—instead of contrasting the technical-constitutional and the social-psychological arguments). But this probably results from the fact that in the quoted context Levi is answering Wechsler's argument (412) that *Brown* was not a sufficiently broad, "principled" decision to cover all possible racial discrimination. See more on this tendency to program the future, from Justinian to the French *arrêts de règlement* to Justice Frankfurter, in Note LXXXVIII.

LXXIV

A doctrinal perspective on the problem of policy is provided by this avant-garde statement published in 1951: There have been "long debates whether policy is proper ground for striking down a rule of law or a line of precedents. But in reality the issue between law and policy is . . . rhetorical. Every rule, every interpretation . . . presupposes one view or another as to public policy" (73)269.

Notes

LXXV

This judicial rule making is, of course, subject to the proposition that the proper task of the judge is in any circumstances to decide the specific case in terms of concrete justice. The organic nature of this axiom imposes itself on any analysis. It can be illustrated also by reference to the contrast between practice and doctrine in Switzerland, where the relations between routine deciding, quasi legislation, and deciding "in equity" are established explicitly in the civil code. As already discussed, Article 1 provides for judicial gap filling through quasi legislation; Article 4 gives the judge the discretion to decide under circumstances "according to law *and equity*."

Germann (168)186 concluded persuasively that the difference between the two forms of gap filling has been largely eliminated in practice and remains rather only a difference between "the point of departure and the gravity center." This conclusion does not make explicit the common purpose of both modes—the just decision of the concrete case. But contrast it with this set of doctrinal dicta taken from the same context in which the quotation from Germann appears (295) Article 4 N.18–21:

> Both activities [under Articles 1 and 4] are forms of the so-called free search or gap filling. They are, however, distinct in that the rule [under Article 1(2)] must be formulated in abstract [*schematiziert*], formally stated as a norm, whereas the equity decision is casuistically arrived at and needs to be justified only as the best solution fitting the special circumstances. Furthermore, there is a material difference in that a decision of a single case needs not to take into consideration the interests of general legal certainty; that must happen when a rule is made under Article 1(2)—not to mention the fact that this rule making in itself promotes certainty of law. For a rule is supposed to assure the predictability of future decisions; gap-filling decisional law may under circumstances have to remain unchanged in consideration of legal certainty [citing cases and doctrine]. . . . The tendency in the doctrine has been to extend the legislative mode to situations envisaged in Article 4. . . . The general formulation under Article 1(2) can vary in its scope. Hence the result can be a very special, narrow rule. Since the decision under Article 1(2) is supposed to be just [this is not explicit in the legislative text!] and there is no absolute *stare decisis*, the general and abstract rule can be corrected in the future if it should prove too broad. Consequently, there is a tendency in the practice—though hidden—to look for the solution that fits best the concrete case, even in the sphere of the [quasi-]legislative method. . . . On the other hand, a decision under Article 4 has an inherent tendency toward generality. . . . Each equity decision contains general criteria. [*Cf.* Radbruch (341)127: "Justice sees the individual case in the perspective of the general norm; equity looks for its own norm in the individual case. But this norm must be eventually also capable of being raised to a general statute (*sic*: *Gesetz*). Equity, just as justice, has in the last analysis a generalizing character."] This tendency toward the general, which equalizes the casuistic and the [quasi-]legislative judicial decisions, is strengthened by the importance that customary law ascribes to doctrine and to decisional law.

I purposely abstained from editorial interpolations in the preceding quotation—except for the absolute minimum—and leave it to the reader to conclude where this analysis stands on the principle of concrete justice, on the distinction between cases of individual hardship and of general, class situations, on teleological gaps, and on possible difference in precedent value between decisions under Article 1 and Article 4.

Compare with the statement of conflict between judicial rule making and certainty in Switzerland this summary of the American practice by Jerome Frank, written about a decade earlier: "In sum, the doctrine of stare decisis seems to mean that certainty outweighs justice; let certainty be achieved though injustice be done and the heavens fall. Since to follow precedents will presumably produce certainty, some courts say they feel obligated to consecrate their former blunders. . . . It is 'of more importance that a rule should be fixed and stable than that it should be strictly just . . .' said an Ohio court" (133)276. But this is certainly not the general contemporary picture. For example, in *The Boys Markets* case (1970), Justice Stewart corrected his "blunder" and helped to overrule five to four the *Sinclair Refining* case (1962), in which he had been on the opposite side. He cited as moral authority the late Felix Frankfurter's dictum that "wisdom often never comes, and so one ought not to reject it merely because it comes late." See Gény's rational position (158)149 at n27.

LXXVI

The terms "creative judge" or "judicial creativity" (see Note LXXI and Boulanger [39]419) are legitimate in contrast to "mechanical jurisprudence." But in the full context of judicial function they are tautological or even out of focus. Compare such expressions as "improperly creative" (141) 842, meaning a formulation of a decisional rule based on values that appear incorrectly applied or otherwise undesirable.

LXXVII

In the type of appellate case that does, or alone should, reach the highest courts, the rate of probing reference to policy is likely to be high, if not total. To explain this phenomenon and to contrast it with routine deciding before lower courts does not require that we equate legislative policy *making* and judicial *deciding on* policy. In cases of original jurisdiction, the fact element should be, on the contrary, more prominent in the mix of decisional factors. But precisely such cases—*e.g.*, *U.S.* v. *Louisiana et al.* (1960)—illustrate the difference between the legislative duty and power to make uniform policy (which the Congress did not do in the Submerged Lands Act of 1953, at issue here) and the judicial task to decide concrete cases on relevant facts and specific policy considerations; this the Court faithfully did here, but it did not generate a uniform policy standard applicable to all states with submerged lands.

The difference between policy making and deciding on policy also lies in the constitutional finality of the event. Even under the system of judicial review in the United States, the overruling of congressional legislation on constitutional grounds is not the ultimate step. It can be corrected by an amendment of the Constitution. An early example of this process is the Sixteenth Amendment (1913), which annulled the decision in *Pollock* v. *Farmers' Loan & Trust Co.* (1895). So much less are ordinary decisions of the U.S. Supreme Court final. In fact, they have been increasingly subject to correction through congressional legislation (79,429).

The scope of judicial review, which looms so large in the dialog about judicial policy and lawmaking, must not be overestimated: over the lifetime of the U.S. Supreme Court, the average is about one case every two years. On the whole, it has been a very careful process. If the great majority of these decisions stuck, it was not for lack of overriding legislative power. Perhaps this was one of the bases for Henry Hart's conclusion that courts are capable of developing law on a "coherent and intelligible fabric of principle" (324)43.

LXXVIII

A perhaps unwitting example of this point is provided by the set of statements selected by the correspondent of a national daily (413) from a twenty-three-page address to the 1976 National Judicial Conference (celebrating the seventieth anniversary of Roscoe Pound's famous speech on the "causes of popular dissatisfaction with the administration of justice") by Edward Levi (253), speaking as the United States attorney general: "Judicial assumption of the social policy making role could . . . have a freezing effect on Congress and the Executive branch. Courts can become not agents of progress, but an obstruction to progress. . . . judicial remedy for social problems is a powerful weapon . . . to be used with care. . . . court policy making may raise expectations and generate dissatisfaction when the expectations are not fulfilled." The quotations come from pages 9 and 19, preceded and followed by many *other* quotables. *Cf.* (310).

If these quotations are set in the context of contemporary dispute, even violence, over busing of children to distant schools to correct unconstitutional segregation—particularly the situation in Boston in the course of the 1975–1976 school year—they add an additional dimension to practice of "separation of powers," but also perpetuate the public misconception of the policy activity of the courts. That was obviously not Levi's intent.

Specifically, the orders of the federal judge in Boston must be contrasted with the apparent "social policy making"—in reality the carrying out of existing, mostly legislative policies, lastly the Esch amendment to the 1964 Civil Rights Act—in the 1971 decision of the Supreme Court in *Swann* v. *Board of Education.* On the facts as reported by a sympathetic correspondent (259), the Boston implementation of *Swann* was not a rational, tailored use of the equity power given the district judges, but a clear excess of judicial power, including intervention in daily administrative routine of the schools involved. Thus neither *Swann* nor its denaturation by the local federal judge had anything to do with judicial social policy making.

The dimension this adds to the realistic perception of the separation of powers in practice is the limitation on the mechanism available to the executive to correct such a judicial excess of power. Either it has the long route of an amendment of standing congressional legislation or it is limited to an application to the judicial branch—in the role of *amicus curiae* if there is an opportunity—to please correct itself.

There is an ample basis in the literature of jurisprudence for the kind of image illustrated in the first paragraph of this note. Note this summary comment by Judge Hutcheson, who at the same time makes his own contribution to the conceptual looseness: "[The] only danger we have to fear from the [Supreme] Court today is the thing that finally killed *Swift v. Tyson* . . . The too complete acceptance of Gray's notion that the judges do not find the law . . . that they make it like the legislators do. . . . When you have this notion in mind very strongly [that] decisions are in reality legislation, a great many judges want to be legislating and not just judging. . . . Of course every decision is legislation in its grounds if it marks out a new way" (382)249.

The wide uncritical acceptance of the undifferentiated concept of judicial policy making shows also in this statement by a political scientist: "One of the basic assumptions which [may] be considered part of the orthodoxy of contemporary public law is . . . that the primary role of the [U.S. Supreme] Court is to make public policy. Our analyses . . . are not directed . . . to the investigation of this hypothesis . . . since we take it for granted" (367)10–11.

The myth of policy *making* is such a part and parcel of judicial psychology that it shows, no doubt unconsciously, even in subtleties of language. See the late Chief Justice Warren's statement: "In some 81 instances since this Court was established it was *determined* that Congressional action exceeded the bounds of the Constitution" (Trop v. Dulles [1958] at 104). I read Warren's word *determine*—distinguished from *declare* or even *decide*—in the sense of settling with finality (without any applicable distinction between the de facto and de jure aspects). Compare also Justice Stewart's shift from "affect" to "make" in the following exchange, in which he could represent the voice of the Court and the questioner, Senator Eastland, the voice of the Congress: "Q. Is [the Supreme Court] a policy making body? A. Insofar as the decision of the cases—and they are difficult cases—necessarily affects policy [correct meaning: requires reference to policy data], it does make policy. [Then followed the exchange already quoted in Note LXXI.] Q. Are you going to be what is termed a 'creative judge' or are you going to follow the law and the precedents? A. Certainly, if I can find precedents that are applicable, I'm happy."

Note how much (if not all) of the conflict language would evaporate if the exchange were predicated on less blunt jurisprudence. The senator would be reduced to asking matter of factly (and perhaps superfluously): Are you always going to decide on all relevant facts, law, and value judgments, so that each concrete case would be solved within acceptable bounds of individual and social justice, and thus the legal order would be best served? A. I will always try. Q. Do you think the Congress could do this job better? A. No, sir.

LXXIX

At least some (probably most) criticism of judicial activism comes from a combination of two *rigid* doctrines, separation of powers and *stare decisis*. Compare Senator Eastland's conception quoted in Note LXXVIII and the position that "the fundamental principle [is] that the judges have no right to fill gaps which they suppose to exist, but must leave it to Parliament to do so," voiced in substantially identical terms by so widely distributed judges as Denning, *London Transport Executive* v. *Betts* (1959) at 247 (from where the verbatim quotation comes); Harlan (for a minority of four), *U.S.* v. *Republic Steel Corp.* (1960) at 493, a public law case; Serrano, concurring in *Rosado* v. *Rivera* (1959), a private law case. A more recent refinement of the English doctrine is by Lord Reid in *Pettit* v. *Pettit* (1969), focusing on an assumed difference in policy power between "lawyers' law and cases" and "matters which directly affect the lives and interests of large sections of the community . . . issues of public controversy . . . on which laymen are as well able to decide as lawyers. [Here] it is not for the courts to proceed on their view of public policy. [This] would be to encroach on the province of the parliament" (323)221–22.

LXXX

The *stare decisis* doctrine comes in all sizes and shapes. The most obvious classification of the various systems would seem to be in two groups: those that practice *stare decisis* openly and those that do it de facto (*tertium non datur*, because no orderly legal system can operate in complete disregard for past decisions, if for no other reason than some minimum reasonable consistency and economy of work). The real differences are along the dogmatic-pragmatic axis.

England was for well over a century prior to 1966 the major jurisdiction with a completely rigid doctrine of *stare decisis*. Although at the end of the eighteenth century "the application of precedent was powerful and constant . . . no judge would have been found to admit that he was 'absolutely bound' by any decision of any tribunal" (3)206. But the "*Beamish* spirit" (Note LXXXVII) was confirmed in the *London Street Tramways* case (1898). Decisions of the House of Lords acting as the supreme court were binding in perpetuity. Practice found its way around this doctrinaire wall. As in Justinian's rescript cited in Note LXXXVIII, the point of control is the determination whether the present case is "like" the one that figured in the "precedent." Thus the decisions of the House never died, but they kept on fading away by means of an art that was labeled "the distinguishing of undistinguished precedents (378)41. The rigid, authoritative doctrine was reversed typically not in the flexible give and take of a decision, but *ex cathedra*, by a declaration by the lord chancellor in his name as well as in that of the lords of appeal in ordinary (26 July 1966), which read in part: "The Lords recognize that a too rigid adhesion to the rule of precedent can cause injustice in a specific case and also impedes the normal evolution of law. They propose therefore to modify their present practice and, while considering the prior decisions of the Chamber binding, will depart from a former decision if they consider it their duty to do so." The new doctrine was first applied in *Conway* v. *Rimmer* (1968). The functioning of *stare decisis* must be seen, in England as well as in any other jurisdiction, in terms of availability of prior decisions. The publication rates of decisions at the various jurisdictional levels have been around 75 percent for the House of Lords, 25 percent for the Court of Appeals, and only 10 percent for the High Court, the higher of the two trial levels (*cf.* the observation about selective publishing of the federal court decisions in Switzerland, Note XXXVIII).

The American doctrine and practice, though prospective and future oriented, has been reasonably functional and functioning. It was not spared dogmatic criticism, *e.g.*, by Oliphant in 1928 (314), for an alleged shift from *stare decisis* to *stare dictis*. This implies an acute perception of the fact that everything in a prior decision is a dictum until the future judge constructs the "true" *ratio decidendi*. But for this insight the author cannot be credited. Twenty years later, an academic (377) 120–122 could still use language such as "the perfidity [of the Supreme Court] to the prior rulings . . . notable reversals," but could add that "most of [these reversals] seem at least justifiable, if not desirable."

One of the most recent restatements of the American variety of *stare decisis* is by the U.S. Supreme Court in *Moragne* v. *States Marine Lines* (1970), per Justice Harlan:

> Very weighty considerations underlie the principle that courts should not lightly overrule past decisions. . . . the mainstay of *stare decisis* is singularly absent in this case. The confidence of people in their ability to predict the legal consequences of their actions and to encourage the settlement of disputes without resort to the courts . . . is threatened least by the announcement of a new remedial rule to effectuate well-established primary rules of behavior. . . . Nor do either of the other relevant strands of *stare decisis* counsel persuasively against overruling [the alleged precedent]. Certainly the courts could not provide expeditious resolution of disputes if every rule were fair game for *de novo* reconsideration in every case. . . . We do not regard the [prior] rule . . . as a closely arguable proposition–it rested on a most dubious foundation when announced [and] has suffered universal criticism and wide repudiation. . . . Finally, a judicious reconsideration of precedent cannot be as threatening to public faith in the judiciary as continued adherence to a rule . . . which produces different results for breaches of duty in situations that cannot be differentiated in policy.

The interest of *Moragne* lies in the fact that it is a common law case; as pointed out at 1790n17, "Congress has largely left to this Court the responsibility for fashioning the . . . rules of admiralty law."

The almost superfluous remark above that *stare decisis* is an integral part of the judicial process anywhere is illustrated for continental Europe by the statutory existence, since 1837, of *jurisprudence constante* built on de jure binding decisions of the full quorum of the Court of Cassation. In Germany, *Gerichtsgebrauch*—decisional law cast as custom—can override legislated law by means of, for example, a consistent judicial interpretation palpably different from the intended thrust of the legislation. In Spain, two identical rulings of the Tribunal Supremo in different cases, which present the same issue of law on similar facts, create *doctrina legal*, an obligatory precedent.

Common to all these practices is their authoritative rigidity. This has been largely supported by the doctrine, though the writers have frequently implied that they understood better. However, the underlying dogmatic matrix invariably shows.

On Switzerland, see the references in Note LVII. The tension between the official ideology and the empirical analysis shows typically in Germann (166). It reads, "absolutely bound by precedent" and "absolute" precedent on pages 237 and 254; by page 262 the distinction is made between "formally" and "not formally" binding precedent. The eventual conclusion, "swathed in obscuring dicta," is that in the last analysis the choice and the responsibility are those of the individual judge reaching the particular decision—a thought that is in its full context almost identical with Cardozo's "Judges have . . . the power, though not the right, to ignore the mandate of the legislature" (61)129.

The kindest thing that can be said about the doctrine of *stare decisis* in France is that it suffers from lack of theoretical homework. Or, in the words of Boulanger (37)22, "We are not very sure that the problem of sources of law has been examined, with respect to decisional law, with a sufficient concern for reality." The result is loose, confused, contradictory language and analysis, *e.g.*, (57)*I* 111–12, (278)40,49; wrong comparisons (358)84; semantic distinctions are either arbitrary (36)91–92 or not useful analytically (*e.g.*, Boulanger (40)82f, *arrêt d'espèce, arrêt de principe*—decision "on the case," on principle; or Carbonnier (57)*I* 122, *jurisprudences assises, j. controversées*—set and controverted decisional law, instead of raising the question why the decisional law is set or not and then analyzing the ingredients of the strong versus weak precedent in the terms suggested above in the text). Or, finally, the doctrine swings from the extreme of ignoring decisions as a source to the other dogmatic extreme of proclaiming—no one less than Ripert—that it would be better if the judge "could render an *arrêt de réglement* and impose himself the rule where the statute has a gap" (42)79. Indeed, the judge does it in concrete cases under Article 4, French Civil Code, no matter what the doctrine says.

A survey of various European conceptions related to the binding nature of prior decision is in (379)480n4.

LXXXI

I suggested the concept "decisional factors" in my first essay on Gény written in 1961–1962 (283)lix,n197, in the context of comparisons of and distinctions between legislative lawmaking and judicial quasi legislation:

> The shared responsibility presupposes that the judge have a full access to the same sources as a base for his [decision]. The judge ought to—and does, if he is a good judge—consider in each case not only the legally relevant established *facts*, but also the *value content* (and context) of the controversy. His decision is based on the projection of these two groups of *decisional factors* against the value system he finds to be legally binding and (or) considers socially objective and desirable. (The classical example of this procedure is the reversal by the U.S. Supreme Court of the *Plessy* doctrine in the *School Segregation Cases* [1954]). Such a decisional framework is also spoken of in terms of policy. The terminology carries the global implication of law making and is therefore not discriminating enough. It tends to distort the picture of routine deciding, which . . . should be based [also] on the full decisional factors rather than the narrower facts. Such a decisional approach is usually spoken of in terms of justice (of the case), equity (in the substantive sense), [concrete justice]. These terms have a wrong exceptional sound. . . . they draw a distinction where there is none.

The functional distinctions implied above (and more explicitly in n250, 255) deserve further refinement. In the first place, both policy and decisional factors have normally also reference to some positive norm (that is, unless the situation to be legislated about or the case to be decided is genuinely first-impression). In the normal case, the legislative policy reference to the norm is for the purpose of some form or degree of change ("How different should the new norm be, and why?"); the decisional reference is primarily for the purpose of application ("How should the case be decided?").

Second, the most obvious measure of the component "facts" for legislative application is relevance; for judicial application it is selection of the "legal" (decisional) facts from the "evidentiary" facts (*i.e.*, facts pleaded *and* proved under the limitations of the available evidence and of the rules of admissibility; the terminology "legal" and "evidentiary" comes from *Dobson*; *cf.* Note LX. But the judicial selection is also a decision about relevance; and the existence of the evidentiary facts is limited by the diligence of the pleaders. Analogously, the legislature does not always have before it all the relevant facts. The limiting factor here is also diligence—staff research, expert and citizen participation in hearings, etc.

Third, there is the obvious difference in the value reference: legislative policy aims (or ought to aim) at general justice, balance of social and individual interests; the value test of the decisional factors is concrete justice between specific parties. Beyond this obvious distinction, the component "values" has a crucial importance in relation to gaps. A verbal gap is the absence of an applicable norm, which is determinable without previous reference to "values." Teleological gap is the absence of an applicable norm determined on the basis of reference to values. Although the term "gap" is used in doctrine normally with reference to judicial decision making only, the act of "formulation" of the norm to fill the gap is similar in both the legislative and the quasi-legislative normative act. Both refer to policy data (*données*, facts and values), although the scope of the goal to be served is different—general rule as against specific ruling.

Both the determination of the relevance of legislative facts and the selection of judicial decisional facts are discretional acts that are, under conditions, subject to judicial review. The legislative discretion is appealable if the constitutionality of the statute is in question. The discretion of the trier of facts is appealable if possible abuse of discretion is at issue. The common denominator is the alleged arbitrariness of the legislator or the lower judge.

The previous analysis, especially the conception of *policy data and decisional factors as interrelated parts of a single system*, deserves additional attention to the central problem of gap. It ought to be analyzed also in these terms: finding a teleological gap is the determination that the legislative norm is, with reference to the concrete case, only a verbal shell. It covers the facts as a category (otherwise there would be a "genuine" verbal gap), but lacks the value content required in function of *the most important vector in the system, the duty of concrete justice.* The filling of the gap, though styled "free search for a rule," is the judicial reading into the verbal norm of the missing or different contemporary value dimension.

The integrated conception has also significant bearing on the analysis of the process of analogy. Beyond Gény's correct classification of analogy as a form of free search, there are important parallels between decision on analogy and legislative lawmaking, which rests on already existing policies—political (including constitutional law doctrines), economic, social. Judicial analogy is also based on an already existing policy, one that underlies a rule governing a comparable fact-value situation or that fashions a solution that can be legitimately related to the case to be decided.

Although Gény's *donné* comes closest to the conception of the decisional factors, various other authors have thought in this direction. Thus we have Heck's "interest situation" (197)110, going back to his and Rümelin's work two decades earlier, at about the same time Gény was writing *Science*; various direct and indirect derivations, *e.g.*, Boehmer, Becker, Lehmann; and Traynor's "all the data pertinent to solution" (324)52. Davis' effort to distinguish legislative and adjudicative facts (99)*II 15.03* would seem to move in the right direction. But in its unreformed conceptual framework it tends to say, at least to me, wrongly that a decision based on a positive norm ought to be the result of applying the positive rule only to facts in the narrow sense (adjudicative facts) rather than to the full-facts-in-their-value context (decisional factors).

The frame of reference of the decisional factors is obviously broader even in comparison with Gény's *donné* and the related "social purpose" of van der Eycken (129): both refer only to "free search," quasi legislation, not to the whole process of the uses of law for the purpose of decision (*cf.* my "unified field theory," pp. 67, 98–100).

The preceding model appears to be applicable to forms of legal process outside the usual private/public law paradigm. It also takes some edge off the sharp distinctions between particular national models. Note the following analysis of the working of United States administrative law. According to the prevailing doctrine and practice, the judiciary does not interfere with administrative fact finding. However, the determination of what is fact and what is law is within the judicial appellate jurisdiction (*cf.* Note LX). No matter what the justifying formula may be, the flexible "middle term"—with the help (mostly unacknowledged) of which the appellate court determines that the administrative "judge" decided a question of law and thus is subject to judicial review—is a value judgment. This reference to values is in function of the outcome; where the appellate court considers the outcome right, it does not have to do more than uphold the administrative jurisdiction on its finding of facts and application of law, without determining where facts end and law begins. Thus it must be concluded that administrative law in the United States is under genuine judicial control, since the courts have the power to reserve for themselves the determination of the most important segment of the decisional factors.

In comparison with, for example, the structurally substantially different French *droit administratif*—where the upper echelons in the administrative hierarchy itself are true judges by status, professional psychology, and technique (including open reliance on prior decisional law) the deep structure of the two processes is similar.

This example adds another item of evidence about the fallacious nature of the still current phrase "facts and law." If the word *law* must be interpreted as extensively as above to make it mean "all the decisional factors other than facts," the phrase does not have much analytical value. Nevertheless, as so many other jurisprudential *bons mots*, it tends to be considered an axiomatic premise. To give a comparative example: Germann's potentially promising argument (167)133 about the relation between gaps and the "teleological interpretation based on values inherent in the legal order" is analytically stillborn because value is here tied to the normative form rather than to the policy foundation (*donné*). Thus Germann's is the conventional facts-and-law model combined with an adorned *analogia juris*, rather than an opening toward fresh analysis in the direction of empirically informed decisional factors. See for a different illustration Reichel (350)281f.

In terms of the preceding analysis, the so-called "mechanical jurisprudence" can be defined more specifically as decisional process that does not pass through the full cycle represented by the above analysis. In particular, it short-circuits the "values" switch. A classical example of such a process in American law, elevated to a constitutional doctrine, is *Adkins* v. *Children's Hospital* (1923). In this case, the majority of the Supreme Court (against Taft, Sandford, and Holmes, with Brandeis not participating) held that the data presented in favor of and against a minimum wage law for women were "proper enough for the consideration of the lawmaking bodies" but without relevance for the determination of the validity of the legislation (at 559–60).

But, as the context of *Adkins* also reminds us, there is not only mechanical jurisprudence, but also mechanical legislation. Boulanger (41) argued that the legislator has the power to promulgate norms without justifying his motives; see Levi (254)31 on legislative facts. In the common law legal culture, mechanical legislation was inevitably fostered by the resistance of courts and doctrine to legislative history as a source of interpretation.

Almost fifty years after *Adkins*, an obituary for Justice Harlan (New York *Times*, 30 December 1971) quoted a law review evaluation in these terms: "Harlan always tried to 'de-emotionalize his decisions, looking to precedent and statutory language and reason rather than to social mores and the spirit of the times.' He thus would have 'greater credibility. [He was] a superb technician.'" It appears permissible to propose that the complete technician is the judge who has mastered the decisional model outlined above, through a combined effort of intellect and intuition; the other judges are just mechanics, no matter how superb.

LXXXII

Even conventional English writers almost two generations ago—*e.g.*, Allen (3) and the "naturalized" Goodhart (174)—made or did not contradict such observations as that the "true ratio decidendi" is determined and the "decisional factors" of the prior and the present cases are compared and defined *ex nunc*. But the necessary conclusions from these observations were not drawn either because of the faulty conceptual matrix or because they would have been too far left of the dogma. Even Stone (385) and, in the United States, Auerbach (15)65 still spoke of the "prior" precedent and the "later" courts. But see Stone's correct analysis (387)44–45.

Comparative literature is rife with implications of the merely potential nature of decisions as future precedents. Thus Radbruch (341)127, Germann (167)133, Meier-Hayoz (295)N.474, and Boulanger (40)79, admitting that even a court of appeals can generate a potential precedent ("decisional law not in technical sense [reserved for the Court of Cassation], but it can serve as the principle for future decisions"). See also such semantics as "We hope that the decision [Court of Cassation] of 21 December 1964, will not be used as precedent" (264); or "Should the decision [*jurisprudence*] in *Lafage* be applied, the principle [decisional doctrine, *système de l'arrêt*] of *Gacon* would" (325).

On the common law side, of course, are Levi (254) and Patton and Derham (323)45,221: "It is impossible to draw a rigorous line a priori between *ratio decidendi* and *obiter dicta*," as well as others already cited.

Montrose (302)16f analyzed correctly the handling of an a priori decision as potential precedent by Judge Roxbury in *In Re House Property & Investment Ltd.* (1954): (1) The judge rejected the "precedent" as automatically binding on grounds of a different conception of liability involved, (2) considered whether the [potential] precedent should be applicable by analogy, (3) considered the dicta of the prior case, and (4) concluded that no *ratio decidendi* for the present case could be constructed from the dicta of the "precedent." Compare Mermin's (298)210f catalog of techniques used in a concrete line of decisions by Wisconsin courts.

A symptomatic example of the influence of traditional concepts as obstacles to rational analysis is Cueto-Rua (90), who comprehensively and correctly summarizes the American practice and doctrine of *stare decisis*, but concludes that even the middle-of-the-road American doctrine (in which the true *ex nunc* nature of the process is clearly implied, though doctrinally buried) cannot be accepted because it violates the principles of (Kelsenian?) logic and symmetry. Contrast Cardozo's "tendency of precedent to extend itself along the lines of logical development . . . powerfully reinforced by . . . an intellectual passion for *elegantia juris*, for symmetry of form and substance" (61)34.

Speaking of acute crisis in the doctrine of *stare decisis* and describing it as unmanageable, Helen Silving proposed a "well defined methodology of precedent," the crux of which is relevant to the analysis of the uses of prior decisions outlined in the text. Silving suggests in essence: (1) "enactment of a statute that would determine . . . what in any authoritative judicial decision should be its 'binding' factor"; and (2) "the imposition of systematic rules on decision writing [which would] require the courts on all levels to make specific findings of fact and conclusions of law. Grounds for decision should be specified in a distinctive part of the decision in brief propositional form; whatever arguments a court or judge chooses to advance should be stated separately . . . concurrence or dissent [should] be formulated in the same style" (375)233,238,241. She warns however that, before the statute above could be more definitely formulated, the present stage of development of decisional law would have to be "discussed," which I read as empirically analyzed. Hence we are back to the theses above, first formulated in a preliminary but indicative form several years before Silving's article in (284) and (283)lx–lxvii.

LXXXIII

A classical statement of this method, "when off the bench," is ascribed to Chancellor Kent (1763–1847, thus a contemporary of Portalis'): "First I made myself master of the facts. [Second], I saw where the justice lay . . . the moral sense decided the court half the time. [Third], the search [for] the authorities [may have caused an occasional embarrassment] by a technical rule, but I almost always found principles suitable to my view of [the justice of] the case" (135)654.

Contrary to the implication of arbitrariness, the "hunch" is "the triumphant presursor of the just judgment" not only in Judge Hutcheson's conception (215). The just result, reached in spite of an apparently indicated positive norm, is the common denominator of Gény's conservative intuitionism and the most open advocates of hunch decision (*cf.* pp. 143–45, Note XIX). Contrast Llewellyn, storming at a conference of state chief justices: "[Are] you . . . in the nature of better-class politicians deciding cases the way you see fit while you just manipulate the authorities to keep it all looking decent. . . . Didn't you go hunting around for authorities after you already knew how you wanted to decide?"

The effort to sweep under the rug the intuitive decision making in law runs counter to the evidence in other disciplines. Here are examples: (*a*) the perception of what is the relevant line of research, so often illustrated by the history of epochal scientific discoveries; (*b*) the well-known intuitive nature of political decision making; (*c*) the "demonstrated correlation between superior management ability and an executive ESP [extrasensory perception]" (426); and (*d*) the phenomenon of "precognition" as a mark of "creative people" (426)—recalling Judge Cardozo's identification of a major coming social problem in the otherwise puny case *McPherson* v. *Buick*. See also Frankfurter's reference to "the finite limitations of disciplined minds and feelings," where "disciplined feelings" must mean value-oriented intuition.

If intuition in complex decision making cannot be eliminated—there is substantial evidence for it, which computer-aided policy and decision making has strengthened, not diminished—the effort in law must be toward making hunch decisions as educated as possible with the help of empirically correct jurisprudence.

LXXXIV

As much as law is a system of rules of conduct, not merely a remedial instrument, the word *use* must be understood broadly. A rule of a single decision may be so categorical that at least for some time its use will be extrajudicial —it will *prevent* litigation—rather than judicial under the rule of *stare decisis.*

LXXXV

I left open earlier (pp. 26, 67) the question relevant here: whether Gény's insistence on the essentially particular normative value of judicial decisions was not analytically correct, although on wrong, formal grounds (157)*85.* In his immediate context and that of his critics, Gény was wrong indeed. The reason was mainly his dogmatic reading of Article 5, French Civil Code, instead of a functional analysis that would have allowed him to examine the roots of his main objection against the uncertainty of decisional law (157)*86.* Note that, proceeding from another kind of formalistic basis, Gény's doctrinal and methodological antipode Kelsen reached comparable conclusions on the status of gap-filling particular decisions (231)153.

Contrary to the common law dogma—in Salmond's words, "We do not look to a decision as evidence of law, it is the law," cited by Hutcheson (382)249—and the civil law dogma about absence of *stare decisis*, Gény correctly notes the continuity in decisional law, stating (157)*223*,s.VII that judicial decisions have force beyond the particular case *rationis imperio*, not *ratione imperii*—because of the force of their principle, not because of their formal authority. He mars his insight in the following paragraph by an overnarrow interpretation of *res judicata* and is not ready to draw the necessary distinctions and comparison between individual decisions and decisional law. Gény's contemporaries made the correct projections that anticipate the analysis of the collective judicial lawmaking above in the text. Planiol (330) 20–21 insisted contemporaneously with Gény (1899) on the transformation of individual decisions into a "customary law of recent origin." See also

Capitant (56)32 and Lambert (241). There is a kinship between Planiol's conception of the *jurisprudence constante* as customary law and the German conception of it as *Gerichtsgebrauch*, the (constant) judicial usage. Lambert's correct analysis did not save him from subscribing, at least by implication, to a rigid *stare decisis* (241)68. Demogue (104) added another refinement in the direction of flexible *stare decisis* when he accepted the need for uniform decisional law, but pointed out that the growth of law is facilitated by the Court of Cassation carefully limiting each decision to the particular case and thus making possible a different decision in later cases where the facts are not sufficiently similar. Compare also Boulanger (37)22.

Only a generation and a half later was "the perhaps unconscious application" (393)134 and "the practical importance of precedent" (40)78 recognized officially: the 1947 law on the reorganization of the Court of Cassation ordered the organization of a card catalog containing the summaries of all the cassation decisions, the publication of a monthly bulletin listing all civil decisions, and a "law clerk" service based on this apparatus. See Note LXV.

Between the two basic sources of modern lawmaking—the "instant" legislative and the "extended" judicial—it is likely that, in terms of the ratio between the norm and the concrete fact-value reference that shapes it, the de facto judicial lawmaking body, separated in time and space, rates substantially higher than the formally convened legislature. This does not invalidate the defensive metaphor of "trial-by-hearing" (208)52, which tried to make legislative lawmaking acceptable in the United States as late as the mid-1930s; but Levi's "Despite much gospel to the contrary, legislature is not a fact-finding body" (254)31 is a more realistic appraisal of the political (as against policy-making) environment of legislation.

LXXXVI

The paradox is curious. On the one hand, judges are cast on both sides of the Atlantic into a subordinate role. Their decisional freedom is formally fettered by the separation doctrine. On the other hand, and equally formally, they are given through the prospective doctrine of *stare decisis* the power to determine policy and make law by a single decision.

The first conception overrates the role of the legislator; the second overrates the role of the judge. Being genuinely paradoxical, the situation does not lack a certain coherence and symmetry. The apparent permissiveness in judicial lawmaking is contingent on the restrictions that the formal subordination imposes on the judges; and in turn it corrects, even overcorrects, them. Such a logical symmetry is not identical with the functional balance required by the social mission of the law.

LXXXVII

The famous *Beamish* non sequitur (1861) stated, "If the rule of law laid down by the House [acting as the court of last resort] were not considered as equally binding on the Lordships, the House of Lords would be giving itself the right to alter the law and thus legislating by its own separate authority."

The reference to Boulanger is to his thesis already quoted in Note LXVII. Typically, Boulanger was contradicted during his lifetime by the Paris Court of Appeals, also quoted in that note.

Compare also the American reference in (395)230–31, a canonization of positive common law a century after *Beamish* and even more extreme than the traditional continental European position toward positive legislated law.

Contrast Gény's sophisticated position two generations earlier: "To evolve is not to change" (158)*162*,374n317, with all the implications for the growth of decisional law—even if Gény did not analytically follow through on his correct instinct.

LXXXVIII

Compare Justice Schaeffer (Supreme Court of Illinois): "One the most pronounced characteristics of work of an [appellate] court is the consciousness . . . that you are writing for the future . . . you are thinking of generations of litigants yet unborn . . . it has to be [so] if a judge is doing his work properly because he has the function not only of deciding the case, but under our system of course it becomes a precedent . . . and you keep guarding your words against this time when you are long gone" (364). Justice Traynor (Supreme Court of California): "A judge should have at least the day after tomorrow in mind" (396)625. But Llewellyn came closer to the past-oriented (retrospective) father than future-oriented conception of *stare decisis* elsewhere (267),52,61,64f,156; and Schaeffer recognized (365)14 that the announcement of a rule for the future is not guaranteed to be followed. (Compare also the Swiss writers cited on p. 61.)

These dicta represent in various degrees the common law version of the *arrêt de réglement*. Compare the already cited critique of Frankfurter's effort to legislate through a decision (p. 91) and a more recent critique of the tendency in the U.S. Supreme Court to legislate into the future through advisory opinions: "The enunciation of an elaborate set of standards governing habeas corpus hearings is in no sense required, or even invited in order to decide the case . . . the many pages [in] the Court's opinion which set these standards further can not be . . . justified even in terms of the normal function of dictum. The reasons against this rule against advisory opinions which purport to decide questions not actually at issue are too well established to need repeating" (Stewart, J. in Townsend v. Sain [1963] at 327).

Another contemporary suggestion in favor of the future-oriented decision was made by Wechsler in his 1959 Harvard lecture on "neutral principles" in constitutional law (412). Levi (256)403f. stripped it with the help of these observations.

> The caliber of a court's opinion is not to be made dependent on its announcement of a principle which . . . will indicate to us how future cases are to be decided . . . to what an extent is it appropriate or necessary for a judge to plot out in the written opinion, as contrasted with the inner process

> of decision, the future course of the law as to those instances and future distinctions which seem feasible to him . . . the process of judicial reasoning is frequently, perhaps basically, retrospective. . . . This in itself involves some projection into the future . . . going beyond the case at hand, but it can [must?] also involve care not to foreclose the considerations of future distinctions . . . even the case which has no articulated theory to support it but seems right . . . has a place in our jurisprudence. . . . the function of articulated judicial reasoning is to help protect the Court's moral power by giving some assurance that private views are not masquerading behind public views. This might lead to the conclusion that the more controversial the issues, the more the Court should endeavor to spell out the future rules of the road. But I doubt if this conclusion follows.

The tendency toward programming the future is a perennial occupational hazard of lawmakers in all sectors. Justinian's rescript of 529 A.D. (Imp. Justinianus Augustus Demostheni, C.1.14.12) reads, "If the imperial majesty has examined a case judicially and has given judgment with the parties personally present, all judges of every sort who are under our sovereignty should know that this is the law not only for that case in which it was issued, but for all like cases." A similar doctrine of eternal precedent was revoked in England only in 1966 (*cf.* Note LXXX). The reaction of legislatures against this kind of judicial legislation was equally extreme: they claimed lawmaking exclusivity. Although it collapsed quickly in its farthest-going form of legislative *référés* (in France by 1837; *cf.* Note LXXII), the doctrine created throughout the nineteenth century the situation against which Gény, among others, raised his pen, though he never overcame the historical overreading of the prohibition of *arrêts de réglement*, Article 5, French Civil Code.

The perhaps best statement of the functional balance comes from Judge Hutcheson (382)273 (1941): "an unduly narrow view . . . of precedent [that] each case contributes only the decision of its own precise facts . . . strips the doctrine of a great part of its useful force. This lies not in controlling, but in directing . . . along the lines of a general principle. . . . courts are not constituted to issue, as the opinion of the court, general sweeping statements of the kind [of *Erie* v. *Tompkins*], as to past or future decisions . . . which have a permissible place as personal view in a dissenting opinion . . . a majority opinion must be devoted to deciding the case before the court." Contrast the insecure and vague language of Boulanger twenty years later: "Court cannot escape at times making decisions in the manner of legislature. But lack of means at their disposal forces them too often to proceed empirically or arbitrarily" (39)433. Empirical means here of course "ad hoc, on the basis of experience only, without the help of theory"—and therein lies the problem, the "lack of means," as I keep on repeating.

LXXXIX

A sample of illustrations: (*a*) Such language as "interpreting binding precedent" (424)149, which is representative of conventional analysis, becomes contradictory; for it is necessary to first examine ("interpret") the prior decisional rule to determine whether or not it will be considered binding. (*b*) The time-worn maxim "Hard cases *make* bad law" has been criticized without the analytical framework suggested here by Frank (133)273 and Traynor (395)231. This analysis can be projected further by pointing out that a just decision in a single hard case makes no law, merely justice; if the hard case represents a class, the law, as Frank suggested, *is* bad. The law will then be *remade* through the development of a decisional doctrine as the first decision is tested and upheld. (*c*) A statement such as "There is naturally less scope for the judge than for the legislator . . . in creative activity" (142)215–made, incidentally, with reference to Gény–is too global and represents functionally an inverted pyramid. (*d*) Conclusions such as "[Judges Breitel, Traynor, etc., stress that] it is a matter of . . . judicial tact . . . whether to fill a legislative gap" or "it is more natural for the courts to develop and modify law in some areas rather than in other" (141)837f. or that a decision may be made on "legislative facts [that] are ordinarily general and do not concern the immediate party" (99)353 do not correspond to the integral pattern that results when one combines the theses on the distribution of powers and on the decisional process with the retrospective doctrine of *stare decisis*.

XC

Obviously if a single decision is only potentially a precedent, the so-called distinguishing is in fact leaving the prior decision in the limbo of potentiality. But this unpretentious, matter-of-fact event is the same when it is labeled "overruling." In other words, when anything less than a decisional doctrine is involved, distinguishing and overruling are the same. When established decisional law is involved, overruling is analogous with a decision *contra legem*–against legislated law as interpreted and applied until then.

XCI

Cardozo actually applied the technique of merely prospective overruling in the *Great Northern Railway Co.* case (1932). It was criticized with reference to the Court's own rules, but upheld in subsequent decisions. In *Linkletter* (1965), the Court per Justice Clark reviewed the whole history and upheld the concept in the unlikely setting of the question whether "purely prospective" ruling, which was actually not prospective in the case–*Mapp* v. *Ohio*–on which Linkletter's petition relied, should apply retrospectively to cases finally decided in the period prior to *Mapp*. Nothing less was in play here than the Hale-Blackstone "declaratory" doctrine versus the doctrine of "interstitial" judicial lawmaking of Austin *et al.* Compare also *Fuller* v. *Alaska* (1968). These are, indeed, criminal cases that put the question of liberal application of decisional changes into a particularly urgent, though not necessarily always meritorious, light.

The problem of "prospective" ruling is entirely the creation of "prospective" *stare decisis.* The problem cannot be solved under this doctrine. The need for overruling arises because of a "bad precedent" (the next item in the text above), or at least one the general acceptance of which is dubious (144). Although it makes a difference whether the "bad precedent" is a single ruling or not, its future use or nonuse is determined, where the facts are substantially similar, by the balance of competing values: (*a*) the *general* utility of selecting another rule for decision than the one that had been applied to the given category of cases; (*b*) the *particular* hardship of not honoring behavior demonstrably guided by the prior decisional rule. The judicial duty to decide this conflict is in principle not different from a number of other choices that determine the individually more or less just result in a given case. The ultimate among these choices has been stated in terms of either applying the words of a statute, which lead to an unjust result, or "fashioning just grounds of decision" (190)708—in other words, practicing free search in a teleological gap situation. Under the postulated theses, the judge has not only the power but also the duty to decide the particular case so as to reach a concretely just result in function of all decisional factors present. These factors include the conflict we are discussing here. The judge has, on the contrary, neither the power nor the right to *bind* another judge deciding another concrete case in the future. All the judge can, and should, do is to indicate the specific circumstances that determined his choice among the available options (*i.e.*, to follow a prior decision, to select another prior rule, or to fashion a new rule). This explanation should be a sufficient notice to potential litigants and future courts. (*Cf.* Silving, Note LXXXII, though not conceived in these specific terms.)

XCII

This was suggested in principle by the conservative del Vecchio (405)16 in 1911, contemporaneous with, though proceeding from premises opposite to, Gray's *Nature and sources of law* (176)*200.*

Even when the judge has available the legislated words of reference, the statutory rule comes to mean increasingly—in proportion to the age of the legislated law, that is of the remoteness in time of the words from the original social-value context—*what the judge decides it means.* I am not saying *should mean* or *should be.* This is not a process of "remolding the world to his heart's desire" (Justice Frankfurter on a temptation that Judge Learned Hand allegedly withstood, as quoted in the New York *Times,* 11 April 1959), but an inexorable, matter-of-fact operational event.

With reference to the postulate of a unified field conception of the legislative and judicial functions of lawmaking and law development, see Pound's tentative and rather unfocused formula of some fifty years ago: "In . . . a conception of judicial decision as a part of a larger process of social engineering, in a sense legislation and judicial decision are put on the same basis" (337)955.

Notes

XCIII

The European profile of the doctrine of interpretation of legislated law, sketched out in the first two essays, indicates the degree of dogmatism involved. The American set of problems and traps is comparable, if one discounts the still-lingering doctrine of narrow construction of statutes in derogation of the common law, which does not have a counterpart on the Continent. See the 1950 Vanderbilt symposium (90,389); for England, where the doctrine has been more difficult to overcome, see (128) and (88)171f.

Radin criticized the American doctrine more than forty years ago (342) 882, saying that "the presence of so many confused . . . and meaningless 'theories' and 'methods' of interpretation creates a turbid atmosphere about courts, which is not conducive to clear thinking." Freund wrote about interpretation with common sense, stimulated by his comparative background, at the time of World War I (138,139). But recent textbooks still substitute litanies of musty Latin phrases (canons) for analysis. In fact, serious analysis would result in eliminating the subject interpretation from the field of legislation, on the grounds that this classification is a corollary of the extreme separation doctrine (Justinian; Prussian code of 1790), or at least would clearly indicate that the subject is enclosed in textbooks on legislation only because there is no other place for it in the conventional law curriculum.

General literature on interpretation lacks vision and interest (*cf.* the staleness of several contributions to the Vanderbilt symposium), is fettered by orthodox doctrines of separation and of prospective *stare decisis*, *e.g.*, (122) 2–3, or at its best remains largely on the level of classification (140)Ch.2, (141)831f. The American doctrine is generally rooted in the notion of judicial finding of the rule from among finished legislative norms—comparable with the European dogmatic approach. Thus it shuts itself off from comprehension of the real nature of interpretation and application of legislated law. It perforce misses the crucial insight about the counterpointlike nature of the relations between the legislature and the courts. The conception of interpretation as search for the "directions" in the statute applicable to the case to be decided (189)1411 is a prelude to analysis. See the virtually identical terminology "directive force," with reference to decisional law, in Cardozo (61)22, quoting Redlich, and in Hutcheson (382)273.

In sum, then, and contrary to the orthodox doctrine:

1. Interpretation is the process by which the judge determines the meaning of *positive law* (legislated *and* decisional) in terms of applicability to the *decisional factors* as he found them. It need not be belabored that in this process the judge will follow the same mental procedure as any intelligent person trying to understand the meaning of a text and to associate this meaning, where indicated, beyond its express semantic confines. From the standpoint of serious analysis these are preliminaries. Yet conventional doctrine has been spending itself on them.

2. If the applicability of positive legislated law is not determined on the basis of grammatical/logical interpretation of the text alone, it follows *a fortiori* that it cannot be determined without any interpretation. Vattel's maxim that what is in no need of interpretation must not be interpreted, still repeated in textbooks on legislation, is contradictory in its terms. But compare the reference to Learned Hand in the text above. The common law version of the maxim two hundred years later is in *Rojas-Gutierrez* v. *Hoy* (U.S. District Court, S.D. California, 1958): decision of one district court is binding on another unless "patently erroneous" and should be followed "without examination." The opinion does not explain how anybody can determine "without examination" whether a prior decision is "patently erroneous"—and in function of what, the prior case or the present case?

3. When the court applies legislated law in a robotlike fashion, literally or mechanically, it has either found the purpose of the statute to be in line with its own value system or it believes erroneously that the original purpose must (or can) remain intact.

4. The concept of certainty in function of interpretation needs to be revised. "Certainty" is a probability that the legislated law as presently interpreted will be applied in a future decision if the facts are substantially similar *and* if the court will base its ruling on the same decisional factors. That presupposes that the future judge will identify himself with the value context of the past interpretation, since the selection of the "legal facts" appears to be the function of value judgments focused on the desired outcome.

It would be incorrect to question the element of certainty in law if claims, relying on past interpretation of legislated law but with a different value reference, were not upheld. A claim that did not take into account the value segment of the decisional factors would be as technically defective as one based on a wrong classification of facts or on inapplicable positive law.

XCIV

Compare Levi (254)Ch.3 and Hart (187)46. The distinction may have been drawn a little too sharply, especially in Hart's context. Both the legislated and the decisional law come in comparable varieties of concreteness. The scale runs from a rule, spelling out its own factual limits of applicability, to general principles. But as much as the traditional *stare decisis* is conceived so that it can (must) draw on any single decision, not only on principles or doctrines that have been elaborated through a number of decisions, there is a difference. As the text following this note further spells out, legislated law comes in a finished verbal form; the decisional rule comes "swathed in obscuring dicta" (61)30. But this does not affect the postulate that in both situations the decision based on full decisional factors is *ex nunc* or the assumptions that underlie the unified theory of the uses of both sources of decision.

See also Silving (375)229, who suggests but does not develop the concept of "general methodology," and—perhaps I am overreading him—Gilmore (169)1045, who seems to imply a fusion of the methods of application of authoritative sources by judges.

APPENDIX A

François Gény (1861–1959)
Biography and bibliography

François Gény was born 17 December 1861, in Baccarat, in the Meurthe-et-Moselle department of Lorraine. He studied law in nearby Nancy. His doctoral theses, presented in 1885, were entitled "De la fiducie" (in Roman law) and "De la responsabilité des locataires en cas d'incendie de la chose louée" (the liability of lessees in the case of fire of the leased property, in French law).

After his *agrégation*, Gény became first lecturer, then professor in Algiers. In 1889 he was called to Dijon. There he continued his intensive writing activities begun already in Algiers. Besides numerous case notes, he published articles in the field of immovable securities and on the law governing the effects of mining operations on surface property and on water sources, as well as the "Essai critique sur la méthode d'interprétation juridique, en vue d'une orientation nouvelle des études de droit privé," published in the *Revue bourguignonne de l'enseignement supérieur* (1897), 307–62, (1898), 119–65, 253–353.

This almost two-hundred-page essay was a warm-up for the work that, finished in Dijon in 1899 when Gény was thirty-seven, made him a classic and a byword among the literati in jurisprudence everywhere: *Méthode d'interprétation et sources en droit privé positif: Essai critique.* The original one-volume edition of 187 sections was updated in the notes (the text was left unchanged) and supplemented by an epilogue (sections 188–224) for a second edition in two volumes (1919). It was reprinted in 1954. The 1963 American translation is the only full translation in any language of the complete second edition.

In 1901, Gény returned to Nancy. He held there the chair of civil law until his retirement in 1931, except for the years 1914–1918 when war forced him to return to Dijon. From 1919 to 1925 he served as dean of the faculty of law. He refused reappointment to gain time for the to him more important scholarly work. After his retirement, Gény remained in Nancy until his death, 16 December 1959, one day before his ninety-eighth birthday.

During his tenure at Nancy, Gény produced the bulk of his scholarship. The list is long, impressive, and important. Among the major items are:

"La technique législative dans la codification moderne," in *Le Code Civil: Livre du centenaire* (1904), 989–1038, translated in American in part as "The legislative technic of modern civil codes," in *Science of legal method* (1917), 498–517.

An annotated translation of Articles 1297–1588 in Volume III of *Code civil allemand* (published by Comité de Législation Étrangère, 1908).

"Les procédés d'élaboration du droit civil," in *Les méthodes juridiques* (1910), 173–96, a study of the method and technique in the current development of codified private law, originally a lecture at the Collège Libre des Sciences Sociales.

Des droits sur les lettres missives principalement en vue du système positif français: Essai d'application d'une méthode critique d'interprétation (1911), a practical application of Gény's doctrine of interpretation to the French law and postal regulations governing private mail, frequently cited by him in the second edition of the *Méthode.*

"La conception générale du droit, de ses sources, de sa méthode dans l'oeuvre de R. Saleilles," in *L'oeuvre juridique de Raymond Saleilles* (1914), 3–63.

Science et technique en droit privé positif: Nouvelle contribution à la critique de la méthode juridique [doctrine and technique in private positive law: a new contribution to the critique of legal method] in four volumes:

I. *Introduction: Position actuelle du problème du droit positif et éléments de sa solution* [the present problem of positive law and the elements of its solution] 1914, 212 p.

II. *Élaboration scientifique du droit positif: (L'irréductible "droit naturel"* [the doctrinal elaboration of positive law (the irreducible "natural law")] 1915, 422 pp.

III. *Élaboration technique du droit positif* (the technical elaboration of positive law), 1921, 522 pp.

IV. *Rapports entre l'élaboration scientifique et l'élaboration technique du droit positif (Le conflict du droit naturel et de la loi positive)* [relation between the doctrinal and the technical elaboration of positive law (the conflict between natural law and positive legislation), 1924, 265 pp.

When the last volume of *Science et technique* was published—the work that Gény considered the crowning effort of his life—he was almost sixty-three. His major productive years were over, but he remained active. This activity continued to show how unusually broad Gény's interests were and how close he kept to concrete problems. In a controlling evaluation,[308] Dean Julliot de la Morandière points out that, for example, in more than thirty articles and comments on decisions in the field of taxation (many of them written in his later years), Gény ranged from such details as income tax on mushroom farming to constitutional-philosophical reflections on the desirable subordination of fiscal law and practice to the principles of civil law as the highest guarantee, in the French context, of individual rights. Gény's article in 1926 on the validity of the gold clause in private contracts even in a period of imposed exchange rate (*Revue trimestrielle de droit civil,* XXV, 557–636) "caused sensation," although its impact on the decisions was not felt until thirty years later.

Other articles, notes, prefaces, and book reviews dealt with paternity, status of women, successions, company law, intellectual property in sound movies, and of course jurisprudence. After several items of routine interest—such as:

"Les bases fondamentales du droit civil en face des théories de L. Duguit," (*Id.,* XXI (1922), 779–820), also appended to *Science,* IV, 159–213;

"Le conflit du droit naturel et de la loi positive" (address, Zurich, 21 March 1929), *Zeitschr. für schweizer. Recht* (1930), 92;

"La notion de droit en France," *Archives de droit et de sociologie juridique* (1931), 9–41;

"La laicité du droit naturel," *Id.* (1933), Gény displayed unfailing freshness and adaptability of his mind when he published in 1938;

"Justice et force: pour l'intégration de la force dans le droit," *Études à la mémoire d' H. Capitant* (1939), 241–57.

This essay ends with a significant thesis: "Everything becomes clear and complete if we admit that force is an essential element of law . . . and that consequently law is constantly changing in response to the shift and conflict of forces in the social environment as well as in the physical world." Although today it sounds axiomatic, if not platitudinous, one may wish that Gény's fertile mind had pursued this line of analysis more rigorously at a time when he was at the peak of his scholarly activity.

A detailed bibliographical list from 1885 to 1938 is in the thesis by M. Toutsakovitch.[394] It is apparently complete except for an early article (1899) on the assignment of debts, mentioned by Gény in his own list of writings between the two editions of the *Méthode* (in the preface to the second edition, n. 2); a note on "Propriété et contrat" (1900), which Gény cites in the last note (*Id.*, 187); the 1930 article in the "Swiss law journal," listed in the bibliography above; and the later notes on court decisions, cited in the already mentioned address by Julliot de la Morandière. (The bibliography on the frontispiece pages of *Science* gives the wrong impression about some items—*e.g.*, the reprints of a 1901 article and of the 1910 lecture—as if they were separate books.)

In 1950–1951, the nonagenarian Gény published his last two works: "Evolution contemporaine de la pensée juridique dans la doctrine française" (contemporary developments in French jurisprudence), in *Études offertes à G. Ripert*, I (1950), 3–8; and *Ultima verba* (1951). With the first he contributed to the *mélanges* for a doctrinal antagonist who, too, was to balance his judgment in his later years—in *Les forces créatrices du droit* (1955)—in a manner not incomparable with Gény's 1938 article. The second is a human rather than jurisprudential testament of a Christian of conviction.

Gény's work was appreciated in many ways. He was an admired and beloved teacher and a spiritual guide to many doctoral candidates. He received the highest French and foreign honors. He became Commander of the Legion of Honor in 1934 and was awarded honorary degrees from the universities of Groningen (1914), Louvain (1927), Bruxelles (1929), Warszawa (1929), Genève (1930), Jassy (1934), Lausanne (1935), Basel (1936), and Athinai (1937). In 1933 he was made honorary member of the American Academy of Arts and Sciences in Boston.

When the *Recueil d'études sur les sources du droit en l'honneur de François Gény* [347] was published in 1935, honoring Gény with some delay on the occasion of his retirement, fifty-seven out of eighty-three contributions were from abroad. Among them were those of Americans, Czechs, Egyptians, Japanese, Romanians, and others attesting the worldwide fame of the master. The eleven North American contributions—by John R. Commons, John Dickinson, Mitchell Franklin, Lon L. Fuller, Fowler V. Harper, Joseph C. Hutcheson, Jr., Albert

Kocourek, Rodney L. Mott, Edwin W. Patterson, Max Radin, and James G. Rogers—were mediated by J. H. Wigmore, who previously had shown his admiration for Gény by including translations from Gény's *Méthode* and *Science et technique* in two volumes of the Modern Legal Philosophy series (1917, 1925).

The latest evidence of Gény's continued importance in the world of law and jurisprudence was a gathering at the Faculty of Law and Economics in Nancy in October, 1962, commemorating the hundredth anniversary of his birth in the preceding December. The papers by Jean Dabin (Louvain), León Julliot de la Morandière (Paris), Pierre Kayser (Aix), Michel Villey (Paris), B. A. Wortley (Manchester), and Walter Yung (Geneva) were gathered in a small memorial volume.[308]

APPENDIX B

Index I *Subjects—Concepts—Ideas*

Where indicated, the order of entries under a main heading is logical rather than alphabetic. The following symbols are used in the index: = is, means; → see; ↔ see also; (→) q.v. (which see).

Index I

Index I

Index I

Index I

Index I

Index I

Index I

APPENDIX C*

Index II
Authors / Sources

(1) Aftalión, E. E., *et al. Introducción al derecho.* Buenos Aires, 1960: *168.*

(2) Allen, C. K. "Justice and expediency." In (362)15: *119. 126. 127. 128.*

(3) ———. *Law in the making.* London, 1927. Cited 3rd ed., 1939: *73/484. 119. 148. 187. 212. 218.*

(4) ———. *Legal duties.* Oxford, 1931: *108.*

(5) Alvarez, A. *Une nouvelle conception des études juridiques et la codification du droit civil.* Paris, 1904: *150.*

(6) American Assembly, The. *Law in a changing America.* Ed. G. Hazard. Englewood Cliffs, N.J., 1968.

(7) American Association of Law Schools. "Papers presented at the Curriculum Committee meeting." *Denver L. J.*, XLIV(1967)1: *108.*

(8) *American Behavioral Scientist.* "Frontiers of legal research." Special issue, VII, 4 (1963): *105.*

(9) Amselek, P. *Méthode phénoménologique et théorie du droit.* Paris, 1964: *112. 133.*

(10) Ancel, M. "Politique législative et droit comparé." *Mélanges Maury,* II (1960)9: *107.*

(11) Archives de Philosophie Du Droit. Paris, 1925f.

(12) Ascarelli, T. *Problemi giuridici.* Milano, 1959: *16*/iii–iv. *107. 153. 154. 157. 158. 160. 161. 201.*

(13) ———. *Studi di diritto comparato e in tema di interpretazione.* Milan, 1952: *16*/202–203. *153. 154. 158. 160.*

(14) Association Henry Capitant. *Travaux.* Vol. V (Semaine internationale de droit, 1949); Paris, 1950. Vol. VI (*Id.*, 1950); Paris, 1954: *143.*

(15) Auerbach, C., *et al. The legal process.* San Francisco, 1961: *193. 218.*

(16) Ballot-Beaupré, A. "Discours." *Le centenaire du code civil.* Paris, 1904: *146.*

*The system of reference and symbols is explained in the Preface, xiii–xiv.

Index II

(17) Barham, M. E. "A rennaissance of the civilian tradition in Louisiana." In (94)38: *69.*

(18) Bartin, E. *Études sur le régime dotal.* Paris, 1892: *140.*

(19) Battaglia, F. "L'interpretazione giuridica nella moderna letteratura francese." *Riv. intern. di filos. del diritto,* IX(1929)185, 376: *128. 130. 134.*

(20) Baudry-Lacantinerie, G., and A. Tissier. *De la prescription.* 2nd ed. Paris, 1923. Louisiana translation, Mayda, 1972: *78.*

(21) Becker, W. G. "Rechtsvergleichende Notizen zur Auslegung." *Festschrift Lehmann.* Berlin, 1956: *155.*

(22) Bel, J. (former director, Service de Documentation et d'Études, Cour de Cassation, Paris). Interviews, correspondence, and an extract from a report "L'automatisation de la documentation à la Cour de Cassation." 1968–76: *195.*

(23) Berner Kommentar zum Schweizerischen Zivilrecht. *Einleitung: Art. 1–10, ZGB.* Bern, 1962: *35.*

(24) Betti, E. *Allgemeine Auslegungslehre als Methodik der Geisteswissenschaften.* German ed., *Teoria generale della interpretazione,* 1955. Tübingen, 1967.

(25) ———. "Ergänzende Rechtsfortbildung als Aufgabe der richterlichen Gesetzauslegung." *Festschrift Rappe.* Hamburg, 1948: *156.*

(26) ———. *Interpretazione della legge e degli atti giuridici: Teoria generale e dogmatica.* Milano, 1949: *156.*

(27) Beutel, F. K. *Some potentialities of experimental jurisprudence as a new branch of social science.* Lincoln, Neb., 1957: *111. 161.*

(28) ———, and T. Negrón-Medero. *The operation of bad check laws in Puerto Rico.* Río Piedras, P.R., 1967: *111. 161.*

(29) Bickel, A. M. *Politics and the Warren court.* New York, 1965: *198. 204.*

(30) Black, H. Dissenting opinion. Katz v. United States. 1967: *193.*

(31) Bobbio, N. *Scienza e tecnica del diritto.* Torino, 1934: *134.*

(32) ———. "Trends in Italian legal theory." *Amer. J. Comp. L.,* VIII(1959) 329: *51. 203.*

(33) Bodenheimer, E. *Jurisprudence: The philosophy and method of the law.* Cambridge, Mass., 1962: *108.*

(34) Boehmer, G. *El derecho a través de la jurisprudencia: Su aplicación y creación.* Trans. Puig-Brutau. Barcelona, 1957: *51. 158. 202. 203. 204.*

(35) Bonnecasse, J. *La pensée juridique française de 1804 à l'heure présente.* Bordeaux, 1933: *128. 129. 156.*

(36) ———. *Précis de pratique judiciaire et extrajudiciaire: éléments de clinique juridique.* Paris, 1927: *196. 214.*

(37) Boulanger, J. "Jurisprudence." *Répertoire de droit civil Dalloz,* III. Paris, 1954: *139. 214. 221.*

(38) ———. "La méthode depuis le code civil de 1804 au point de vue de l'interpretation judiciaire." In (14)329, 528: *54*/336f. *107. 168. 169. 184. 188.*

(39) ———. "Notations sur le pouvoir créateur de la jurisprudence civile." *Rev. trim. de droit civ.,* LX(1961)417: *12*/441. *64*/428. *115. 140. 142. 197. 209. 223.*

(40) ———. "Le précédent judiciaire dans le droit privé français contemporain." *Rev. du Barreau,* XXI(1961)65: *71*/68–85. *74*/87. *99*/85. *197. 207. 214. 221.*

(41) ———. "Principes généraux du droit et le droit positif." *Études Ripert,* I (1950), 51: *178. 217.*

(42) ———. "Rôle du juge en cas de silence ou d'insuffisance de la loi." In (14) V61 (general report): *64*/64. *165. 175. 214.*

Index II

Index II

(72) ———, and D. M. Trubek. "The creative role of the judge: Restraint and freedom in the common law tradition." *Yale L. J.*, LXXI(1961), 255: *146.*

(73) Cohen, F. S. "Field theory and judicial logic." In *Structure, method, and meaning: Essays in honor of H. M. Sheffer.* New York, 1951, p. 255: *207.*

(74) Cohen, M. R. *Law and the social order.* New York, 1933: *13*/287, 385n24. *14*/287. *119. 130. 135. 149.*

(75) ———. *Reason and nature.* New York, 1931: *104. 133.*

(76) ———, and E. Nagel. *Introduction to logic and scientific method.* Washington, D.C., 1934: *114.*

(77) Colin, A., and H. Capitant. *Traité de droit civil.* Ed. L. J. de La Morandière. Paris, 1937: *146.*

(78) Commons, J. R. "The problem of correlating law, economics, and ethics: Comments on Gény's *Méthode.*" In (347)III124: *148.*

(79) "Congressional reversal of Supreme Court decisions, 1945–1957." *Harv. L. R.*, LXXI(1958)1324: *210.*

(80) Cossio, C. *El derecho en el derecho judicial.* Buenos Aires, 1944: *15*/114. *130.*

(81) Cowan, T. A. "Decision theory in law, science, and technology." *Rutgers L. R.*, XVII(1963)499: *193.*

(82) ———. "Jurisprudence: Method and trends." *Intern. Encycl. Soc. Sciences*, 1967: *108.*

(83) ———. "Notes on the teaching of jurisprudence." *J. Leg. Educ.*, XV(1962)1: *105. 108.*

(84) ———. "Postulates for experimental jurisprudence." *Rutgers L. R.*, IX(1954), 404: *112.*

(85) ———. "Some problems common to law, jurisprudence and technology." *G. Washington L. R.*, XXXIII(1964)3.

(86) Cox, A. "Foreword: Constitutional adjudication and the promotion of human rights." *Harv. L. R.*, LXXX(1966)91: *194.*

(87) Croce, B. *Filosofia nella practica economica ed etica.* Bari, 1923: *12*/328. *128.*

(88) Cross, R. *Precedent in English law.* Oxford, 1961: *226.*

(89) Crosskey, W. W. *Politics and the Constitution in the history of the United States.* Chicago, 1953: *193.*

(90) Cueto-Rua, J. "El common law (stare decisis)." *Rev. Fac. Derecho* [Univ. Central, Caracas] 12(1957)69: *218.*

(91) Curtis, C. P. "A better theory of legal interpretation." *Vanderbilt L. R.*, III(1950), 407: *226.*

(92) Dabin, J. "François Gény, le savant." In (308)5: *12*/16. *128. 129. 133. 135. 159.*

(93) ———. *Théorie générale du droit.* Bruxelles, 1943: *127. 129. 132.*

(94) Dainow, J., ed. *Judicial decisions and doctrine in civil law and in mixed jurisdictions.* Baton Rouge, 1974: *69*/311f.

(95) ———. "Louisiana." In (14)VI411: *168.*

(96) David, R. *French law: Its structure and sources.* Trans. Kindred. Baton Rouge, 1972.

(97) ———. *Les grands systèmes de droit contemporain.* 5th ed. Paris, 1973. Also trans. Brierly. London, 1968.: *99*/341. *184. 193. 196.*

(98) ———, and H. de Vries. *The French legal system.* New York, 1958: *129.*

(99) Davis, K. C. *Administrative law treatise.* St. Paul, 1958: *216. 224.*

(100) ———. "The future of judge-made public law in England: A problem of practical justice." *Columb. L. R.*, LXI(1961)201.

(101) Davitt, T. E. *The elements of law.* Boston, 1959: *108. 153.*

Index II

(102) Dawson, J. P. *The oracles of the law*. Ann Arbor, Mich., 1968: *119. 128. 141.*

(103) Degni, F. *L'interpretazione della legge*. Napoli, 1909: *155.*

(104) Demogue, R. *Les notions fondamentales du droit privé*. Paris, 1911: *221.*

(105) Dewey, J. "Legal method and the law." *Cornell L.Q.*, X(1924)17: *3.*

(106) Dias, R. H. W. "Jurisprudence." *Encycl. Brit.* XIII. 1965: *108.*

(107) Dickinson, E. B. "The problem of the unprovided case." In (347)II503: *116. 133. 135.*

(108) Djuvara, M. "Droit rationnel et droit positif." In (347)I220: *16*/253, 282. *154. 158.*

(109) Dualde, J. *Una revolución en la lógica del derecho*. Barcelona, 1933: *13*/178. *15*/45. *27*/180f. *32*/178. *128. 145. 154. 156.*

(110) Duguit, L. *Traité de droit constitutionel*. Paris, 1921: *137.*

(111) Dupeyroux, O. "La jurisprudence: Source abusive de droit." *Mélanges Maury*, II (1960)349: *196. 197.*

(112) Durkheim, E. *Les règles de la méthode sociologique*. Paris, 1895: *111.*

(113) Egger, A. *Kommentar zum schweizerischen ZGB: Einleitung*. 2nd ed. Zurich, 1928: *183. 188.*

(114) ———. *Schweizerische Rechtsprechung und Rechtswissenshaft*. Berlin, 1913: *166. 170.*

(115) Ehrenzweig, A. A. *Psychoanalytic jurisprudence*. Dobbs Ferry, N.Y., 1971: *97.*

(116) ———. "Psychoanalytic jurisprudence: A common language for Babylon." *Columb. L. R.*, LXV(1965)1331: *54*/1342.

(117) Ehrlich, E. *Freie Rechtsfindung und freie Rechtswissenschaft*. Leipzig, 1903. American trans. in (369)70. *21*/v. *110. 116. 148.*

(118) ———. *Grundlegung der Soziologie des Rechts*. München, 1913: *143.*

(119) ———. *Die juristische Logik*. Tübingen, 1918. Originally "Arch. für die civilistische." Praxis, CXV(1917)125: *149. 154.*

(120) ———. *Die stillschweigende Willenserklärung*. Berlin, 1893: *148.*

(121) ———. "Ueber Lücken im Rechte." *Jurist. Blätter*, 1888. Summarized in (117)iii–iv: *148.*

(122) Elliot, S. D. "Statutory construction," in Karlen, ed. *Anglo-American appeals study*. New York, 1962: *226.*

(123) Esmein, A. "La jurisprudence et la doctrine." *Rev. trim. de droit civ.*, I (1902)5: *141.*

(124) Esmein, P. "La jurisprudence et la loi." *Id.*, L(1952)17: *86. 107. 141.*

(125) Esser, J. "Book review (Meier-Hayoz)." *Zeitschr. für ausländ. u. internat. Privatrecht*, XXVIII(1953)170: *53*/172. *59*/171–72.

(126) ———. "Book review (du Pasquier)." *Id.*, 167: *55*/167. *163. 178.*

(127) ———. *Grundsatz und Norm in der richterlichen Rechtsfindung*. Tübingen, 1956: *15*/290. *119. 127. 129. 149. 154. 155. 156. 163.*

(128) Evershed, R. "The judicial process in twentieth-century England." *Columb. L. R.*, LXI(1961)761: *154. 192. 226.*

(129) Eycken, P. van der. *Méthode positive de l'interprétation juridique*. Bruxelles, 1907: *216.*

(130) Fellmann, D. "The essential nature of American constitutional law." In Forkosh, ed. *Essays in legal history in honor of Felix Frankfurter*. Indianapolis, 1966: *68.*

(131) Fenet, P. A. *Recueil complet des travaux préparatoires du code civil*. Paris, 1827–28: *121.*

(132) Frank, J. "A sketch of an influence." In (362)189: *155.*

(133) ———. *Courts on trial*. Princeton, 1949: *96*/270. *209. 224.*

(159) ———. *Science et technique en droit privé positif: nouvelle contribution à la critique de la méthode juridique*. 4 vols. Paris, 1914–24: *1*/2. *8*/3.302. *9*/1–6,303. *11*/45, 61,167–177,196,197,302,303. *19*/II 121–22. *26*/301,par. XVIII–XIX. *29*/12; 26. *72*/I 10n1. *104*. *107*. *110*. *115*. *122*. *124*. *125*. *126*. *127*. *131*. *132*. *133*. *134*. *138*. *139*. *141*. *148*. *150*. *151*. *156*. *159*.
(160) ———. "The legislative technics of modern civil codes." Trans. Bruncken. In (369)498: *123*.
(161) Germann, O. A. *Die methodische Grundfragen*. Basel, 1946: *15*/38. *59*/142. *128*. *145*. *153*. *154*. *157*. *160*. *170*. *176*. *186*. *187*.
(162) ———. *Grundlagen der Rechtswissenschaft*. Bern, 1950: *170*.
(163) ———. "Neuere Judikatur des Schweizerischen Bundesgerichtes zur Frage der Gesetzesauslegung nach den Vorarbeiten, insbesondere nach dem darin geäusserten Willen des Gesetzgebers." *Zeitschr. für schweiz. Recht*, LXXXI (1962)207: *37*/209n8. *38*/213n23; 214n26; 220,225. *45*/212n19. *49*/216–26. *53*/225n64. *63*/215n28. *74*. *172*. *176*. *181*. *182*. *183*. *184*.
(164) ———. "Präjudizielle Tragweite höchstinstanzlichen Urteile." *Id.*, LXVIII (1949)297, 423: *36*. *62*/306. *190*.
(165) ———. *Präjudizien als Rechtsquelle*. Stockholm, 1960: *62*/46. *190*.
(166) ———. *Probleme und Methoden der Rechtsfindung*. Bern, 1965: *51*/75. *53*/236n23. *54*/401n31. *55*/396. *58*. *170*. *175*. *176*. *177*. *178*. *181*. *184*. *187*. *190*. *214*.
(167) ———. "Zum sogennanten Analogieverbot." *Festgabe Hafter*. Bern, 1946: *44*/n163. *183*. *185*. *217*. *218*.
(168) ———. "Zur Problematik der Ermessensentscheide." *Festgabe Ruck*. Basel 1952: *165*. *208*.
(169) Gilmore, G. "Legal realism: Its cause and cure." *Yale L. J.*, LXX(1961) 1037: *157*. *228*.
(170) Gmür, M. *Die Anwendung der Rechts nach Art. 1 des schweizerischen Zivilgesetzbuches*. Bern, 1908: *61*/125. *163*.
(171) Gnaeus Flavius [H. Kantorowicz]. *Der Kampf um die Rechtswissenschaft*. Heidelberg, 1906: *143*. *144*.
(172) Gomez, H. *Judicial function—a source of law*. Dallas, 1958: *155*.
(173) González, J. *Estudios de derecho hipotecario y derecho civil*. Madrid, 1948: *154*.
(174) Goodhart, A. L. *Essays on jurisprudence and the common law*. Cambridge, 1931: *69*. *218*.
(175) Graham, F. P. "Lowering voting age." New York *Times*, 29 March 1970: *175*.
(176) Gray, J. C. *The nature and sources of law*. 2nd ed. Boston, 1921: *225*.
(177) Green, L. *Judge and jury*. Kansas City, 1930: *105*.
(178) Grisoli, A. *Guide to foreign legal materials: Italy*. Dobbs Ferry, N.Y., 1965.
(179) Gurvitch, G. *L'idée du droit social*. Paris, 1931: *133*. *148*.
(180) Gutzwiller, M. "Book review (Berner Kommentar)." *Zeitschr. für schweiz. Recht*, LXXXI(1962)I 142: *58*/147. *59*/149. *171*. *174*. *176*.
(181) Haines, C. G. *American doctrine of judicial supremacy: Renaissance of natural law*. New York, 1930: *133*.
(182) Hall, J. *Foundations of jurisprudence*. Indianapolis, 1973: *105*.
(183) ———. "From legal theory to integrative jurisprudence." *U. Cincinnati L. R.*, XXXIII(1964)153: *105*. *106*. *109*.
(184) ———. "Integrative jurisprudence." In (362)313: *109*.
(185) ———. *Reason and reality in jurisprudence*. Buffalo, 1958: *109*.
(186) ———. *Studies in jurisprudence and criminal theory*. New York, 1958: *105*.

(187) Hart, H. M. "Comments." In (324)40: *105. 227.*
(188) ———, and J. T. McNaughton. "Evidence and inference in the law." *Daedalus,* LXXXVII(1958)40.
(189) ———, and A. M. Sachs. *The legal process: Basic problems in the making and application of law.* Cambridge, Mass., 1958: *74. 226.*
(190) ———, and H. Wechsler. *Federal courts and federal system.* Brooklyn, 1954: *91*/659. *225.*
(191) Hart, H. L. A. *The concept of law.* Oxford, 1961: *108.*
(192) ———. "Definition and theory in jurisprudence." *L. Q. R.,* LXX(1954)37: *108.*
(193) Hartmann, R. E. "General theory of value." In Klibansky, ed. *Philosophy in the mid-century.* Milano, 1958: *103. 111. 161.*
(194) Hauriau, M. "La théorie de l'institution." *Cahiers de la Nouvelle Journée,* IV(1925)10: *142.*
(195) Hauser, M. Letter on behalf of A. Meier-Hayoz. Zürich, 1963: *48. 50.*
(196) Hazeltine, H. D. "Preface." In W. Ullman, *The medieval idea of law.* London, 1946: *205.*
(197) Heck, P. *Begriffsbildung und Interessenjurisprudenz.* Tübingen, 1932: *155. 157. 161. 216.*
(198) ———. *Interessenjurisprudenz.* Tübingen, 1933: *34.*
(199) Hernández-Gil, A. *Metodología del derecho.* Madrid, 1945: *123. 128. 133. 146. 156.*
(200) Hohfeld, W. N. "Some fundamental legal conceptions as applied to judicial reasoning." *Yale L. J.,* XXIII(1913), 16: XXVI(1917), 710: *161.*
(201) Holland, T. E. *The elements of jurisprudence.* 1880. Cited 12th ed. Oxford, 1917: *116.*
(202) Holmes, O. W. *The common law.* Boston, 1881: *118.*
(203) ———. "Natural law." *Harv. L. R.,* XXXII(1918)40: *129. 134.*
(204) ———. "The path of law." *Id.,* X(1897), 457: *61. 116.*
(205) ———. "The profession of law." In *Collected legal papers.* Boston, 1920: *116.*
(206) ———. *Speeches.* Boston, 1921: *116.*
(207) Hook, S., ed. *Law and philosophy: A symposium.* New York, 1964: *109. 161.*
(208) Horack, F. E. "The common law of legislation." *Iowa L. R.,* XXIII(1937) 41: *190. 221.*
(209) Huber, E. *Recht und Rechtsverwirklichung.* Basel, 1921. *72. 175.*
(210) ———. *Schweizerisches Zivilgesetzbuch: Erläuterungen zum Vorentwurf.* Bern, 1902. Cited 2nd ed. 1914: *51*/37–38. *60*/38.
(211) Huber, H. "Die Staats- und Verwaltungsrechtliche Rechtsprechung des Bundesgerichts im Jahre 1957." *Zeitschr. d. Bernischen Juristenvereins,* XCIV(1958)457: *38*/467. *49*/467. *63*/466. *191.*
(212) Hurst, J. W. *The growth of American law.* Boston, 1950.
(213) ———. "Perspective upon research into legal order." *Wis. L. R.* (1961)356: *192. 193. 204.*
(214) Husson, L. *Les transformations de la responsabilité: Étude sur la pensée juridique.* Paris, 1947: *128.*
(215) Hutcheson, J. C. "The judgment intuitive: The function of 'hunch' in judicial process." *Cornell L. Q.,* XIV(1929), 274. Also in (347)II 531: *145. 219.*
(216) Isay, H. *Rechtsnorm und Entscheidung.* Berlin, 1930.
(217) Jeanneau, J. "Les principes généraux du droit dans la jurisprudence administrative." Thesis, University of Paris, 1954.

Index II

(218) Jhering, R. von. *Geist des römischen Rechts.* 3 vols. 1852–65: *111. 117.*

(219) ———. *Über den Grund des Besitzschutzes.* Jena, 1869.

(220) ———. *Kampf ums Recht.* Berlin, 1872.

(221) ———. *Der Zweck im Recht.* Leipzig, 1877.

(222) Jones, H. W. "A view from the bridge." *Law and society* (Summer, 1965) 39: *110.*

(223) ———. "The creative power and function of law in historical perspective." *Vanderbilt L. R.*, XVII(1953)135: *110.*

(224) Jones, J. W. "Cino da Pistoria." In (362)376: *155.*

(225) ———. "Modern discussion of the aims and methods of legal science." *L. Q. R.*, XLVII(1931)62: *111. 119. 129.*

Julliot de La Morandière. See Morandière, L. J. de La.

(226) Kalven, H. "The quest for the middle range: Empirical inquiry and legal policy." In (6)56: *111. 112.*

(227) ———, and H. Zeisel. *The American jury.* Boston, 1966: *105. 111. 112. 161.*

(228) Kantorowicz, H. U. "Legal science—a summary of its methodology." *Columb. L. R.*, XXVIII(1928)679: *193.*

(229) Katzenbach, N. de B. "Address." Supreme Court of the United States: In memory of Honorable Felix Frankfurter. 86 *S.Ct.* xxxi–xxxix (1965): *70/xxxv.*

(230) Kayser, M. P. "François Gény, le professeur et l'homme." In (308)1: *76/7. 135.*

(231) Kelsen, H. *General theory of law and state.* Trans. Wedberg. Boston, 1945: *220.*

(232) Knapp, V. "La création du droit par le judge dans les pays socialistes." In E. von Cammerer *et al.*, eds. *Ius privatum gentium* (Festschrift Rheinstein). Tübingen, 1969.

(233) ———. Personal communication. Praha, 1965: *77.*

(234) Kocourek, A. "Libre recherche in America." In (347)459: *144. 154.*

(235) Kohler, J. "Die Freirechtsbewegung in den Vereinigten Staaten." *Deutsche Jurist. Zeitung*, XVI(1911), 918: *144.*

(236) ———. "Die schöpferische Kraft der Jurisprudenz." *Jahrb. f.d. Dogmatik*, XXV(1887), 262: *148.*

(237) ———. "Ueber die Interpretation der Gesetze." *Zeitschr. f.d. Privatund öffentl. Recht*, XIII(1886), 1: *148.*

(238) Korzybski, A. *Science and sanity: An introduction to non-Aristotelian and general semantics.* Lakeville, Conn., 1959: *21. 83.*

(239) *La logique juridique.* Paris, 1967: *105. 109. 130. 161.*

(240) Lambert, E. *Du contrat en faveur de tiers.* Paris, 1893: *140.*

(241) ———. *Études de droit commun législatif. Introduction, Vol. I: La fonction du droit civil comparé.* Paris, 1903: *12/34. 14. 18/30–32. 22. 112. 128. 141. 143. 146. 156. 221.*

(242) ———. "Une réforme nécessaire des études de droit civil." *Rev. internat. de l'enseignement*, XL(1900)216: *141.*

———, ed. *Recueil Gény.* See *Recueil.*

(243) Langdell, C. C. *Selection of cases on the law of contracts.* Boston, 1971.

(244) Language of law, The. Symposium. *West. Reserve L. R.*, IX(1958)115.

(245) Lasswell, H. D., and A. Kaplan. *The decision process.* New Haven, Conn., 1950: *112.*

(246) ———, and M. S. McDougal. "Criteria for a theory about law." *So. Calif. L. R.*, XLIV(1971)362: *161.*

(247) ———, and *Id.* "Trends in theories about law: Comprehensiveness in conceptions of the constitutive process." *G. Washington L. R.*, XLI(1972)1: *161.*

Index II

(248) *Law and philosophy: A symposium.* Ed. Hook. New York, 1964: *109. 161.*

(249) Lawlor, R. C. *Fact content of cases and precedent: A modern theory of precedent.* Los Angeles, 1971: *112.*

Le centenaire Gény. See Nancy, University of.

(250) Legaz y Lacambra, L. *Introducción a la ciencia de derecho.* Barcelona, 1943: *126. 128.*

(251) Lehmann, H. "Wirkungsstärke des Naturrechts." *Festschrift Raape* (1948) 370.: *131.*

(252) Lehmann-Haupt, C. "Book review (Steiner)." New York *Times,* 7 May 1975.

(253) Levi, E. H. "Address." National conference on the causes of popular dissatisfaction with the administration of justice. St. Paul, Minn., 9 April 1976: *206. 210.*

(254) ———. *An introduction to legal reasoning.* Chicago, 1962. Originally *U. Chicago L. R.,* XV(1948)501: *154. 206. 217. 218. 221. 227.*

(255) ———. *The crisis in the nature of law.* New York, 1970: *204.*

(256) ———. "The nature of judicial reasoning." In (207) and *U. Chicago L. R.,* XXXII(1965)395: *207. 222.*

(257) ———. *Some aspects of separation of powers.* New York, 1975: *68. 204.*

(258) Lévy-Bruhl, H. *Sociologie de droit.* Paris, 1961: *107.*

(259) Lewis, A. "The Boston schools, II." New York *Times,* 24 May 1976: *85. 210.*

(260) Liard, L. *L'enseignement supérieur en France, 1789–1893.* Paris, 1894: *150. 151.*

(261) Librairie Larousse. *Grand Larousse.* Paris: *125.*

(262) ———. *Petit Larousse Illustré.* Paris: *125.*

(263) Lichnerowitz, A. "Celui qui veut tout changer." *L'express* [Paris], 8–14 January 1968, p. 74: *196.*

(264) Liet-Veaux, G. "Un anachronisme: La mitoyenneté des murs." *Juris-Classeur Périodique* I (1966), 1991: *218.*

(265) Liver, P. "Der Begriff der Rechtsquelle." In *Rechtsquellen-probleme.* Bern, 1955: *16/40. 145. 169. 170. 183. 186. 187.*

(266) ———. "Einleitung." In (23)7: *34/N.58,61. 36/N.157–58. 162. 190.*

(267) Llewellyn, K. N. *The bramble bush.* New York, 1951. 1st ed., 1930. *222.*

(268) ———. *Common law tradition.* Boston, 1960: *13/422n46. 104. 117. 123. 128. 135. 148. 150. 189.*

(269) ———. *Law in our society: Topical syllabus.* Chicago, 1950: *117.*

(270) Loevinger, L. "Law and science as rival systems." *U. Florida L. R.,* XIX (1967), 530: *112.*

(271) Loussouarn, Y. "Relative importance of legislation, custom, doctrine, and precedent in French law." *Louisiana L. R.,* XVIII(1958), 235: *155. 157. 206.*

(272) Lowe, A. "Comment on Jonas, 'The practical uses of theory.'" *Social research,* XXVI(1959)127: *114.*

(273) Lucien-Brun, P. "Le rôle et les pouvoirs du juge dans le code civil suisse." Thesis, University of Grenoble, 1920.

(274) Lundberg, G. A. *Foundations of sociology.* New York, 1939: *104. 106. 114.*

(275) MacKaay, E. "Jurimétrie, informatique juridique, droit de l'informatique: Un résumé de la litérature." *Rev. jurid. Thémis,* VI, 1 (1971): *112.*

(276) Maggiore, G. "La dottrina del metodo giuridico e la sua revisione critica." *Riv. internat. di filos. del diritto,* VI(1926)364: *133.*

(277) Makkonen, K. "Der Stand der finnischen Rechtstheorie." *Rechtstheorie,* I(1970)96: *108.*

Index II

(278) Maury, J. "Observations sur la jurisprudence en tant que source du droit." *Études Ripert*, I (1950)28: *64*/38–39. *144. 145. 189. 196. 197. 214.*

(279) Mayda, J. "Book review (Centenaire Gény)." *Amer. J. Comp. L.*, XIV (1965)713: *152. 188.*

(280) ———. "Book review (Friedrich)." *Tulane L. R.*, XXXV(1960)290: *20*/292. *110. 127.*

(281) ———. "Book review (Hierro, *El derecho en Ortega*)." *Asomante* [San Juan] 3 (1967)58: *110. 123. 205.*

(282) ———. *Environment & resources: From conservation to ecomanagement.* Río Piedras, P.R., 1967, 1968: *80*/112–44. *89*/75f. *114. 203.*

(283) ———. "Gény's *Méthode* after 60 years: A critical introduction." In (158) i–lxxvi: *34*/xlii n155. *41*/xlix n170. *113. 115. 119. 126. 134. 193. 214. 219.*

(284) ———. *Introduction to law: A preliminary edition.* Río Piedras, P.R., 1959, 1963, 1969. Cited 1969 ed.: *92*/572, 598–603. *219.*

(285) ———. "The Korean repatriation problem and international law." *Amer. J. Intern. L.*, XXXVII(1953), 414: *157.*

(286) ———. "Lawyers and ecomanagement." *Louisiana L. R.*, XXXIV(1974)975: *80*/983. *114.*

(287) ———. "Problems of legal education in Latin America." *J. Leg. Educ.*, XII (1960)407: *192.*

(288) ———. "Montesquieu's *Esprit des lois.*" Seminar paper, Faculty of Law, Masaryk U., 1939: *203.*

(289) ———. "Some critical reflections on contemporary comparative law." *Rev. Juríd. U.Pto.Rico*, XXXIX(1970), 431. (In French, in *Rev. intern. dr. comp.*, XXI(1970)57; Reprinted (in English) in K. Zweigert and H. J. Puttfarken (eds.), *Rechtsvergleichung–Die Wege der Forschung.* Darmstadt, 1978): *27. 58. 81*/438. *104. 106. 110. 123. 132.*

(290) ———. Syllabus. Seminar of Louisiana appellate judges. Baton Rouge, 1973.

———. Translation of Gény, *Méthode.* See Gény, F.

(291) McDougal, M. S. "Jurisprudence for a free society." *Georgia L. R.*, I (1966)1: *105. 113.*

(292) ———, H. D. Lasswell, and W. M. Riesman. "Theories about international law: Prologue to a configurative jurisprudence." *Virginia J. Intern. L.*, VIII(1968)188: *109. 112. 113. 161.*

(293) McWhinney, E. "Judicial restraint and the West German constitutional court." *Harv. L. R.*, LXXV(1961)5: *191.*

(294) Mehren, A. T. von. *The civil law system.* Englewood Cliffs, N.J., 1957: *128.*

(295) Meier-Hayoz, A. "Art[ikel] 1 [ZGB]." "Art. 4." In (23)78; 421: *34*/N.2. *37*/N.151–78. *38*/N.164; 168–73; 162,170. *41*/N.33. *52*/N.164f. *58*/–; N.465. *59*/N.344. *60*/N.33. *61*/N.499; 478. *62*/N.522,523; 481. *163. 164. 165. 168. 169. 170. 172. 173. 174. 175. 176. 177. 179. 180. 189. 208. 218.*

(296) ———. *Der Richter als Gesetzgeber.* Zurich, 1951: *34*/243n12. *163. 170. 180. 184. 187.*

(297) ———. "Der Richter als Gesetzgeber: Zum rechtspolitischen Komponente der richterlichen Tätigkeit." *Festschrift Guldener* (1973), p. 189: *71*/200.

(298) Mermin, S. "Concerning the ways of courts." *Wis. L. R.* (1963)192: *218.*

(299) Merryman, J. H. *The civil law tradition.* Stanford, 1969: *71*/49.

(300) Mezger, M. "Discussion." In (14)V66: *165.*

(301) Mishan, E. J. *The cost of economic development.* London, 1967: *114.*

(302) Montrose, J. L. *Precedent in English law and other essays.* Ed. Hanbury. Belfast, 1968: *218.*

(303) Moore, U. and C. C. Calahan. *Law and learning theory: A study in legal control.* New Haven, 1943: *111. 161.*

(304) Morandière, L. J. de la. "François Gény et la jurisprudence française." In (308)67: *151.*
(305) Morrison, F. L. "Judicial process in Switzerland: A study of the Swiss Federal Court." Thesis, Princeton University, 1966: *52*/Ch.V. *53*/56. *54*/193. *56*/194,256–79. *63*/231; 325–26. *173. 181. 182. 184. 185.*
(306) Morrow, C. J. "Louisiana blueprint." *Tulane L. R.*, XVII(1943)351, 556. *28*/556. *119. 130.*
(307) Müller-Erzbach, R. *Die Rechtswissenschaft im Umbau.* München, 1950: *161.*
(308) Nancy, University of. Faculté de droit et des sciences économiques. *Le centenaire du doyen François Gény.* Paris, 1963: *4*/iii. *25. 38*/78. *105. 130. 150. 152.*
(309) ———. *Fêtes universitaires des 28, 29 et 30 novembre 1934 à l'occasion du jubilé universitaire de Monsieur F. Gény.* Nancy, 1935: *33*/64. *166.*
(310) Oelsner, L. "Unlike 1906, A.B.A. meeting is receptive to reform." New York *Times*, 11 April 1976: *210.*
(311) Oertmann, P. "Book review (Gény)." *Arch. f. bürgerl. Recht*, XVIII(1900) 348: *153.*
(312) Ogden, C. K., and I. A. Richards. *The meaning of meaning.* New York, 1923: *104.*
(313) Olgiatti, F. *Il concetto di giuridicità nella scienza moderna del diritto.* Milan, 1943: *15*/287. *128. 133.*
(314) Oliphant, H. "A return to stare decisis." *Amer. Bar Assn. J.*, XIV(1928), 71: *213.*
(315) O'Toole, T. J. "Jurisprudence of François Gény." *Villanova L. R.*, III(1958), 455: *119. 126. 129.*
(316) *Oxford English Dictionary.* Compact ed. Oxford, 1971: *113. 162.*
(317) Pascal, R. "Book review (Capelletti)." *Amer. J. Comp. L.*, XV(1967)829.
(318) Pasquier, C. Du. *Introduction à la théorie générale et à la philosophie du droit.* 3rd ed. Neuchâtel, 1948. 1st ed., 1928: *166. 188.*
(319) ———. "La méthode depuis le code civil de 1804: Suisse." In (14)VI500: *44*/509; 504. *172.*
(320) ———. *Les lacunes de la loi et la jurisprudence du tribunal fédéral suisse sur l'Art. ler CCS.* Basel, 1951: *35*/26–28. *42*/21. *51*/21. *61*/68–72. *163. 170. 172. 173. 175. 178. 183. 184. 186. 190. 191.*
(321) ———. "Modernisme judiciaire et jurisprudence suisse." *Recueil trav. Fac. droit Neuchâtel* (1929)193: *170.*
(322) Patterson, E. *Jurisprudence: Men and ideas of the law.* Brooklyn, 1953: *126. 135. 196.*
(323) Patton, G. W., and D. P. Derham. *A textbook of jurisprudence.* 4th ed. Oxford, 1972: *212. 218.*
(324) Paulsen, M. G., ed. *Legal institutions today and tomorrow.* New York, 1959: *74*/46. *194. 203. 210. 216.*
(325) Peiser, N. "Note under C.E., 10 June 1966, Affaire Brasselet." *Jur.-Classeur Périod*, 1966.II.4845: *218.*
(326) Pelagius, A. *De planeta ecclesiae. Ca.* 1540: *205.*
(327) Perick, A. "The Swiss code." In A. Alvarez, ed. *Continental legal series.* Vol. XI, 1918: *163.*
(328) Perreau, E. H. *Technique de la jurisprudence en droit privé.* Paris, 1923: *145.*
(329) Picot, A. "De l'interprétation du Code Napoléon à celle du code civil suisse." *Rev. suisse de jurispr.* (1909)243: *170.*

Index II

(330) Planiol, M. *Traité élémentaire de droit civil.* Paris, 1899: American trans. of 12th ed.; 1959: *17/14.B.n. 140. 142. 220.*

(331) Posner, R. A. "The birth of a journal [Journal of Legal Studies]." *U. Chicago L. School Record* (Spring, 1971), 26: *105.*

(332) Pound, R. "Fifty years of jurisprudence." *Harv. L. R.*, L(1937)557; LI (1938)444, 777: *123. 128. 129.*

(333) ———. "Hierarchy of sources and forms in different systems of law." *Tulane L. R.*, VII(1933)475: *121.*

(334) ———. *An introduction to the philosophy of law.* New Haven, Conn., 1922: *129.*

(335) ———. "Jurisprudence." *Enc. Soc. Sciences.* VII. 1932: *108.*

(336) ———. *Jurisprudence.* St. Paul, Minn., 1959: *14/I 181–83. 123.*

(337) ———. "The theory of judicial decision." *Harv. L. R.*, XXXVI(1923)641, 802, 940: *68/958. 70/940. 225.*

(338) Puig-Brutau, J. "Book review (Mehren)." *Tulane L. R.*, XXXVII(1958), 340: *71.*

(339) ———. *La jurisprudencia como fuente de derecho.* Barcelona, 1950. *150.*

(340) Radbruch, G. *Einführung in die Rechtswissenschaft.* 9th ed. Stuttgart, 1952: *156. 174. 184.*

(341) ———. *Rechtsphilosophie.* Ed. Wolf. 4th ed. 1950: *174. 208. 218.*

(342) Radin, M. "Statutory interpretation." *Harv. L. R.*, XLIII(1930), 863: *145. 226.*

(343) ———. "The theory of judicial decision: Or how judges think." *Amer. Bar Assn. J.*, XI(1925), 357.

(344) Random House. *Dictionary of the English Language.* New York, 1966: *96. 113.*

(345) Reale, M. *Teoria tridimensional do direito.* Saõ Paulo, 1968: *109.*

(346) Recaséns-Siches, L. *La nueva filosofía de la interpretación del derecho.* México D.F., 1956: *129.*

(347) *Recueil d'études sur les sources du droit en honneur de François Gény.* Ed. Lambert. Paris, 1935: *100. 130. 133. 145. 232.*

(348) Rehnquist, W. Dissenting opinion in *Taylor* v. *Louisiana*: *194.*

(349) Reichel, H. *Gesetz und Richteramt.* Zürich, 1915: *59. 163. 164. 166.*

(350) ———. "Zu den Einleitungsartikeln des schweizerischen Zivilgesetzbuches." *Festgabe Stammler* (1926)281: *34/283. 170. 186. 217.*

(351) Reichenbach, H. *The rise of scientific philosophy.* Berkeley, 1959: *71/117. 109.*

(352) Ripert, G. "Droit naturel et positivisme juridique." *Annales Fac. droit d'Aix*, n.s., 1(1918), 35: *132.*

(353) ———. *Les forces créatrices du droit.* Paris, 1955: *14/82. 15/424. 23/18. 28/393. 129. 155. 157. 197.*

(354) ———. "Preface." In (330): *22. 139.*

(355) ———, and J. Boulanger. *Traité de droit civil.* Paris, 1956: *133.*

(356) Rodriguez-Ramos, M. " 'Equity' in the civil law: A comparative essay." *Tulane L. R.*, XLIV(1970), 720.

(357) Rogers, J. "A scientific approach to free judicial decision." In (347)II552: *135.*

(358) Roubier, P. *Théorie générale du droit.* 2nd ed. Paris, 1951: *110. 129. 132. 145. 156. 214.*

(359) Rümelin, M. *Der Vorentwurf des schweizerischen Zivilgesetzbuches und seine Bedeutung für uns.* Tübingen, 1908: *34.*

(360) Saleilles, R. *De la personalité juridique.* Paris, 1902: *144.*

(361) ———. *École historique et droit naturel.* Originally in *Rev. trim. de droit civil.* Paris, 1902: *14. 131.*
(362) Sayre, P. L., ed. *Interpretations of modern legal philosophies.* New York, 1947.
(363) Schaeffer, W. V. "Chief Justice Traynor and the judicial process." *Calif. L. R.*, LIII(1965), 11.
(364) ———. "Panel remarks." A.B.A. Section of Legal Education. August 23, 1955: *192. 222.*
(365) ———. *Precedent and policy.* Chicago, 1956: *222.*
(366) Schick, R. P., trans. *The Swiss civil code.* Boston, 1915: *162.*
(367) Schubert, G. A. *Quantitative analysis of judicial behavior.* Glencoe, Ill., 1959: *86. 112. 190. 211.*
(368) *Schweizerisches Zivilgesetzbuch: Der Vorentwurf des Eidgenössischen Justiz- und Polizeidepartments vom 15. November 1900.* Bern, 1901: *34.*
(369) *Science of legal method.* Trans. E. Bruncken and L. B. Register. New York, 1917: *22*/263n12.
(370) Seagle, W. *Men of law, from Hammurabi to Holmes.* New York, 1947: *117.*
(371) Sedláček, J. "L'oeuvre de François Gény et la science du droit pure." In (347)I277: *130.*
(372) Selznick, P. "Sociology and natural law." *Natur. L. Forum,* VI(1961)84: *132.*
(373) Sethna, M. J., ed. *Contributions to synthetic jurisprudence.* Bombay, 1962: *109.*
(374) Shalev, G., and S. Herman. "A source of study of Israel's contract codification." *Louisiana L. R.*, XXXV(1975), 1091: *193.*
(375) Silving, H. "Stare decisis." *Rev. Jur. U. Puerto Rico,* XXXV(1966)195: *99. 191. 219. 228.*
(376) ———. "The twilight zone of positive and natural law." *Calif. L. R.*, XLIII (1955)477.
(377) Small, B. F. "Stare decisis on two continents: A saga of gain and loss." *Rocky Mount. L. R.*, XVIII(1946), 97: *213.*
(378) Smith, S. A. de. *Judicial review of administrative action.* New York, 1959: *212.*
(379) Spiro, K. *Über den Gerichtsgebrauch zum allgemeinen Teil des revidierten Obligationsrecht.* Basel, 1948: *150. 170. 187. 204. 214.*
(380) Stammler, R. *Die Lehre von dem richtigen Rechte.* Halle, 1926 (1st ed., 1902): *34.*
(381) ———. *Wirtschaft und Recht nach der materialistischen Geschichtsauffassung.* 1896: *131.*
St. Clair, J. A. See Clair, J. A. St.
(382) "Status of the rule of judicial precedent, The." *U. Cincinnatti L. R.*, XIV (1940)203: *211. 220. 223. 226.*
(383) Stone, J. "Fallacies of the logical form in English law." In (362)696: *119.*
(384) ———. *Legal system and lawyers' reasoning.* Stanford, 1964: *145. 189.*
(385) ———. *The province and function of law.* Cambridge, Mass., 1946: *26*/159 n63. *119. 129. 149. 158. 178. 218.*
(386) ———. "The ratio of the ratio decidendi." *Modern L. R.*, XXII(1959)597: *145.*
(387) ———. *Recent trends in English precedent.* Sydney, 1945: *202. 218.*
(388) Sugiyama, N. "La loi du 8 juin 1875 sur l'administration de justice et les sources de droit privé." In (347)II 446: *158.*
(389) "Symposium on statutory construction." *Vanderbilt L. R.*, III(1950)365: *153. 226.*

Index II

(390) Tate, A. "Civilian methodology in Louisiana." *Tulane L. R.*, XLIV(1970) 673: *99/680.*

(391) ———. "The Louisiana action for unjustified enrichment." *Tulane L. R.*, L(1976)883: *77/904.*

(392) ———."The role of the judge in mixed jurisdictions: The Louisiana experience." In (94)23: *69.*

(393) Terré, F. "En relisant Gény." *Arch. philos. de droit*, VI(1961)125: *129. 130. 135. 159. 184. 221.*

(394) Toutsakovitch, M. "Publications de F. Gény." *Elaboration scientifique du droit positif dans la conception de François Gény.* Paris, 1939. Pp. 177–80: *232.*

(395) Traynor, R. J. "*La rude vita, la dolce giustizia*: Or hard cases can make good law." *U. Chicago L. R.*, XXIX(1961)223: *222. 224.*

(396) ———. "No magic words can do it justice." *Calif. L. R.*, XLIX(1961)615: *222.*

(397) Troller, A. *Ueberall gültige Prinzipien der Rechtswissenschaft.* Frankfurt/M., 1965: *112. 133.*

(398) Tunc, A. "Book review (Lawson)." *Amer. J. Comp. L.*, VI(1957)357: *157.*

(399) ———, and S. Tunc. *Le droit des États-Unis d'Amérique: Sources et techniques.* Paris, 1955: *107.*

(400) Tuor, P. *Das schweizerische Zivilgesetzbuch.* 6th ed. Zurich, 1953. (1st ed., 1912): *129. 166. 170. 188.*

(401) Ulam, S. M. *Adventures of a mathematician.* New York, 1976: *79. 203.*

(402) Ulman, J. N. *A judge takes stand.* New York, 1933: *145.*

(403) Vasilesco, P. "L'oeuvre de M. Gény et ses résultats." In (347)II 49: *156.*

(404) Vecchio, G. del. *Filosofia del derecho.* Trans. L. Recaséns-Siches. 2 vols. Barcelona, 1935–36: *64/I* 587. *189.*

(405) ———. "Sulla positività come carattere di diritto." *Riv. di filos*, III(1911) 16: *225.*

(406) Villey, M. "François Gény et la renaissance du droit naturel." In (308)39: *14/48. 24/43. 118. 130. 135. 136.*

(407) ———. *Leçons d'histoire de la philosophie du droit.* Paris, 1957: *130.*

(408) Voirin, P. "François Gény [Necrology]." *Riv. diritto commerc.* (1960), 234: *151.*

(409) Voorhis, J. van. "Cardozo and the judicial process today." *Yale L. J.*, LXXI (1961), 202: *153.*

(410) Waline, M. "Le pouvoir normative de la jurisprudence." *Mélanges Scelle*, II(1950) 613: *64.*

(411) Wasserström, R. A. *The judicial decision: Toward a theory of legal justification.* Stanford, 1961: *189.*

(412) Wechsler, H. "Toward neutral principles of constitutional law." *Harv. L. R.*, LXXIII(1959), 1: *194. 207. 222.*

(413) Wehrwein, A. "Levi warns on courts' social role." Washington *Post*, 10 April 1976: *210.*

(414) Whitehead, A. N. *Essays in science and philosophy.* New York, 1947: *117.*

(415) ———. *Science and the modern world.* New York, 1948. (1st ed., 1925): *104. 115.*

(416) Whorf, B. L. *Language, thought, and reality.* New York, 1956: *104.*

(417) Wieacker, F. *Gesetz und Richterkunst: Zum Problem der aussergesetzlicher Rechtsordnung.* Karlsruhe, 1958.

(418) Wigmore, J. H. "The judicial function." In (369) Introduction: *96*/xxvi, xxxviii.

Index II

(419) Wilk, K., trans. *The legal theories of Lask, Radbruch, and Dabin.* Cambridge, Mass., 1948: *126.*
(420) Williams, G. "Language and the law." *L. Q. R.*, LXI(1947)71; LXII (1948)387: *159.*
(421) Williams, I. *The sources of law in the Swiss civil code.* Oxford, 1923: *166.*
(422) Wittgenstein, L. *Philosophical investigations.* Oxford, 1953: *71. 104. 108.*
(423) ———. *Tractatus logico-philosophicus.* Trans. Pears and McGuiness. New York, 1961: *71.*
(424) Wortley, B. A. "François Gény." In Jennings, ed. *Modern theories of law.* London, 1933, p. 139: *129. 223.*
(425) ———. "La théorie des sources." In (347)II 16: *150.*
(426) Wright, R. A. "E.S.P., not science, rules decisions." New York *Times*, 31 August 1969: *220.*
(427) Wu, J. C. *Cases and materials on jurisprudence.* St. Paul, Minn., 1959: *126. 135. 150.*
(428) Wurzel, K. G. *Das juristische Denken.* Wien, 1904. Trans. in (369)286: *155.*
(429) Wyzanski, C. E. "History and law." *U. Chicago L. R.*, XXVI(1960)237: *210.*
(430) Yntema, H. "The jurisprudence of codification." In Rappy, ed. *David Dudley Field Centenary Essays.* New York, 1949, p. 251: *104.*
(431) Yung, W. "Eugène Huber et l'ésprit du code civil suisse." In Faculté de droit de Genève. *Grandes figures et grandes oeuvres juridiques.* Geneva, 1948, p. 187: *164. 165. 167.*
(432) ———. "F. Gény et la jurisprudence en Suisse." In (308)85: *33*/87. *34*/87; 97. *37*/89. *42*/95. *45*/95. *49*/90. *52*/93. *53*/92. *55*/86. *59*/97. *135. 166. 170. 183. 188. 189. 191.*
(433) ———. "Le code suisse et nous." *Zeitschr. für schweiz. Recht*, LXXX(1961), 323: *58. 64*/342. *166. 190.*
(434) Zweigert, K., and H. J. Puttfarken. "Statutory interpretation–civil style." *Tulane L. R.*, XLIV(1970)704: *117.*
(435) ———, and K. Siehr. "Jhering's influence on the development of comparative legal method." *Amer. J. Comp. L.*, XIX(1971)215.

APPENDIX D

Index III
Judicial Decisions

United States and England

Abortion Cases. *See* Doe v. Bolton; Roe v. Wade.
Adams v. Lindsell (K.B., 1818) 106 Engl. Rep. 250.
Adkins v. Children's Hospital (U.S. Supreme Court,1923) 261 U.S. 525.
Beamish v. Beamish (H.L., 1861) 9 H.L.C. 274.
Brown v. Board (U.S. Supr. Ct., 1953) 349 U.S. 235.
Conway v. Rimmer (1968) All-Engl. L. Rep. 874.
De Gregory v. Attorney-General (U.S. Supr. Ct.,1965) 383 U.S. 825.
Dobson v. U.S. (U.S. Supr. Ct.,1943) 320 U.S. 489.
Doe v. Bolton (U.S. Supr. Ct., 1973) 410 U.S. 179.
Fuller v. Alaska (U.S. Supr. Ct., 1968) 393 U.S. 80.
Great Northern Ry. Co. v. Sunburst Oil (U.S. Supr. Ct., 1932) 287 U.S. 358.
Guaranty Trust v. York (U.S. Supr. Ct., 1945) 326 U.S. 99.
Harris v. Commissioner (2. Cir., 1949) 178 F.2d 861.
Hynes v. N.Y. Central R. Co. (N.Y. App., 1921) 231 N.Y. 229; 131 N.E. 898.
Jones v. A. H. Mayer Co. (U.S. Supr. Ct., 1968) 392 U.S. 409.
Katz v. U. S. (U.S. Supr. Ct., 1967) 389 U.S. 347.
Linkletter v. Walker (U.S. Supr. Ct., 1965) 381 U.S. 618.
London Street Tramways Co. v. London City Council (1898) A. C. 375.
McPherson v. Buick (N.Y. App., 1916) 217 N.Y. 382.
Mapp v. Ohio (U.S. Supr. Ct., 1961) 367 U.S. 643.
Miller v. Oregon (U.S. Supr. Ct., 1908) 208 U.S. 412.
Minyard v. Curtis Products (Supr. Ct., La, 1967) 251 La 624; 205 So2d 422.
Miranda v. Arizona (U.S. Supr. Ct., 1966) 384 U.S. 436.
Moragne v. States Marine Lines (U.S. Supr. Ct., 1970) 398 U.S. 375.
Paddock Woods Case. *See* Jones v. Mayer.
Plessy v. Ferguson (U.S. Supr. Ct., 1896) 163 U.S. 537.
Pollock v. Farmer Loan & Trust Co. (U.S. Supr. Ct., 1895) 158 U.S. 601.
Roe v. Wade (U.S. Supr. Ct., 1973) 410 U.S. 113.

Index III

*Switzerland**

*Only "leading cases" are cited in Switzerland by name, frequently that of the plaintiff or petitioner alone. The reference in court opinions or literature is then in the form of "the *Suisa* case," "judgment *Torre*" or "the *Pantet* decision." BGE is the acronym for the official collection of court decisions in German. Volume I reports public law cases, II private law, IV criminal law. *See also* Note XXXVIII.